Explaining Explanation

David-Hillel Ruben offers a discussion of some of the main historical attempts to explain the concept of explanation, examining the works of Plato, Aristotle, John Stuart Mill, and Carl Hempel. Building on and developing the insights of these historical figures, he introduces an elaboration and defense of his own solution.

In this volume, Ruben relates the concept of explanation to both epistemological and metaphysical issues. Not content to confine the concept to the realm of philosophy of science, he examines it within a far more broadly conceived theory of knowledge. He concludes with his own original and challenging explanation of explanation.

Explaining Explanation will be read with interest by students of general philosophy as well as those specializing in the philosophy of science and scholars with a more advanced level of interest.

The Problems of Philosophy:
Their Past and Present

General Editor: Ted Honderich
Grote Professor of the Philosophy of Mind and Logic
University College
London

Each book in this series deals with a great or significant problem of philosophy. The series is intended to be easily accessible to under-graduates in philosophy, as well as to other readers at a more advanced level.

The first part of each book presents an introduction to and history of the problem in question. The second part, of a contemporary and analytical kind, defends the author's preferred solution.

Already published

Religious Belief and the Will   Louis P. Pojman
Private Ownership   James O. Grunebaum
The Rational Foundations of Ethics   T.L.S. Sprigge
Moral Knowledge   Alan H. Goldman
Rationality   Harold I. Brown
Personal Identity   Harold Noonan
Practical Reasoning   Robert Audi
Mind-Body Identity Theories   Cynthia Macdonald
If P, Then Q   David Sanford
Thought and Language   Julius Moravcsik
The Infinite   A.W. Moore
Human Consciousness   Alastair Hannay
The Weakness of the Will   Justin Gosling

Forthcoming

The Nature of Art   Anthony Cothey
Scepticism   Christopher Hookway

Explaining Explanation

David-Hillel Ruben
Senior Lecturer in Philosophy
The London School of Economics and Political Science

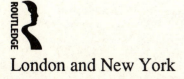

London and New York

First published 1990
by Routledge
11 New Fetter Lane, London EC4P 4EE

Simultaneously published in the USA and Canada
by Routledge
a division of Routledge, Chapman and Hall, Inc.
29 West 35th Street, New York, NY 10001

© 1990 David-Hillel Ruben

Typeset in 10/12 Times by LaserScript Limited, Mitcham, Surrey
Printed in Great Britain by T.J. Press (Padstow) Ltd, Padstow, Cornwall

British Library Cataloguing in Publication Data

Ruben, David-Hillel.
Explaining explanation. – (The problems of philosophy)
1. Explanation
I. Title II. Series
160

Library of Congress Cataloging in Publication Data

also available

ISBN 0-415-03269-5

For my parents
Blair S. Ruben
Sylvia Ginsberg Ruben

שְׁמַע בְּנִי מוּסַר אָבִיךָ
וְאַל־תִּטֹּשׁ תּוֹרַת אִמֶּךָ:

Hear, my son, the instruction of
thy father,
And forsake not the teaching of thy mother

Contents

Preface and Acknowledgements

This book is written in the conviction that the concept of explanation should not be exclusively hijacked by the philosophy of the natural sciences. As I repeat often in the following, like knowledge, explanation is an epistemic concept, and therefore has a philosophical location within the theory of knowledge, widely conceived. The philosophy of science has great relevance for a theory of explanation, just as it does for discussions of knowledge. But it is not the sole proprietor of either concept.

It is a pleasure to acknowledge the many debts I have incurred in the writing of this book. A Nuffield Foundation Fellowship for the period of January–April 1988, and a grant from the Suntory-Toyota International Centre for Economics and Related Disciplines which funded a period of leave from January to April 1989, were both invaluable in providing me with time to write the book. I am extremely grateful for their help, and wish to thank them publicly for it. In addition to funding leave, both also provided me with a small sum of money for the purchase of books, which I found immensely helpful in ensuring that I had all that I needed to work and write efficiently.

My intellectual debts are many. Peter Milne read ancestors of chapters II and V, and generously helped me with some of the more technical parts of chapter II. Jonathan Barnes read and commented on an ancestor of chapter III. Graham Macdonald and Mark Sainsbury commented on, and made many helpful suggestions for the improvement of, early versions of chapters I and V. Peter Lipton provided me with many fruitful discussions of explanation generally, and also commented in detail on chapters I, IV, V, and VI. Gary Clarke and Paul Noordhof read over the whole manuscript in an almost final form; both made many useful suggestions throughout the manuscript, and saved me from numerous errors. It would, perhaps, not be inappropriate in a paragraph on intellectual debts to mention my deep respect for the literature I discuss (even when I argue with it), and the extent to which I have learned and profited from it. This is obvious in the case of the historical figures, but, obvious or not, it is similarly the case with the contemporary literature on explanation which I cite (and some which I do not have space or time to cite). Whatever I have been able to discern has only been by standing on their shoulders. I have learned a great deal from everything I have read, but perhaps the greatest single influence on my thinking has been the work of Peter Achinstein.

It is so self-evident that only the writer himself can be responsible for any remaining mistakes and errors, that writers often attempt to discover increasingly novel or amusing ways in which to say this. I shall not try; I know that the philosophical influence of all these people made the book much better than it would otherwise have been, and it cannot be the fault of any of them that they were unable to detect all of the errors I made, or unable to ensure that I was capable of making good every error they pointed out to me.

In each of my previously published books and articles, I have thanked Mark Sainsbury for philosophical conversation, which – all too often – has been one-sided, with him as teacher and me as pupil. I, like most philosophers, cannot work without constant philosophical discussion, and I have him principally to thank for bringing it about that I live in a philosophically acceptable environment.

The strategy of the book is almost, but not quite, straightforward. In the historical portion of the book, chapters II, III, and IV, I discuss the theories of explanation of Plato, Aristotle, John Stuart Mill, and Carl Hempel. Although there is little *explicit* philosophical work on explanation between Aristotle and Mill – a gap of over two thousand years – there is much implicit in the writings of Bacon, Berkeley, and many other philosophers that is relevant to explanation, but which considerations of space have forced me to neglect. I discuss and state my view on some issues as I move through these historical chapters, but in the main I reserve chapters V, VI, and VII for the elaboration of my own views on explanation.

I have not yet mentioned the purpose of chapter I. The placement of this chapter has given me some pause. As I began my discussions of the historical figures, I found myself in constant need of a technical vocabulary with which to make the issues they treat clear and precise. I therefore decided to devote an opening, non-historical chapter to questions of terminology, and to classification of kinds of theories of explanation. The danger in this strategy is that the reader will not really see the point of chapter I, until much later in the book. I might suggest, for readers who begin to tire of chapter I, that they proceed to chapter II, and return to chapter I only when they find a need for a discussion of the issues it deals with. I decided not to relocate chapter I to a later position in the book, but to leave it in place, allowing readers to decide when the reading of the chapter would be appropriate.

David-Hillel Ruben
London, 1990

CHAPTER I

Getting our Bearings

The series in which this book is appearing is called 'The Problems of Philosophy: Their Past and Present'; this volume, since it is about the concept of explanation, discusses some of the philosophical problems about explanation, as they arise in the writings of past philosophers.

It is necessary to introduce certain distinctions, and settle a few substantive matters, before beginning the discussion of explanation in the succeeding chapters. One possible consequence of this approach is that readers will not always see the motive for the distinction or decision; I can only ask them to be patient, for the discussion in the following chapters returns to these issues time and time again. I engage in a separate, introductory treatment of these common and recurring themes, rather than weave them into the body of the ensuing text. But perhaps a 'map' of what this chapter contains will help.

First, it is essential to identify more precisely the concept I shall be discussing. Which concept does the term 'explanation' designate? The literature is somewhat remiss in this respect. Usually, the author presupposes that the audience will have no difficulty in identifying which concept it is, about which the author wishes to raise certain problems. This may be an acceptable presupposition in discussions of concepts like causation and knowledge. It does not seem to me to be an acceptable presupposition in the case of explanation (or, for that matter, in the case of the concept of a person). Hence, it is not a presupposition that I shall make. One of my main motives, in the sections entitled 'Some explanations', 'Process and product', 'Restricting the scope of the analysis', 'Scientific and ordinary explanation', 'Partial and full explanation', and 'Bad explanations and no explanations', is to specify as precisely as I can *which* concept it is that I shall be discussing, by distinguishing it from others with which it might easily be confused.

I also use this chapter to introduce some terminology and draw various distinctions that I need for my later discussion. One needs a perspicuous terminology in which to raise the central questions properly. The philosophical implications (for surely there are such) of choice of terminology are not always apparent to the writer; it is therefore especially incumbent on the writer to be as clear about this as possible, so that others may be able to see those implicit and unnoticed ramifications, which may escape notice. Introduction of terminology, and drawing of pertinent distinctions, occur in the sections mentioned above, but also in the sections entitled 'Some terminology', 'Theories of explanation', and 'Dispensing with contrastives'. In the last section, 'Dispensing with contrastives', I discuss a certain view about what it is that one explains in an explanation. I discuss explanation in a 'traditional' terminology, which the contrastive view seeks to overturn; hence, my motive for taking on the contrastive view in this introductory chapter.

The section on theories of explanation is the longest in the chapter. It offers a typology by which to identify and describe specific theories of explanation. In order to help the reader see what is going on in that section, I introduce its own 'map' at the beginning of the section. But I would stress that the motive for drawing the distinctions in the way I do can only emerge in the subsequent chapters, in which the distinctions are applied to specific theories.

Many writers on explanation fail to make the 'ground rules' of the discussion of explanation at all clear. One is presented, in the literature on explanation, with many extremely plausible but competing accounts of explanation. In virtue of what features is one account better than another? What acceptance tests should an account of explanation be prepared to meet? I address this question in the section entitled 'The methodology of explaining explanation'.

Throughout the book, I make use of a contrast between epistemology and metaphysics, and the various concepts whose analyses belong to one or the other of these two branches of philosophy. For example, a theme that recurs throughout the book is that explanation is an epistemological concept, but one which requires a metaphysical 'backing'.

I am content for this contrast to be understood in a rough and ready way. Metaphysics is the study of what there is, and what it is like, quite apart from questions about our knowledge of these matters. Typical metaphysical questions include: are there universals?; what is an event?;

does every event have a cause?; is the concept of causation a deterministic concept? Epistemology is the study of knowledge, belief, reasons, and evidence. Typical epistemological questions include: must all beliefs be justified by other beliefs?; is all knowledge certain?; which, if any, non-deductive arguments with true premises provide reasons for belief in their conclusions? I am quite prepared to admit that there are some concepts which do not fit easily into one category rather than the other (perhaps the concepts of truth and of fact are examples), but this does not, I think, detract from the usefulness of the distinction.

I do occasionally refer to the views of Carl Hempel throughout this chapter. I discuss Hempel fully in chapter IV. However, since his writings on explanation have proved to be so central to contemporary discussions, reference to him here is intended to be merely a useful illustration of whatever specific question is at hand.

Some explanations

Giving explanations is a common activity, engaged in by layman and scientific specialist alike. Most books about explanations begin by giving examples of scientific explanation. The following are representative cases of the sort of explanations that scientists offer:

(a) Two kilograms of copper at 60 degrees C are placed in three kilograms of water at 20 degrees C. After a while, water and copper reach the same equilibrium temperature, 22.5 degrees C, and then cool down together to the temperature of the surrounding atmosphere. Why is the equilibrium temperature 22.5 degrees C? Since the specific heats of water and copper are 1 and 0.1 respectively, and since the conservation of energy requires that the total amount of heat be neither increased or diminished, the heat loss of copper, namely, $0.1 \times 2 \times (60-T)$ must be the same as the heat gain of water, namely, $1 \times 3 \times (T-20)$, where T is the final equilibrium temperature. And this yields 22.5 degrees C as the value of T.

(b) Two nerve impulses, I_1 and I_2, in close physical proximity in a neuron, arrive within 0.3 milliseconds of each other at the synapse of that neuron. Neither has a local potential quite strong enough to fire a certain adjacent dendrite. Nevertheless, the dendrite in question fired. Why? Because the local potentials of I_1 and I_2 have summated to a degree high enough

3

to evoke a spike potential in the adjacent dendrite, a phenomenon that will occur in the described circumstances provided that the arrival time of the distinct nerve impulses does not exceed 0.5 milliseconds.

(c) It is observed that certain human beings suffering from extreme fatigue and lengthy food deprivation show little or no desire to eat when presented with food. The explanation for this is that extreme fatigue inhibits the rhythmic contractions in the duodenum that initiate blood chemistry changes which in turn trip off the central mechanisms leading to eating behaviour.[1]

The three examples of scientific explanation cited above are picked almost at random from many equally good ones with which the reader would be presented in any adequate book on the concept of scientific explanation.

The third example is an example of the explanation of a generalization (well, almost a generalization; the point is that it does not concern a specific or particular case): 'certain human beings suffering from extreme fatigue and lengthy food deprivation show little or no desire to eat when presented with food'. The first and second examples are examples of the explanation of particular cases: two specific nerve impulses which fire a dendrite, and a specific sample of copper weighing two kilograms placed in a container with three kilograms of water. Carl Hempel cites a particular case explanation in the opening pages of his *Aspects of Scientific Explanation*:

> John Dewey describes a phenomenon he observed one day while washing dishes. Having removed some glass tumblers from the hot suds and placed them upside down on a plate, he noticed that soap bubbles emerged from under the tumblers' rims, grew for a while, came to a standstill and finally receded into the tumblers. Why did this happen? Dewey outlines an explanation....[2]

I have relatively little to say in this book about the explanation of laws and generalizations; I concentrate on what I call 'singular explanation'. Some writers, for instance Michael Friedman, have claimed that explanation in science is almost always explanation of laws:

> ...what is explained is a general regularity or pattern of behavior – a law if you like .... Although most of the philosophical

literature deals with the explanation of particular events, the type of explanation illustrated by the account above seems much more typical of the physical sciences. Explanations of particular events are comparatively rare – found only perhaps in geology and astronomy.[3]

I think Friedman's claim is exaggerated. Two of the cases which I cited above, which are taken from scientific journals, are examples of the explanation of particular events (and neither is from geology or astronomy). It is true that science often – perhaps always – has explanatory interest in particular cases only in so far as they are examples of a general sort. It would not really have mattered if the above explanations had been of two similar impulses firing a similar dendrite, or of a similar sample of copper placed in a similar amount of water. As Raimo Tuomela says: 'Singular facts, events, etc., are not *per se* of any interest to at least pure science. All interest in them is ultimately interest in their being instantiations of some universal rather than another. . ., for indeed there are no bare particulars.'[4]

This may have something to do with the nature of explanation itself. *Whenever* a particular case is explained, perhaps the same explanation could be given for any relevantly similar example, and so the explanatory interest is never in the particular case as such, but only in it in so far as it is a particular case *of a general sort*. But this, if true, is *not* the same thing as having little or no interest in particular cases. In any event, if my neglect of the explanation of laws is a weakness of the book, at least I can claim that what I have to say is consistent with the truth about the explanation of laws or generalizations, whatever it may be.

A theory of explanation does not only address itself to cases of explanation in science. It must address itself to other cases as well, in which non-specialists explain things to one another. I am not thinking of explanations of human action, about which I will have very little to say in this book. Rather, I have in mind the perfectly acceptable ordinary explanations we are able to give one another of natural occurrences: the onset of warm weather explains the melting of the snow; overexposure to the sun explains my painful burn; my match lit because I struck it. The person who explains the melting of the snow by the onset of warm weather may not be able to explain how or why higher air temperature causes the snow to melt; for this latter, they may need a microtheory which only scientific specialists possess. But inability to explain how or

5

why an air temperature increase leads to the melting of the snow does not imply inability to explain the snow's melting on the basis of an increase in the air temperature. Nearly everyone, whether or not they have a degree in a natural science, knows that the snow melts *because* spring has come.

The analysis of explanation, then, belongs to general epistemology, in the same way as the analysis of knowledge does, and not just to the philosophy of science, narrowly conceived. Scientific explanation, like scientific knowledge, has a special importance and pride of place in a general theory of knowledge. But just as there is more to knowledge than scientific knowledge, so too there is more to explanation than scientific explanation. The knowledge that I now have that I am sitting at my desk and writing is not scientific knowledge. The explanation that I can give of the snow's melting in terms of the warmer weather is not scientific explanation. Ordinary explanations, like ordinary knowledge, are not impervious to error, and it may sometimes happen that science overturns what we wrongly took to be an example of ordinary know-ledge or of acceptable ordinary explanation. But, when not so over-turned, such ordinary explanation or knowledge is not, *per se*, scientific explanation or knowledge. I do not intend these introductory remarks to beg any questions about the nature of the distinction between ordinary and scientific explanation, nor to suggest that there is some hard and fast contrast between them. I deal with these issues in the course of the chapter. Rather, these remarks are intended only to serve as a reminder about the scope of our topic. Far too many discussions of explanation assume that what can be said about scientific explanation exhausts what of interest there is that can be said about explanation *tout court*, and this is, in my view, simply not so.

For the present, I shall move rather cavalierly between 'explanation' and 'scientific explanation'. I ask the reader's temporary indulgence. I deal with this (alleged) distinction later in the chapter.

Process and product

'Explanation' itself is susceptible to a well-known process–product ambiguity, as are many other words ending in '-ion'. 'In the process–product shift, a word, often one ending in "-ion" or "-tion", may signify an activity or its result.'[5] A simple example is this: 'I saw the destruction at Rotterdam.' The sentence might mean either that I saw the act of Rotterdam being destroyed or that I saw the results of such an act.

'Explanation' is ambiguous in the same way as 'destruction'. As Bromberger points out, in one sense

> an explanation may be something about which it makes sense to ask: How long did it take? Was it interrupted at any point? Who gave it? When? Where? What were the exact words used? For whose benefit was it given?[6]

On the other hand, an explanation 'may be something about which none of [the previous] questions make sense, but about which it makes sense to ask: Does anyone know it? Who thought of it first? Is it very complicated?'

The linguistic evidence points to two different senses of 'explanation'. The first suggested by Bromberger's evidence is the process or act sense; the second, the product sense. Other examples of words which have this ambiguity range from philosophically uninteresting ones like 'simulation' and 'destruction' (Clark and Welsh's example) to ones which raise philosophical issues similar to those raised by 'explanation': 'prediction', 'deduction', 'derivation', 'proposition', 'argument', 'statement', and 'analysis' (although the last three do not end in '-ion').

So, in speaking of an explanation, one might be referring to an act of explaining, or to the product of such an act. How are these two senses related? There seem to be just four possibilities:

(1) The idea of an explanatory act can only be analysed by using the idea of an explanatory product, but not vice versa.
(2) The idea of an explanatory product can only be analysed by using the idea of an explanatory act, but not vice versa.
(3) The ideas of explanatory act and explanatory product mutually depend on one another.
(4) The ideas of explanatory act and explanatory product are independent of one another.

Most of the literature on explanation, and certainly the four writers on explanation whom I shall be discussing, Plato, Aristotle, Mill, and Hempel, were interested only in the idea of an explanatory product. They believed (and I agree with them) that an explanatory product can be characterized solely in terms of the kind of information it conveys, no reference to the act of explaining being required. Hence, each would have rejected (2) and (3). Their question was this: what information has to be conveyed in order to have explained something?

One recent writer, Peter Achinstein, has advanced (2).[7] If (2) were true, then the idea of an explanatory act would have a far more central position in the analysis of explanation than it has previously been given. According to Achinstein, an explanatory product is neither just an argument (the Hempelian view) of a certain sort nor just a proposition of a specific kind, nor any other entity which can be characterized *solely* in terms of its syntactic form and/or the type of information that it conveys. Rather, according to him, an explanatory product is an ordered pair, in part consisting of a proposition, but also including an explaining act type (e.g. the type, explaining that such-and-such). For example, on Achinstein's view, the explanation of why Nero fiddled might be the ordered pair, {'Nero fiddled because he was happy seeing Rome burn'; the act type, explaining why Nero fiddled}.

Why does Achinstein think that an explanatory product cannot be characterized solely in terms of its information content? His argument rests on the uncontroversial fact that the same information content might be conveyed by both an act of explaining and an act of another type,[8] e.g. an act of criticizing. For instance, in saying that Nero fiddled because he was happy seeing Rome burn, Achinstein claims that I could be either criticizing Nero or explaining his action (Achinstein 1983: 88–9). Achinstein reasons that since the same information content can be conveyed in two different kinds of acts, and since no product of an explaining act could be identical with, for example, the product of a criticizing act, the explanation product (and the criticism product) must be more than just the information conveyed.

But why can't the product of an act of criticizing and an act of explaining be identical? Achinstein relies on the following sorts of principles to show that they cannot be:

(5) The product of S's act is an explanation only if S explained.

(6) The product of S's act is a criticism only if S criticized.

These principles will lead to the conclusion that Achinstein wants. If I am explaining Nero's actions but *not* criticizing them, and you are criticizing them but *not* explaining them, then the explanation product of my act cannot be identical with any criticism product and the criticism product of your act cannot be identical with any explanation product. If explanation and criticism products are to be distinguished in this case, the products ought to be distinguished even in the case in which one person is engaging in two or more acts[9] at one and the same time. Each of the acts will have its own 'internal' product.

But what reason is there to think that (5), (6), and other analogous principles, which claim that a necessary condition for something to be a person's product[10] of a certain kind is that *he* has *actually* produced it in an act of that kind, are true? These principles simply presume what they are used to prove. I can see no good reason to deny that objectively speaking, quite apart from whatever intention you (or anyone else) may have had in acting, the information you impart in criticizing (explaining) Nero may also be an explanation (criticism) of what he did, in the product sense. One can, in criticizing Nero, convey information which is also an explanation (in the product sense) of why he fiddled, whether the criticizer or indeed anyone else has *ever* engaged in an act of explaining what he did. There can be explanations (in the product sense), even if no one has ever explained anything; (5) and (6) are false.

Explanatory products can be fully characterized in terms of their information content independently of explanatory acts, so (2) and (3) are false. (I do not wish to pronounce on the choice between (1) and (4).) Of course, we may tend to *call* such information 'an explanation' (in the product sense) as opposed to a criticism or an argument only if it figures as the product of an explaining act. But that gives us no more reason to deny that an explanation product may be the same as a criticism product than there is to deny that the Morning Star = the Evening Star on the grounds that we tend to call the heavenly body the latter only when it appears in the evening, and the former only when it appears in the morning.

The methodology of explaining explanation

The title of this book is *Explaining Explanation*. The suspicious might think that there is something self-defeating in such a title. How, one might ask, if one were genuinely in need of enlightenment about the concept of explanation, could one undertake to explain what explanation is? Would it not be rather like trying to pull oneself up by one's own bootstraps?

Of course, there is no real difficulty here. In offering a philosophical analysis of any concept, one must attribute to oneself an (at least partial) implicit understanding of that concept, which the analysis is attempting to make explicit. Some sophistication or other of this basic idea of what it is to offer an analysis is necessary if one is to escape the paradox of analysis. The alleged paradox asserts: if one knew what was involved in the concept, one would not need the analysis; if one did not know what was involved in the concept, no analysis could be forthcoming. The escape is through some implicit/explicit distinction. One can know implicitly, but need the analysis to make the knowledge explicit.

Moreover, there is a second reason why explaining explanation offers no difficulty. What we are explaining is the concept of explanation, as employed not only in science, but also in ordinary life. But the explaining that we are undertaking is specifically philosophical explication or analysis (I use these terms interchangeably) of a concept. Carl Hempel, for example, repeats in several passages that what he is doing is offering an explication, and that the purpose of an explication or analysis is to lay bare the 'logical structure of the concept'. Hempel often speaks of the analysis of a concept as 'a model', as he does when he says that there are three 'models' of explanation.[11] On his view, there are really three distinct concepts of explanation, and the three 'models' make clear in what ways the three differ.

The literature abounds with competing and incompatible explications, or analyses, of explanation. Optimally, we should like to be able to choose rationally one from amongst them. We need to know, then, what constraints there are on such a choice. Should the best analysis 'fit' the way in which we ordinarily use the term 'explanation'? Should it, rather, meet some more technical requirements of science or philosophy? I wish below to draw a contrast between two different ways of answering these questions.

I intend the following general remarks on methodology to be as anodyne and uncontroversial as possible, for they are not intended as an excursus into the philosophy of language or philosophical logic. I do not think one needs to take them as a serious contribution to the understanding of the nature of concepts. I will also assume in the discussion the view of analysis or explication adopted explicitly by Hempel, when he said that he is engaged in laying bare the logical structure of a concept. Although Hempel does not say so, it would seem to follow from this view that the truths so exposed about a concept have the status of analytic or necessary truths. I do not here distinguish between analyticity and necessity, for nothing of importance for my discussion hangs on that distinction.

Perhaps a brief comparison with the philosophical literature on the analysis of knowledge will help us to understand the idea of the two different ways of judging competing analyses. I gesture to this other literature, only as a way of drawing the contrast in philosophical method that I will then apply to the case of the analysis of explanation. These different ways of proceeding philosophically, whether in discussing knowledge or explanation, arise out of different traditions of what it is to do philosophy.

First, some discussions of knowledge proceed in this way. Various complicated situations are described, for instance a situation in which a person has justified true belief but there is no causal connection between the fact the belief is about and the belief itself. We are then asked whether we would apply 'knows' in such a situation. 'So, all three conditions for knowledge . . . are fulfilled; but we still do not want to say that S knows. . . .' 'Surely we do not want to say that his friend's wild guess endows S with knowledge.'[12]

The idea is that our analysis of knowledge should capture all and only, or (in a weaker and more plausible version) most of, those situations in which we would prephilosophically be prepared to use the term 'knows'. I am, of course, thinking of the vast literature inspired by Gettier's famous article.[13] For better or worse, I call this method 'the language users' approach'. Notice that this language users' approach might not be wedded to everyone's use of the word at all times (it is important to see that this approach need not be wedded to the idea of *ordinary* language). It is open to an exponent of this view to designate some subset of users of the word as having a special status. For instance, the philosopher of knowledge might only be interested in how scientists employ the concept of knowledge, and perhaps only while they are engaged in some specific scientific activity. I still think of this as the same view, but with the class of users cut down in size and scope.

Michael Friedman adopts this language users' approach in his account of explanation:

> . . .most, if not all, scientific theories that we all consider to be explanatory should come out as such according to our theory. . . . Although it is unreasonable to demand that a philosophical account of explanation should show that every theory that has ever been thought to be explanatory really is explanatory, it must at least square with most of the important, central cases.'[14]

Friedman does not say why his requirement is plausible. Isn't it logically possible that all or most of the central and important cases of theories we thought were explanatory fail really to be so? Perhaps Friedman has in mind here some version of the paradigm case argument; if so, the prospects for his view seem dim.[15]

It is more difficult to give a succinct general characterization of the alternative method which I wish to describe. I call it 'the technical approach'. In one way or another, it dispenses with such reliance on the way in which terms are actually used or employed. As far as the analysis of knowledge is concerned, a good example of this approach is Karl Popper's 'Epistemology Without a Knowing Subject': '... scientific knowledge simply is not knowledge in the sense of the ordinary usage of the words "I know".'

> ... ordinary language ... has no separate terms for the corresponding two senses of 'know'. ... My quoting The Oxford English Dictionary should not be interpreted as either a concession to language analysis or as an attempt to appease its adherents. It is not quoted in an attempt to prove that 'ordinary usage' covers 'knowledge' in the objective sense of my third world.'[16]

Popper's characterization of knowledge must meet some constraints, and his article goes on to specify just what they are. But whatever they are, they do not include 'fit' with the way in which we (or even just scientists) employ or use the term 'knows'.

My names for these two positions, the language users' approach and the technical approach, are not especially happy ones, but they do at least suggest the sort of position intended. Different philosophical orientations have tended to favour one or the other of these positions, but of course these are 'ideal types', and the actual practice of many philosophers is more complicated, combining elements of both of these approaches, and perhaps others besides.

Even on the language users' approach, one might regard usage as vague, ambiguous, imprecise, even inconsistent or incoherent; the philosopher may say that there is no single concept that is expressed by all of the ordinary uses of some term. He then may single out a subset of those uses as a way to disambiguate and to focus on one concept at a time. Or the concept as used may be vague (it is not strictly true that one can speak of *the* concept in such a circumstance); there may be general agreement about the paradigm cases, but dispute about cases in the concept's penumbra. The language users' approach should permit us to depart from ordinary usage at least to the extent of eliminating vagueness in a concept's application and disambiguating. Let's call this 'tidying up a discourse'. But, in all versions of this approach, actual language-use is where one at least begins one's analysis.

The other approach I called 'the technical approach'. A philosopher engaged on some project might eschew interest in the concepts used by the speakers of a language. The philosopher might see as part of his task the introduction of some quite novel concept, whose criteria are given by stipulative specification. Examples of this include some of the technical concepts of philosophy: sense data, the distinction between essence and accident, the ideas of a metalanguage, and material implication. The great philosophical systems, e.g. the Platonic, Kantian, and Hegelian philosophies, provide examples of this technical concept introduction: Forms, the distinction between reason and understanding, the synthesis of the understanding, noumena and phenomena, transcendental arguments, the Absolute in and for itself. The philosopher might think that such a concept plays an important role in coming to understand something that we simply failed to understand before. I call this 'simple introduction'.

The above examples of the technical approach are cases of straight-forward concept introduction. But there are other cases in which the introduced concept is intended to replace or improve upon one already in use by the common man. Hume's 'reformed' concept of the self, Berkeley's idea of a physical object which excludes the commitment to unperceived existence, Hobbes's redefinition of desire and aversion in terms of internal motions, and the idea of truth-in-a-language, are examples of concept replacement. Many scientific reductions involve concept replacement in the reduced science; arguably, the pre-reduction concept of water is not the same as the concept of water after its identification with H_2O. The latter would then be a replacement for the former.

Suppose a philosopher practising this technical approach decides that there are good reasons for the introduction of a new concept of X, to replace the old one. The new replacing and old replaced concepts will sometimes have very similar extensions, and their analyses (or, 'models') may have many features in common. But this is hardly essential. Replacing concepts might differ dramatically in intension from the concepts that they replace.[17] Moreover, the new and old concepts of X may differ in extension. We might even come to believe that nothing correctly called 'X' before, when the old concept was in use, can be correctly so-called now that it is the new concept that is in service, and vice versa.

I have stressed the intensional and extensional discontinuities there might be between replacing and replaced concepts of something. But surely there are limits here. There must be some difference between (a) replacing the old concept of X with the new concept *of X*; (b) eliminating the concept of X and simply introducing the concept of Y, as two separate exercises in improving our discourse. How could we account for this difference if not by introducing some sort of continuity between the old and new concepts?

Indeed, it is true that there must be some sort of continuity. There is, by and large, a point in having the concepts we do. For example, at least part of the point and purpose of explanation is that we should come to understand why things happen.[18] That is the *function* that explanation has for us. If a replacing concept of explanation is a replacement *for* the standard or ordinary concept of explanation, it surely must serve at least this function. The requisite continuity between the old and new concept of X might be provided by continuity of function.

Some philosophers may believe that these 'functional' facts about a concept have no place in its logical analysis. They will say, in the case of explanation, that although it is true that explanations do or should lead us to *understand*, that this is so is not a logically or conceptually necessary truth about explanation. Hempel, for example, says that 'such expressions as "realm of understanding" and "comprehensible" do not belong to the vocabulary of logic, for they refer to psychological or pragmatic aspects of explanation'.[19] These facts about what explanations do for us have, on his account, no place within the analysis of explanation itself. For such philosophers, there could be a complete intensional and extensional discontinuity between the old and new concepts of explanation, with only the sameness of contingent functional facts linking the two concepts as two concepts of *explanation*.

Other philosophers will find room for these functional facts within the analysis of the concept.[20] The analysis of explanation will include some mention of understanding. For these philosophers, there will after all have to be some, at least minimal, intensional continuity between replaced and replacing concepts of explanation.

I have great sympathy for the technical approach, rather than the language users' approach in any of its possible refinements. However, if the technical approach is adopted, one needs to consider arguments which attempt to justify the new replacing concept one has introduced. Many new concepts might be introduced, which could be said to have the same point as the old replaced one. How can we justify one candidate over the others as the replacing concept, if language use does not constrain that choice? How can we show that the replacing concept we select is not just arbitrary, *ad hoc*?

Suppose concepts a, b . . . n are all put forward by different philosophers as competing new replacement concepts of explanation. Each might plausibly be thought of as *a* concept of explanation. For each, its philosophical champion can produce a set of necessary or analytic truths. That by itself is wholly uninteresting. Which of a, b, c . . . n is the best replacement for the old concept of explanation? It is only when we can answer that question that we will know which set of analytic truths has any real claim to be of interest to us, and what it is that we are trying to do when we offer an analysis of explanation. This is an issue which I will want to raise when I look at Aristotle, Mill, and Hempel, and which will provide a thread of continuity that runs throughout the book.

Restricting the scope of the analysis

The Hempelian models are not intended as models of *all* explanations. Hempel contrasts the cases of explanation covered by his models of scientific explanation with others in which we do not explain why such-and-such or that such-and-such: 'explaining the rules of a contest, explaining the meaning of a cuneiform inscription or of a complex legal clause or of a passage in a symbolist poem, explaining how to bake a Sacher torte or how to repair a radio' (Hempel 1965: 412–13). In the cases of explaining the meaning of something, 'the explanandum will be specified by means of a noun phrase . . . whereas explanations of the kind we have been considering . . . are characterized by means of a sentence' (Hempel 1965: 414). Hempel would consider none of these above mentioned sorts of explanation as scientific in his sense, and none constitutes a reasonable objection to his account of explanation:

> Similarly, to put forward the covering-law models of scientific explanation is not to deny that there are other contexts in which we speak of explanation, nor is it to assert that the corresponding uses of the word 'explain' conform to one or another of our models. Obviously, those models are not intended to reflect the various senses of 'explain' that are involved. . . . Hence to deplore, as one critic does, the 'hopelessness' of the deductive-nomological model on the ground that it does not fit the case of explaining or understanding the rules of Hanoverian succession is simply to miss the intent of our model.
>
> (Hempel 1965: 412–13)

15

Hempel indicates two ways by which to delimit the explanations for which he seeks to offer an analysis. The first is grammatical: '... explanations of the kind we have been considering are concerned with ... [whatever] is properly characterized by means of a sentence' (Hempel 1965: 414). Elsewhere, he speaks, rather circularly, of the explanations in which he is interested as being answers to 'explanation-seeking why-questions' (Hempel 1965: 412). Fully and completely explaining how to ride a bike is not a case of explanation to which Hempel would consider his models of scientific explanation appropriate; it fails both the grammatical and the 'why-question' tests. In chapter III, I return to the question of the adequacy of these two ways of characterizing the subset of explanations to which Hempel restricts his analysis.

Since Hempel, in the above quotation, speaks of 'the various senses of "explain"', he seems to commit himself to the thesis that 'explain' in 'explain that p', 'explain how', and 'explain the meaning...' is ambiguous. That thesis seems to me dubious, but we do not need to decide the matter one way or the other, in order to delimit the instances of 'explain' in which Hempel is interested.

Scientific and ordinary explanation

As my opening remarks suggested, there are, or are thought to be, such things as scientific explanations. The contrast is usually with ordinary explanations. What does this contrast come to? Is 'scientific explanation' anything more than a pleonasm for 'explanation'?

There are at least two possible senses of 'scientific explanation'. In the first sense, it refers to explanations which are actually given in science. As we shall see, this is *not* the sense of the expression in which Hempel is primarily interested. In the second sense, the meaning of 'scientific explanation' is commendatory, or honorific, in some way. In any event, in this second sense, it is an open question whether any of the explanations actually given in science are scientific explanations at all.

There is without doubt a distinction between ordinary explanations and scientific explanations in the first sense, since it is simply a fact that some explanations are given in the course of life's ordinary affairs and others are given by scientists when they do science. But Hempel uses 'scientific explanation' in the second sense. Consequently, the question

I address in this section is whether there is a distinction between ordinary explanations (and also scientific explanations in the first sense) on the one hand and scientific explanations in this second sense on the other.

In my view, the only distinction that can usefully be drawn is that between full and partial explanations, and the distinction between scientific (in the second sense) and ordinary explanations is either that distinction or no distinction at all. As I indicated before, although I discuss Hempel's views on explanation fully in a later chapter, I use him here as a way of sharpening the issue (and in this case, actually stating my own position).

To begin with, Hempel does not think of scientific explanations as explanations actually given by scientists: 'these models are not meant to describe how working scientists actually formulate their explanatory accounts'.[21] The practising scientist may use 'explanation' in as loose or vague a way as the ordinary man on the street. What the scientist calls 'an explanation', *and indeed his actual explanatory practices too*, how he actually goes about explaining things, may fall woefully short of what Hempel requires of an explanation. Actual explanations in science may suffer from the same deficiencies as do explanations offered by the non-scientist on the Clapham bus.

Perhaps, then, the term 'scientific explanation' is meant to conjure up the fact that there is a goal or ideal of precision and completeness, explicated by Hempel's models, which explanations in science can aspire to and can actually meet if so required. 'The construction of our models therefore involves some measure of abstraction and of logical schematization' (Hempel 1965: 412); 'we have found ... that the explanatory accounts actually formulated in science and in everyday contexts ... diverge more or less markedly from the idealized and schematized covering-law models' (Hempel 1965: 424). Hempel compares his models of explanation with the 'ideal' (this is his term) metamathematical standards of proof theory (Hempel 1965: 414). So, the models are 'ideals', in some sense. Actual explanations in science may fall short of the ideal by being elliptic, incomplete, partial, or mere sketches of an explanation. Hempel describes these various forms of incompleteness at some length (Hempel 1965: 412–25).

In what sense does Hempel use the terms 'ideal' and 'idealized'? The models are surely not ideals for Hempel in the sense that explainers *should* always strive to do their best to make their explanations complete; there is no doubt that circumstances can justify explainers in explaining only incompletely, by omitting information known by their audience. In normal circumstances in which no one doubts the prevalent atmospheric conditions, a scientist would be a bore if he attempted to explain the fire by adducing both the short circuit and the presence of oxygen. It is not true that even scientists always ought to give as full an explanation as is possible.

Rather, the models Hempel introduces are ideals for him simply in the sense that they are complete; they specify a type of complete or full explanation. In fact, Hempel believes that such complete explanations are rarely given even in science. It is *possible*, and it would not matter to his argument if it were so, that no one, not even a scientist, actually ever offers such a complete and full explanation, which includes exceptionless laws needing no further qualification and *all* relevant initial conditions. Moreover, it could even be that every actual explanation ever given was *justifiably* incomplete, due to the pragmatic constraints on providing explanations. However, and this is surely the important point for him, incomplete explanations explain only in virtue of there being such complete explanations, whether or not anyone ever gives or should give one. One might draw the necessary distinction in Kantian terms. Hempel's requirements provide a *constitutive* ideal for full explanation; they are not intended as a regulative ideal.

A consequence of this interpretation of what Hempel has in mind is that, if these models provide an ideal or goal for explanations in science ('scientific explanations' in the first sense), there is no reason why they should not equally provide an ideal for explanations in ordinary life too. The ideal sets a standard for explanation, *tout court*. Indeed, Hempel discusses quite explicitly the application of his model to historical events, to the actions of agents, and to functional systems. In science, a scientist might give some explanation that, because of the constraints of time or the interests of his audience, fails to live up to Hempelian standards. However, exactly the same is true in ordinary life. We normally are happy to explain why the chicken crossed the road by saying that it wanted to get to the other side, but if required, we could impose all of the Hempelian requirements, to obtain a full explanation of what the chicken did. On several occasions, Hempel explicitly couples scientific (in the first sense) and everyday explanations together, as both being subject to the same 'idealized and schematized . . . models' (Hempel 1965: 424–5). As he told us above, explanations in science *and* everyday contexts 'diverge more or less markedly' from the ideals set by his models.

18

So a 'scientific explanation' (in the second sense) doesn't seem to be either an explanation actually offered in science, or an ideal appropriate only for explanations offered in science or by scientists. The truth is that, as far as Hempel is concerned, the Hempelian models of scientific explanation, if they provide an ideal for *any* explanations, provide an ideal for *all* explanations (subject only to the restriction described in the preceding section on the range of cases for which the analysis is offered). They are models of complete explanation, in science and in ordinary affairs. By 'scientific explanation' (in the second sense), Hempel means only 'a complete or full explanation', and nothing more.

I have developed my discussion of 'scientific explanation' around remarks of Hempel's. But I think that the lesson is general. 'Scientific explanation' is an expression that repeatedly occurs in most discussions of explanation. If 'scientific explanation' does not mean 'explanation actually offered in science', the sense of the expression is far from obvious, and needs to be made clear. Many philosophers of explanation use it merely in the sense of 'an ideally complete explanation'. Much of the potentially mesmerizing mystique of 'scientific explanation' will vanish, if this is kept in mind.

Partial and full explanation

The key, then, to unlocking the idea of a scientific explanation (in the second sense) is the distinction between complete or full and incomplete or partial explanation.[22] The distinction between partial and full explanations is a distinction between two different sorts of explanatory products; presumably, the activity of explanation-giving can at least sometimes justify giving partial rather than full ones.

It is not possible to draw the distinction between full and partial explanations in a neutral way, equally agreeable to all theories of explanation. Different theories disagree about what counts as a full explanation. Some will hold that explanations, as given in the ordinary way, are full explanations in their own right; others (like Hempel) will argue that full explanations are only those which meet some ideal, rarely if ever achieved in practice. A partial explanation is simply a full explanation (whatever that is) with some part of it left out. On any theory of explanation, we sometimes do not say all that we should say if we were explaining in full. Sometimes we assume that the audience is in possession of facts which do not stand in need of repetition. At other times, our ignorance does not allow us to fill some of the explanatory gaps that we admit occur. In such cases, in which we omit information for pragmatic or epistemic reasons, we give partial explanations.

Partiality is sometimes related to falsity. Laws may be omitted entirely from a partial explanation. Sometimes they are not omitted, but rather are given an incomplete formulation which ignores certain exceptions. If a law is an exceptionless generalization, an incompletely formulated law is a generalization with exceptions, and which is therefore not strictly true. Something not strictly true is just false. On other occasions, strictly relevant initial conditions might be too marginally relevant to the explanandum outcome to include in the explanans, and so the explanation, in order to present itself as if it were complete rather than only partial, may make a closure assumption about the environment in which the outcome occurs which is not strictly true.

Of course, whether some particular explanation is partial or not may be contentious. Since theorists will disagree on standards for full explanation, they are bound to disagree about which explanations are partial. All I assert is that every theory of explanation must draw some distinction between full and partial explanation, and that the idea of a partial explanation is parasitic on the idea of a full one.

Recall that in the first sense of the term, 'scientific explanation' refers to the explanations actually given in science. Most or all of these explanations are, like their ordinary counterparts, merely partial explanations for Hempel. It is consistent with my interpretation of Hempel that the way in which explanations actually given in science are partial may generally differ from the way in which actual ordinary explanations are partial. For example, typically ordinary explanations omit all mention of laws, and this may not be so in at least some areas of science. For example, in the first example of a scientific explanation given at the beginning of this chapter, even if it were to count as partial on some grounds, it does mention the law of the conservation of energy. In the second example, although a law is not explicitly mentioned, it proffers all the materials for the formulation of one in the concluding sentence. I return to the question of the place of laws in explanation, and the idea of a full explanation, in chapter VI.

In what follows, unless I otherwise indicate, I mean to be speaking of full explanation. If I want to speak of partial explanation, I explicitly use the qualifying adjective. I sometimes add 'full' as a qualification, if the qualification is especially important and stands in need of emphasis.

20

Bad explanations and no explanations

Is the concept of explanation for which we are seeking an explication the same as the concept of a good explanation? This question is highly contentious (e.g. it involves the distinction between semantics and pragmatics), and is inextricably bound up with other questions about explanation. I will have something more to say about this in chapter V. Whatever the right answer, it is important for a philosopher to be clear about how he would answer it.

Consider the following remarks by Hilary Putnam:

> Explanation is an interest-relative notion ... explanation has to be partly a pragmatic concept. To regard the 'pragmatics' of explanation as no part of the concept is to abdicate the job of figuring out what makes the explanation good. More precisely: the issue is not whether we count the pragmatic features as 'part of the meaning' – that is a silly kind of issue in the case of such notions as 'explanation' – but whether our theory does justice to them or relegates them to mere 'psychology'.[23]

Let's call Putnam an 'explanatory pragmatist'. I take that to mean that what counts, for him, as a full explanation of something (and not just as a *good* explanation of that thing) is audience-variant; the interests of audiences differ, and therefore what counts as a full explanation differs as a function of differences in interest. *Every* theorist of explanation can admit that the idea of a good explanation is audience-variant. Putnam is refusing to draw a sharp distinction between explanation and good explanation, and therefore argues that the idea of full explanation, not just that of good explanation, is audience-variant.

From my point of view, Putnam unjustifiably conflates the analysis of explanation with the pragmatics of giving explanations (or the pragmatics of information giving, for, following David Lewis,[24] I think that the requirements for explaining well are included in the requirements for conveying information well). Nor do I see why Putnam thinks this is a silly kind of issue. In this, I follow Hempel and others, in thinking that there is a clear distinction between the analysis of explanation and the pragmatics of explanation-giving. It will be my view that we can mark out what counts as an explanation by the information content of what is said. For example, on one specific sort of non-pragmatic view, a causal theory of explanation (this is not my view, but I use it for the purpose of illustrating the point), an explanation of an event e is always in terms of its cause, c. Perhaps not just any true statement of the form, 'c is the cause of e', would be an explanation. But to try to explain e in terms of some event that is not its cause would be, on this view, to produce no explanation at all. It would be to cite something simply irrelevant from the point of view of explanation. Such a requirement for explanatory relevance would *not* be audience-variant.

What a causal theorist, indeed any non-pragmatist about explanation, can concede is that how we select from the full list of explanatory relevant features in order to obtain the ones required in a particular (partial) explanation we may offer is a pragmatic and audience-variant question. A partial explanation is one that omits certain relevant factors; a full explanation is one that includes all relevant factors. In 'c causally explains e', one might be citing what is in fact only part of the cause (or, the cause only partially described, if one prefers). *The* cause of the match's lighting was its being struck. But if I say this, I assume that my audience knows or assumes that the match was dry and that oxygen was present, and that my audience has no further interest in having the dryness of the match or the presence of the oxygen mentioned. That is a matter of pragmatics. A partial explanation may be good relative to one set of circumstances, but bad relative to another, in which interests, beliefs, or whatever differ.

There are additional ways in which an explanation can be bad other than by being partial in its selection of relevant factors in the wrong way. A full explanation can be bad too, if it conveys more information than is required (suppose it sends the listener to sleep). A partial explanation can also be bad for other reasons. The cause could be described in a causally relevant but too general or too specific a way. In a history textbook, the occurrence of a plague can explain a population decline, but the explanation might be bad if it included a detailed microbiological description of the disease. Putnam himself contrasts the goodness of the simple explanation of why a 1 inch square peg will not pass through a 1 inch round hole in terms of geometry, compared with the awfulness of the far more complex and detailed explanation in terms of a complete enumeration of all the possible trajectories of the elementary particles making up the peg, obtained by applying forces, and the fact that no combination of them takes the peg through the round hole.[25]

But the non-pragmatist will insist that all of these remarks are about the *goodness* of explanations, and relate to ill-advised choices concerning selection from or description of *relevant* features. None of these concessions shows that there are no audience-invariant constraints on what could count as a relevant feature (for the purposes of explanation) and hence on what could count as an explanation.

In this book, I take it that the topic is the analysis or explication of the concept of explanation. I have nothing to say directly about pragmatic issues. That one can produce, contrary to Putnam's remarks, an account of explanation that distinguishes between explanations (whether good or bad) and non-explanations on the basis of information content, is best argued for not in the abstract, but by producing just such an account. It is this that I hope to do in chapter VII.

Some terminology

The expressions 'explanans' (i.e. that which does the explaining) and 'explanandum' (i.e. that which is explained) – and their plurals 'explanantia' and 'explananda' – occur repeatedly in this book. They also occur ambiguously, and this is intentional on my part.

If explanation is a relation, one can refer to its relata, whatever they may be, as 'the explanans' and 'the explanandum'. What ontological sort of entities are these explanantia and explananda? We shall discuss this issue fully in chapter V. Obvious candidates include: phenomena, events, facts, and true propositions (or beliefs or statements). Whichever candidate is selected, we can call this 'non-sentence explanation'. If events can explain events, then chunks or bits of reality (like the match's striking and the match's lighting) literally explain and are explained. Or perhaps it is the fact that some event occurred which explains the fact that some other event occurred.

On the other hand, another possibility is that it is true statements which explain true statements rather than events which explain events. (Propositions and statements are not sentences.) Even if this is so, statements explain and are explained only in virtue of the way the things in the world which they are about really are. If it is the statement that there is a short circuit that explains the statement that there is a fire, the explanation only works in virtue of the real short circuit bringing about the real fire (and although it would not be true, strictly speaking, that it is the short circuit that *explains* the fire).

On one well known theory we will be examining, we explain only if we can deduce a sentence describing the explained phenomenon from a sentence that describes the explaining reality and a lawlike generalization. In this way, then, one might also think of 'explanantia' and 'explananda' as sentences (which should be sharply distinguished from statements or propositions); e.g. 'the explanans entails the explanandum'. We can call this 'sentence explanation'.[26]

But if there is sentence explanation, it is conceptually dependent on the primary idea of non-sentence explanation (whether the right choice of relata for that relation is events, or facts, or true statements). This is, I hold, uncontroversial.[27] Even a theory that seeks to analyse explanation in terms of the logical form of, and logical relations between, various sentences is analysing the idea of explanation in the primary, non-sentence sense. The theory may attempt to 'reduce' the idea of non-sentence explanation to some facts about sentences, but it does not reduce non-sentence explanation to the idea of sentence explanation.

In this intentional ambiguity of 'explanans' and 'explanandum', I follow Hempel himself (except that he conflates 'sentence' and 'statement'):

> The conclusion E of the argument is a sentence describing the explanandum-phenomenon; I will call E the explanandum sentence, or explanandum statement; the word 'explanandum' alone will be used to refer either to the explanandum-phenomenon or the explanandum-sentence: the context will show which is meant.[28]

Context will also determine whether I am using 'explanans' or 'explanandum' in the sentence or non-sentence sense.

So, I variously employ these expressions to refer to *sentences, statements* (or *beliefs*), the *facts* and the *actual worldly events* the statements are about. The ambiguity is harmless; it often lets me say less clumsily what would otherwise involve cumbersome expression. In any event, even if we wished, it would not be possible to sort out fully the ambiguity, beyond what I have said here, in advance of the discussion in chapter V concerning the relata of the explanation relation.

Salmon introduces all three obvious non-sentence categories: statements, events, and facts:

> It is customary, nowadays, to refer to the event-to-be-explained as the *explanandum event*, and to the statement that such an event has occurred as the *explanandum statement*. Those facts – both particular and general – that are invoked to provide the explanation are known as the *explanans*. If we want to refer specifically to statements that express such facts, we may speak of the

explanans statements. The explanans and explanandum taken
together constitute the explanation.[29]

What the quotation appears to say is that the explanation relation *per se*
relates facts. The events such facts are about are the explanans event(s)
and the explanandum event. The statements which express such facts
are the explanans statement(s) and the explanandum statement. On
Salmon's view, we explain facts, which are about events, by means of
making various statements. One consequence of this view is that there
must be a significant distinction between facts and statements. In
chapter V, I return to these questions, and especially to the theme of
facts, and the role they might play in a theory of explanation.

Theories of explanation

Let me introduce what shall prove to be some useful distinctions
between different types of theories of full explanation, although the
extent of that usefulness can only be apparent as those distinctions are
applied in subsequent chapters. I stress that these are theories of *full*
explanation; I shall try and add some remarks about partial explanation
as I go along. The distinctions provide allegedly necessary conditions
for explanation, not sufficient conditions. Thus, these distinctions do not
themselves yield specific theories of explanation, but rather permit us to
catalogue specific theories as being of one or another of the types.[30]

The distinctions make use of concepts such as: event, causation,
determinism, indeterminism, certainty, probability, deductive and
non-deductive argument. In a book on explanation, it will be
unnecessary to offer analyses of these concepts. The purpose of
introducing them is only to show how they relate to explanation. I use
them, hopefully in ways uncontroversial to the matters at hand.

I introduce three sets of distinctions by which to categorize theories
of explanation, (A), (B), and (C). The typology which these three sets of
distinctions produce permits us to categorize theories of explanation in
two different ways: epistemologically and metaphysically. The first two
sets of distinctions, (A) and (B), are epistemological. Hempel, for
example, says that we explain something when we see that it 'was to be
expected; and it is in this sense that the explanation enables us to
understand why the phenomenon occurred'.[31] An expectation is a belief.
Must our belief about the occurrence of the explained phenomenon be
certain, or might it only be likely? Under (A), I distinguish between

theories of explanation which offer different answers to these questions.

Theories also differ about the form an explanation may take. I discuss these distinctions under (B). Must an explanation be an argument? I distinguish between argument theories of explanation (which answer the preceding question in the affirmative) and non-argument theories (which answer it in the negative). Argument and non-argument theories give somewhat different answers to the epistemological question of the certainty or probability of one's belief about the explanandum phenomenon. Argument theories can use the ideas of deductive and non-deductive arguments, as a way of giving substance to the ideas of certainty and epistemic probability; non-argument theories do not have this manoeuvre available to them.

The third set of distinctions which I use to classify theories of explanation is metaphysical, and I discuss this under (C). The relevant metaphysical distinctions involve, among other things, the ideas of causation, determinism, indeterminism, and nondeterminism. That is, different theories of explanation presuppose different things about the nature and extent of causation. A theme that runs throughout this book is the way in which an epistemic concept like explanation requires or presupposes a 'metaphysical backing'. I try to show how those differing metaphysical commitments partially motivate different epistemic views about explanation.

Probability is a highly ambiguous term, and although there are many kinds of probability, and various further distinctions one can draw within the two broad kinds of probability I distinguish, I want simply to separate epistemic or inductive probability from physical or objective or descriptive probability.[32] There are many competing accounts of each (e.g. frequency and propensity theories are competing accounts of physical probability; logical and Bayesian theories are competing accounts of epistemic probability). Epistemic probability is concerned in some way with support or degree of rational belief; physical probability is meant to be a matter of objective fact about the world. Obviously the two concepts of probability are related, although distinct. (Another term that can have both an epistemic and a metaphysical sense is the concept of what is necessary. 'Necessary' can either be construed as 'certain', or as 'objectively necessary'.)

(A) I begin, now, drawing the epistemological distinctions between different theories of explanation. There are certainty, high epistemic probability, and low epistemic probability models of explanation.

(These are three rival accounts.) On a certainty model of explanation, an explanans can explain an explanandum only if the explanandum is certain, given the information contained in the explanans. This is what we might call relative or conditional rather than absolute certainty; something may be certain, given something else, without being certain or indubitable *per se*. This is one of the ways in which one might interpret von Wright's remark: what makes an explanation explanatory is that 'it tells us why [an event] E *had* to be (occur), why E was *necessary* once the basis is there and the laws are accepted'.[33] 'Necessary' here might be construed as an epistemic idea; it is certain that E would occur, given knowledge of the basis and the laws.

On the other hand, one might only require of an explanation that the explanandum be (epistemically) probable, given the explanans information. '. . . we might try to salvage what we can by demanding that an explanation that does not necessitate its explanandum must make it highly probable.'[34] Salmon, in this passage, is suggesting that an explanans need only to make its explanandum epistemically probable (we need not discuss just yet whether highly so or not), but need not make it certain. An epistemic probability model says that there can be more kinds of full explanations than the certainty model allows. The former allows that there can be full explanations which meet the certainty model, and others beside. So they are rival accounts.

An epistemic probability model comes in a stronger and a weaker form. The strong model is a high epistemic probability model. It requires that in a full explanation the explanandum is at least highly likely, given the explanans information (or, the explanans highly supports the explanandum). Given the information in the explanans, we have good reason to believe that the explanandum is true, but perhaps not conclusive reason. It is true that the strong model has a certain vagueness about it, but it is not clear whether vagueness here is a strength or a weakness. What is highly likely? Any cut-off we select will appear arbitrary and unmotivated. But we might argue that this captures accurately the vagueness of explanation itself. The higher the probability of the explanandum, given the explanans, the more clearly we have an explanation. We have no clear intuitions, the strong modellist might say, about at precisely what point we cease having even a poor explanation and have instead no explanation at all. Moreover, this is entirely consistent with the non-pragmatic view that there is a distinction between poor explanations and no explanations.

Is 'explanation' genuinely ambiguous according to the epistemic probability model? This depends on the way in which the certainty-conferring and probability-conferring models of explanation are set out. The high epistemic probability model need not hold that there is a radical difference between the two kinds of explanation, since certainty is the limiting case of high probability. On the other hand, Hempel often speaks of these as two different types or kinds of explanation. That on its own is no more evidence for ambiguity than the fact that there are vertebrate and invertebrate kinds of animals is evidence for the ambiguity of 'animal'. However, Hempel says that there are different models for explanation, and given his views on models and analysis, this ought to mean that 'explanation' for him is ambiguous and stands for no single concept. Thus, he says: 'we have to acknowledge that they [explanations conforming to the I-S model] constitute explanations of a distinct logical character, reflecting, as we might say, a different sense of the word "because"' (Hempel 1965: 393).

The weaker version of an epistemic probability model does not even require that, in a full explanation, the explanans information provide good, although not necessarily conclusive, reason to believe that the explanandum is true. On this weaker version, the explanans information may only give some, albeit small, reason to believe that the explanandum is true; in one sense of 'expectation', the explanandum phenomenon was not to be expected at all. As Peter Railton says, the explanation 'does not explain . . . why the decay *could be expected to* take place. And a good thing, too; . . . there is no *could be expected to* about the decay to explain – it is not only a chance event, but a very improbable one'.[35]

Wesley Salmon has also argued that the explanandum might have a low probability, given the explanans. The quote from him four paragraphs back continues: '. . . even this demand [for high probability] is excessive . . . we must accept explanations in which the explanandum event ends up with a low posterior weight' (Salmon *et al.* 1971: 64).

There are two sorts of arguments for a low epistemic probability model of explanation. The first is simply the presentation of cases of explanation which appear to support such a theory. The most convincing examples are indeterminisitic ones, since they ground the low epistemic probability of the explanandum statement on the objective low conditional probability of the corresponding event. Both Salmon and van Fraassen use this example:

. . .a uranium nucleus may have a probability as low as 10^{-38} of decaying by spontaneously ejecting an alpha-particle at a particular moment. When decay does occur, we explain it in terms of the 'tunnel effect', which assigns a low probability to that event.

(Salmon *et al.* 1971: 152)

The thought here is that in both cases, the decay's occurring and the decay's not occurring, precisely the same information is relevant to the outcome. It seems arbitrary to allow that the information has explanatory force in the case of one outcome, but to deny that the information has any explanatory force in the case of the other.

This question should be considered by anyone who is inclined to accept a high epistemic probability model and deny a low epistemic probability model: why should exactly the same information, which intuitively seems equally relevant to both events, explain one but not the other? Of course, the convinced high epistemic probability modellist can always reply: because the information makes what is to be explained highly probable or likely in one case but not in the other. What is wrong with the reply is that it seems as arbitrary and unmotivated as the original doctrine. So the conclusion would seem to be: if explanations meeting the high epistemic probability model are acceptable, then we should sometimes be in a position to explain an explanandum on the basis of an explanans on which the explanandum is only improbable or unlikely.

A second argument that Salmon uses for the low epistemic probability model derives from a famous argument due to Kyburg.[36] Kyburg's argument concerned the class of reasonably accepted statements, 'an idealized body of scientific knowledge'. The question he raises is this: is the class of reasonably accepted statements closed under conjunction? Closure of the set under conjunction would amount to this: If S is a body of reasonably accepted statements, then the conjunction of any finite number of members of S belongs to S. Suppose p and q are members of the set of statements which are reasonably accepted by me. Closure under conjunction means that, for any p and q, if p and q are reasonably accepted, then (p&q) is reasonably accepted.

Now, a statement need not be certain (have a probability of 1) in order to gain admittance to S. Suppose that we decide to admit to the body of our reasonably held beliefs only those beliefs which are either certain or highly probable, say, with a probability of at least 0.85. We admit p and q (which we assume throughout are statistically independent), each of which has a probability of 0.9, and therefore qualifies for admission. Because of the basic multiplicative rule of the probability calculus, the belief (p&q) will have a probability of 0.81, below the bottom limit of acceptability. For whatever lower limit of acceptability that we set, some conjunction of what is accepted will itself be unacceptable. This seems in contradiction to the intuitively plausible closure principle, but Kyburg himself, in his article, counsels abandoning the principle despite its original appeal: 'It is difficult to give an argument against the conjunction principle, partly because it is so obvious to me that it is false, and partly because it is so obvious to certain other people that it is true' (Kyburg 1970: 77).

One implication of the conjunction principle that Kyburg thinks is false is that one has a right to believe the conjunction of all the statements one has a right to believe. Even if one has good reasons for believing each and every statement that one believes, one may still have a general argument for believing that some (but of course one would not know which) of the things one believes are false. If such a general argument were sound, then one would not have the right to believe the conjunction of all the statements that one has a right to believe.

Salmon has used this same basic argument in several of his writings,[37] but applied it to explanation rather than reasonable acceptance, to link the fates of the high and low probability models. Suppose S is now taken to be the body of explained statements (a statement is explained iff there is some explanans that explains it). Let's pretend we are high epistemic probability modellists, and say that a statement gains admittance to this set S only if there is some information on which the statement has a probability of at least 0.85. Again, suppose that p and q each have a probability of 0.9. If we accept the following conjunctive closure principle for explanation,

If S is the body of statements which have an explanation, then the conjunction of any finite number of members of S belongs to S,

then we can argue that (p&q) has an explanation which confers on it a probability below the required level. Whatever lower probability limit we set for explanation, an application of this argument (Salmon 1971: 80–1) will force us to admit as an explained statement some statement whose probability, given the explanans, is lower than the intended lowest limit. Hence, a low epistemic probability model of explanation must be true. Unlike Kyburg, Salmon holds fast to the conjunction principle, and accepts the consequence that there is no lowest limit to the epistemic probability an explanans must confer on the explanandum in order for the former to explain the latter.

Salmon, as far as I know, has never given any argument for holding on to the conjunctive closure principle for explanation, which is odd given the fact that Kyburg seeks to resolve his own puzzle by denying the parallel conjunctive closure principle for reasonable acceptance. Colin Howson has suggested rejecting the conjunctive closure principle for explanation, in order to hold on to a high epistemic probability model without being thereby saddled with a low epistemic probability model.[38] He points out that 'there is no general support for such a closure principle'. In view of the havoc conjunctive closure rules would bring in an example such as the set of reasonably accepted statements, Howson counsels arguing case by case for their use, and not assuming universally, as Salmon seems to do, that conjunctive closure rules are reasonable. However, even if we do not accept Salmon's second argument for a low epistemic probability model of explanation, adapted from Kyburg, the sorts of examples he and van Fraassen cite still constitute some evidence in favour of such a theory.

There is even a strong and a weak version of a low epistemic probability model of explanation. A strong low epistemic probability model will require that the explanans raise the probability of the explanandum from some prior probability, even though the resulting probability may still be low. The weak low epistemic probability model allows an explanation to further lower the explanandum's probability from some already low prior probability. (There is an analogous variant of the high epistemic probability model, according to which an explanation can lower an explanandum's high probability.) Salmon, for example, admits into an explanation explanatory factors which have such a negative effect on the epistemic probability of the explanandum.[39]

An example of such a low epistemic probability explanation which even further lowers the probability of the explanandum, according to Salmon, is this: consider a mixture of uranium 238 atoms, with a very long half-life, and polonium 214 atoms, with a very short half-life.[40] The epistemic probability of an atom's disintegrating if one knows that it was uranium is low; the epistemic probability if one knows that it was polonium is high. The epistemic probability that some unspecified atom in the mixture will disintegrate is somewhere between that for uranium 238 and polonium 214 atoms. This gives the epistemic probability of disintegration for an unspecified atom in the mixture, which we can assume is low.

Suppose some atom disintegrates in a short space of time, and we wish to explain this. If we learn that it was a uranium atom that disintegrated, then the explanans is: it was an atom of uranium 238. Its being an atom of uranium 238 explains the disintegration. (Note that the explanans is *not*: an atom of uranium 238 disintegrated, for that entails the explanandum.) One might object to this example, on the grounds that *simply* learning that it was a uranium 238 atom could hardly explain the disintegration. That would almost be like trying to explain something simply by assigning a name to it. But it is easy to remedy this defect. Suppose there are at least two different nondeterministic causal mechanisms leading to disintegration, one in the case of uranium and the other in the case of polonium, and what one learns is that one of the mechanisms rather than the other leads to the disintegration being explained.

The difficulty then is this. The epistemic probability of its disintegration given that it is uranium 238 is *less* than the epistemic probability of its disintegration given that it was merely an unspecified atom in the mixture, and yet we can explain why the unspecified atom disintegrated by saying that it was an atom of uranium 238. So, according to Salmon, 'the transition from the reference class of a mixture of atoms of the two types to a reference class of atoms of U 238 may result in a considerable lowering of the weight'.[41]

The epistemic probability models admit that there are different kinds of full explanation (certainty-conferring explanations and epistemic probability-conferring explanations). They might even admit that there can be these two different kinds of full explanation for the *same* explanandum. Suppose that there is an explanation for something that meets the certainty requirement, and another (full) explanation for the same thing, which only meets the weaker epistemic probability requirement. Must the high or low epistemic probability modellist admit that the explanation meeting the certainty requirement is necessarily the *better*? I do not think that they need to admit this. A *good* explanation is one that meets the interests, and assumes what it should assume about the beliefs, of the audience. We may prefer the epistemic probability-conferring explanation, as being simpler, less unwieldy, and more intuitive; in short, a better explanation, given what we want.

(B) Specific theories of explanation can also be distinguished by their views on the form an explanation must take: argument theories and non-argument theories of explanation. The three examples of explanation at the beginning of this chapter did not appear to be arguments, but appearances might be deceptive. Perhaps the examples should be recast in the form of an argument, or perhaps they are parts of arguments, the rest of the argument being implicitly understood.

An argument theory of explanation uses the idea of an argument to give substance to the ideas of both certainty and epistemic probability. Obviously, on no specific argument theory of explanation does just any argument count as an explanation. Different theories will add different further necessary conditions for explanation.

On an argument theory, what kind of argument is an explanation? Deductivism and probabilism differ about what sorts of arguments explanations can be. Deductivists are certainty modellists who hold an argument theory; probabilists are epistemic probability modellists who hold an argument theory. If an explanans can fully explain an explanandum only when the explanandum is certain, given the explanans information, and if all full explanations are arguments, full explanations must be deductive arguments. Deductivist theories require that all full explanations be, *inter alia*, deductively valid arguments. This is Karl Popper's view of causal explanation.[42] On a theory of this type, *only* a deductively valid argument could count as a full explanation.

On a probabilist theory, since an explanans can fully explain an explanandum even if the explanandum is only probable (to a degree less than 1) given the explanans information, inductive arguments provide another sort of argument that fits the bill (*in addition to deductive arguments*). Hempel's theory of explanation, since it admits both D-N and I-S explanations, is of this type. For the probabilist, some explanations are good non-deductive arguments whose premises support or make probable (to a degree less than 1) their conclusion. It is important to recall that the claim is about full explanation, since even a deductivist can allow a non-deductive relation between the explanans and explanandum in a *partial* explanation. The probabilist will accept that if there is sufficient information from which an explanandum can be deduced, then there will be an explanation that meets the deductivist requirement. But if there is insufficient information for a deduction, then we may have a full explanation which shows that the explanandum was epistemically probable, given the relevant information in the explanans.

Note that since there is no such thing as a valid non-deductive argument whose conclusion is improbable on the premises, the only viable sort of argument variety of the epistemic probability model is one which claims that an explanation may be a non-deductive argument whose premises render the conclusion highly probable. There is no argument version of a low epistemic probability model of explanation.[43]

Suppose that the assumption that all explanations are arguments were rejected. An explanation of something is constituted by a certain kind of information about the thing, but such information may not necessarily, or may even never, have the form of an argument. There are various possible non-argument theories: explanations are single sentences, or 'a story', or the conjunction of an argument and an addendum sentence, or a list or assemblage of statistically relevant factors,[44] or an answer,[45] and so on. The only thing such non-argument theories have in common is that they reject the assumption that all explanations are arguments. Wesley Salmon was one of the first contemporary philosophers to question the view that explanations are arguments;[46] historically, the argument view is entirely absent in Plato's writings, and only first makes its appearance with Aristotle.

On the non-argument view, there can still be relative certainty and epistemic probability models of explanation; it is just that these ideas cannot be cashed out by means of the idea of an argument of a certain sort. A non-argument (relative) certainty theorist might say, for example, that an explanation is a *sentence* which states that the explanandum is certain (has an epistemic probability of 1), given the explanans; a non-argument epistemic probability theorist (a high or low epistemic probability theorist, or a HEP or a LEP theorist) says that an explanation, in addition to the above, can be a *sentence* that assigns an epistemic probability of less than 1 to an explanandum, given the explanans. Such non-argument theorists would take explanations to be *sentences* which attribute conditional epistemic certainty or probability. Of course, there are many other non-argument theory possibilities; I mention these only by way of illustration.

I have called the general ideas of certainty and high and low probability conferring explanations 'models' of explanation. These models have both argument and non-argument forms. I now reserve the terms relative certainty theory, high epistemic theory, and low epistemic theory (HEP theory and LEP theory) for the specifically non-argument forms of these general doctrines. The relative certainty theory is the non-argument analogue of deductivism; high epistemic probability theory (HEP theory), the non-argument analogue of probabilism; low epistemic probability theory (LEP theory) has no argument analogue.

(C) An explanation is a piece of information, and the above distinctions have been concerned with the form in which such information has to be presented, and its epistemic status. I now want to concentrate on what such information must be *about*. We can distinguish theories of explanations by the metaphysical presuppositions they make about the reality they seek to explain.

It will be helpful in introducing this typology to assume something that I regard as false: *all explanations of singular events or states of affairs are causal explanations*. I will discuss this assumption in chapter VII, and broaden the kinds of singular explanations that there can be. It will then be easy to broaden the typology to take account of this, having already introduced it on the narrower assumption. But, in the interim, I will be making this (admittedly false) assumption.

Is causation (the idea of the whole or full cause) a deterministic concept? Some accounts of causation hold that it is, and others deny this. I do not wish, in this book, to become entangled in questions about the correct analysis of causation (if indeed there is one to be had at all!). So my discussion allows for the possibility that the idea of causation is not deterministic, and hence that some events may have nondeterministic causes, without assuming that this is so.

'Indeterminism' might name either of two doctrines: (1) some events have no cause; (2) some events have a nondeterministic cause (whether or not there are events with no cause of any kind). A nondeterministic cause, if such there be, is a cause, but of a special sort. To keep doctrines straight, I use 'indeterminism' as the name of the doctrine that asserts that some events have no cause of any kind; 'nondeterminism' as the name of the doctrine that claims that the idea of causation is not deterministic, and that some events have nondeterministic causes.

The idea of a deterministic cause is that the cause necessitates the outcome, that only one outcome is possible, given the cause (and the relevant laws of nature). Different theories will spell out the idea of determinism and necessitation differently. A constant conjunction theory might explain the idea of a deterministic cause in one way (it might add that the idea of necessitation, if it goes beyond constant conjunction, is illicit); a counterfactual analysis will provide an alternative way in which to understand determinism and necessitation. If we remember the earlier quote from von Wright, his use of 'necessary' might also be taken in this metaphysical sense: an explanation 'tells us why [an event] E *had* to be (occur), why E was *necessary* once the basis is there and the laws are accepted' (von Wright 1971: 13).

But many philosophers believe that some cases of causation are not deterministic, and hence that causation is not itself a deterministic concept. The nondeterministic view of causation has been argued by philosophers otherwise as different as David Lewis, John Mackie, Patrick Suppes, and Wesley Salmon, although these philosophers have tried to capture the idea of nondeterministic causation in different ways.[47] A cause, as Mackie argues, is not necessarily strongly sufficient for its effect.[48] If c causes e, Mackie says that it does *not* follow that if e had not been going to occur, c would not have occurred. A cause, on the Suppes view, raises the objective probability or likelihood of the occurrence of its effect from what it would have been had the cause not occurred, but it does not necessarily confer a probability of 1 on its occurrence. On Lewis's account, nondeterminism affects the necessity of a cause for its effect, not just its sufficiency. In Lewis's parlance, causation is chancy: if the cause had not been, the effect would have had less of a chance of occurring. For all of these writers, effects *depend* on their causes, without being determined by them.

Proponents of these nondeterministic views of causation are often responding to cases from quantum physics, but cite quite ordinary cases as well as supporting this nondeterministic analysis.[49] The kind of chance or probability needed by a nondeterministic view of causation is objective physical probability, although it is open to such a view to adopt any one of a number of competing theories about how such chance or probability is to be understood (relative frequencies, single-case propensities, and so on).

Given our earlier assumption that all explanation of singular events is causal explanation, theories of explanation can be classified as determinative, high, or low dependency theories of explanation. A determinative theory asserts that a necessary condition for a cause c fully to explain its effect e is that c physically determine or necessitate e. A high dependency theory asserts that a necessary condition for a cause c fully to explain its effect e is either that c necessitate e or that e highly depend on c (given the cause, its effect has a high physical or objective probability). A low dependency theory claims that, in a full explanation, an effect e might depend only slightly on its cause c (given the cause, its effect has only a low chance or physical probability of occurring).

Suppose that the outcomes that result from flipping a coin were objectively nondeterministic. If I flip such a coin which is heavily biased for heads and obtain a heads, and if my flipping of the coin was the cause of its landing heads, my flipping caused the landing of heads without necessitating it. Its landing heads highly depended on, but was not determined by, the flipping. On the other hand, if I flip such a coin and obtain the improbable outcome of a tails, and if my flipping of the coin was the cause of its landing tails, then its landing tails, although caused by the flipping, was improbable or unlikely, given the flipping.

Note that a determinative theorist need not deny that there are nondeterministic causes, or deny that there are some events with no cause in any sense. A determinative theorist can accept indeterminism and nondeterminism. He has only to deny that nondeterministic causes explain their effects, and deny that there are explanations for whatever is uncaused. For him, the nondeterministically caused and the uncaused are inexplicable.

Plato and Mill are proponents of a determinative view of explanation. For Plato, an explanans is the cause of its explanandum, and the causation is a form of compulsion or forcing. Mill (at least on the standard view of him) also holds that all explanation of singular events or conditions is by way of causal explanation, and that all causes are deterministic.

The determinative theorist will subscribe to some version of the certainty model of (full) explanation. If we explain only by citing causes, and if all explanatory causes are deterministic, then *full* explanations are always relative certainty-conferring. A full explanation must give the whole cause, and since the effect is the only possible outcome, given the whole cause, we can be certain that the effect will occur, if we know that the cause has occurred. Ignorance may mean that we do not know an effect's full cause, or for the sorts of pragmatic reasons discussed above, we may think it worthwhile to cite only some part of the cause (or some part of the cause's relevant description). When this is so, there can be partial explanations that do not meet the certainty-requirement. But the explanation would be only partial.[50]

High and low dependency theories of explanation allow explanation on the basis of nondeterministic causes. Statistical information, on this view, has explanatory relevance only when that information relates to the mechanisms that produce that outcome. Such mechanisms can be nondeterministic ones whose outcomes are highly likely but not necessary, or may even be unlikely (as in the example above of flipping the nondeterministic coin and getting the improbable tails). I agree with the spirit of Salmon's recent judgement, according to which the relevance of statistical relations for explanation can only be indirect.

Statistical relations are evidence for causation, but the causation for which they are evidence may itself be of a probabilistic or nondeterministic sort.[51]

What relation is there between high and low dependency theories of explanation, and the two epistemic probability models of explanation (in either an argument or non-argument version)? The high dependency theorist need not deny that there can be a full cause c of an effect e, such that the conditional probability of e on c is low. Such a theorist needs only to assert that such a cause is unable to explain its effect. However, neither a high nor a low dependency theorist will adopt a certainty model of explanation. *Their commitment to physical chance will be reflected in their commitment to an epistemic probability model of full explanation.* If some full causes are nondeterministic, and if we can sometimes explain by citing them, then on the basis of the laws of nature and the occurrence of the cause, it will sometimes be only highly epistemically probable (on one version) or even epistemically improbable (on the other version) that the effect will occur.

Although the view that some (unexplanatory) causes are nondeterministic is consistent with a determinative theory of explanation (as I argued above), the sole convincing motive, as far as I can see, for holding either a low or a high dependency theory of full explanation, and hence any version of the high or the low epistemic probability model of full explanation (in either an argument or a non-argument form), is a belief that the world contains, in some measure, nondeterministic causes, and that explanations are sometimes possible in spite of this. Since both of those beliefs seem eminently plausible, the motive is a good one.

If Hempel had said that all singular explanation was causal explanation (he does not hold this view, and we shall want to look at this very carefully in chapters IV and VII), we could have classified him as a proponent of a high dependency theory of explanation. The case for a low dependency theory of explanation has been made both by van Fraassen and Salmon.[52] The example of the improbable decay of the uranium nucleus, cited earlier as evidence for a low epistemic probability theory of explanation, can also be used as evidence for a low dependency theory of explanation.

Determinative, high, and low dependency theories of explanation have implications for inexplicability, as well as explicability. We would expect that the higher the demands for explanation, the more will turn out to be inexplicable. So, on a determinative theory, events with no

38

causes or with only nondeterministic causes are inexplicable, whatever else we might know about their occurrence. That may seem to make too much inexplicable.

On the other hand, one might wonder whether a low dependency theory does not set the standards for explicability too low, and make too little inexplicable. Let's accept that the tunnel effect causes the uranium nucleus's decay when it does decay, even though it has a low conditional probability of decay given that effect. But it does not follow from the fact that the tunnel effect was the cause of its decay, that the tunnel effect explains its decay.

Finally, a high dependency theory might seem to divide explicability from inexplicability in an ad hoc way. Salmon's arguments discussed above bring out one of the oddities of a high dependency theory for the question of inexplicability. In the case of the tossing of a coin with a strong bias for heads, the coin's landing heads is explicable, but its landing tails is inexplicable, although the same information is relevant in both cases.

The classifications I have introduced may seem overcomplicated, but I think they are necessary, to make sense of the literature on explanation. On the one hand, the classification shows how metaphysical beliefs, especially about determinism and nondeterminism, play an essential role in one's theory of explanation. On the other, explanation is an epistemic notion, and the classifications show how metaphysical commitments have consequences for the epistemology of explanation.

Dispensing with contrastives

The 'traditional' view, to which I subscribe, holds that, in an explanation, one explains facts such as, the fact that p (I shall conduct the discussion in terms of facts, but there are analogous statements of the view in terms of events: in an explanation, one explains, for example, an event e).[53] A number of writers have disputed the traditional view, and argued that what is explained in *every* explanation (including full ones) is something with a contrastive form: the contrastive fact that p rather than q (or, the event e rather than the event f).[54] The contrastive theory claims that a question, such as 'Why p?', is *always* implicitly of the contrastive form, 'Why p rather than q?', and that a question such as 'Why p?' typically will be ambiguous, for there are likely to be several different contrasts with 'p' which are possible.

Moreover, the contrastive suggestion is that whatever insights are contained in the contrastive idiom cannot be captured by the traditional theories of explanation which ignore that idiom. The contrastive view utilizes contrast spaces (Garfinkel) or contrast classes or a set of alternatives (van Fraassen), and these are unaccounted for on the traditional theories.[55]

This contrastive view should not be conflated with a distinct view, argued for by David Lewis, that links contrast to the pragmatics of explanation-giving. He claims that contrastive stress or explicit contrastive formulation is or can be a good way to indicate what part of a maximally true answer to a question is the part one wants to hear on a particular occasion.[56] On Lewis's view, a maximally true answer to an unambiguous question is non-contrastive. Lewis's view is not my target.

An anecdote about the American bank robber, Willy Sutton, is intended to illustrate the contrastive view that I have in mind. When asked by a priest why he robbed banks, Sutton replied that it was because that was where the money was kept. The contrastive diagnosis of this anecdote is that the fact to be explained, that Sutton robs banks, is merely elliptical for some contrastive fact, and that there is more than one contrastive fact for which it might be elliptical. The priest was no doubt wishing for an explanation of Sutton's robbing banks rather than not robbing at all; Sutton replied with an explanation of why he robbed banks rather than other institutions.

Although I have no objection to the contrastive terminology (and indeed will occasionally use it), I have two points of dispute with the contrastive view I have described. First, I do not believe that *all* explananda are contrastive. Second, even when contrastive terminology is appropriate, it seems to me that whatever insight it makes can be set out just as well in traditional terms, using non-contrastive facts (or, events and event failures). To simplify my discussion, I will hereafter speak only in terms of the explanation of facts; the extension of the argument to event explanation is straightforward.

The first question is whether all explained facts are contrastive. Suppose I want to explain the fact that Carl is a good philosopher. I do so by describing his excellent philosophical training, in the company of great philosophical masters. Sometimes I might have contrasts in mind: why he is a good philosopher rather than a good carpenter; why he rather than Hans is a good philosopher. But sometimes at least there is no obvious contrast, and, in the example I have mentioned, the information about his training seems to explain why he is a great philosopher, *tout court*. There is no obvious 'rather than' about it.

A contrast theorist has a ready reply to this. In such a case, I explain the fact that Carl is a good philosopher rather than his not being a good philosopher. Sometimes, the contrastive fact is this: the fact that p rather than ~p. This was the contrastive strategy in the Sutton example: 'The priest was no doubt wishing for an explanation of Sutton's robbing banks rather than not robbing at all.'

However, the fact that p rather than ~p, is just a tedious pleonasm for the fact that p. I do not claim that if one explains p, then one has *ipso facto* explained every proposition logically equivalent to p. But if it is a fact that p, it follows, by double negation, which only those bordering on idiocy could fail to appreciate, that it is not a fact that ~p. There is nothing more here to explain: a person explains the fact that p rather than ~p iff he explains the fact that p. So some explanations are not contrastive. I think that the priest wanted such a non-contrastive explanation from Sutton. In truth, what the priest wanted to know was why Sutton robbed, no non-pleonastic contrast being required.

There is no doubt that some explanations are contrastive. What is involved in explaining genuine contrastives, e.g. why event e rather than event f, or explaining the fact that p rather than q? One plausible-seeming thought is this: to explain the fact that p rather than q is just to explain the fact that p&~q. This view makes the pleonastic nature of 'the fact that p rather than ~p' clear, for it would be equivalent to 'the fact that p&~~p'.

Dennis Temple believes that this is the correct analysis for contrastives.[57] To explain a contrastive fact is to explain a certain type of conjunctive fact. Thus, in explaining why he robbed banks rather than other institutions, Sutton was explaining why he robbed banks *and* did not rob other institutions. If I explain why I live in London rather than Boston, I explain why I live in London and do not live in Boston.

One argument against Temple's plausible-seeming view runs as follows. For any arbitrary p and ~q, suppose I explain the fact that p and then I explain the fact that ~q. Let 'p' be 'snow is white' and let '~q' be 'it is not the case that grass is red'. *If* it then followed that I had explained the fact that snow is white and grass is not red, we would have a simple argument against Temple's suggestion. Even if I have explained the fact that snow is white and grass is not red, I certainly have not explained the fact that snow is white rather than grass is red.

In order to save Temple's analysis, we cannot allow that explanation is closed under conjunction. That seems independently plausible, since Kyburg's conjunctivitis seemed to teach the same lesson. So, if I explain

41

the fact that p and I explain the fact that ~q, it does not follow that I have explained the fact that p and ~q. The argument against Temple's suggestion is blocked, if explanation is not closed under conjunction. Let (a) be: '. . . explained the fact that p rather than q'; let (b) be '. . . explained the fact that p&~q'; let (c) be: '. . . explained the fact that p & explained the fact that ~q'. Temple's claim would be that (b) is the analysis of (a). For Temple's analysis to stand, (c) cannot be sufficient for (b), since (c) is certainly not sufficient for (a).

(c) cannot be necessary for (b) either. Untreated latent syphilis is the only cause of paresis, but only a small number of those who have untreated latent syphilis develop paresis. Suppose Jones but not Smith has untreated latent syphilis, and Jones gets paresis. I can (fully) explain why Jones rather than Smith developed paresis, on the grounds that Jones but not Smith had untreated latent syphilis. But, in view of the small number of those with untreated latent syphilis who develop paresis, I might not have fully, if at all (depending on one's view of explanation), explained why Jones got paresis.

On Temple's view, if I explain the fact that Jones rather than Smith developed paresis, I have explained the fact that Jones developed paresis and Smith did not develop paresis. But, in view of the above argument, it does not follow that I have explained the fact that Jones develops paresis. If Temple's analysis is to stand, explanation cannot be closed under simplification either. If I explain the fact that p&~q (p rather than q), it does not follow that I have explained the fact that p, and *a fortiori* it does not follow that I have explained the fact that p & explained the fact that ~q.

It is not so much that Temple's analysis is faulty. Rather, it is that (b), 'explains the fact that p&~q', does not really illuminate (a), 'explains the fact that p rather than q'. We cannot understand the conjunction sign within the 'explains' context in the normal, truth-functional way. Neither the conjunction nor the simplification rule holds. It is not then clear what 'explains the fact that p&~q' is supposed to mean, and the suspicion is that we can only understand the purported analysans, 'explains the fact that p&~q', in so far as we understand 'explains the fact that p rather than q', which is supposed to be the analysandum.

A difference (perhaps there are others) between (a), 'explaining the fact that p rather than q', and (c), 'explaining the fact that p and explaining the fact that ~q', seems to be that (a) requires some sort of relevance or connection between 'p' and '~q', and that (c) does not require this. I am doubtful that there is a single way in which to capture the relevance relation between the fact that p and the fact that ~q in all cases of explaining the fact that p rather than q. *One* way, which I described in an earlier article, is this: the fact that p 'eclipses' the fact that q. In some cases in which the explanation of the fact that p rather than q is more than the explanation of the fact that p and the fact that ~q, the 'more' has to do with this eclipsing.

For example, suppose I want to explain why a certain stone was in London rather than Boston in the late evening of 7 January 1986. It is insufficient to explain only why it was in London in that late evening, because – for all we know so far – the stone might have been in both places during the course of that late evening.

Often what is needed in order to explain why the fact that p rather than q (why the stone was in London rather than in Boston) is an explanation of how or why the fact that p (its being in London) is physically inconsistent with the fact that q (its being in Boston at that time). As I shall say, the fact that p eclipses the fact that q, where 'eclipses' means 'causally or physically prevents'. In many cases, like that of being in London rather than Boston, a person explains why the fact that p rather than q iff that person explains how or why the fact that p eclipsed or prevented the occurrence of the fact that q. The additional information needed is sometimes minimal, indeed often quite trivial. In the case of the presence of the stone in London rather than Boston, it is merely the information that its being in London physically prevents its being in Boston in the course of the same late evening.

Peter Lipton argues that cases of choice, surprise, and discrimination cannot be handled by my 'eclipsing' analysis. The paresis case discussed above is a case of explaining a discrimination. Jones's getting paresis does not eclipse, and is not physically inconsistent with, Smith's getting paresis as well. In this case, to explain why the fact that p rather than q is to show that a causally necessary circumstance for the fact that p was absent in the circumstances that led up to the non-occurrence of the fact that q. For example, untreated latent syphilis, present in Jones's case, was absent in Smith's. The analysis of this example will not replace my eclipsing analysis, but will have to be added to it.

I do not assert that the cases of eclipsing and of the presence–absence of causally necessary circumstances between them exhaust the content of all genuinely contrastive fact explanations (I have not discussed cases of choice and surprise, also mentioned by Lipton). There may be others. But if these two are indicative, I think that we can say that there are no explanations of *irreducibly* contrastive facts. These facts are reducible to (perhaps relational) non-contrastive facts: the fact that one thing prevented another; or the fact that something was present in one case but absent in another. It seems to me that such explanations can all be handled by techniques available to standard (non-contrastive) theories of explanation. So I stick to the traditional terminology in which to discuss explanation.

CHAPTER II

Plato on Explanation

In one sense, the whole of Plato's theory of the Forms can be read as an extended discussion of the requirements for explanation. However, what Plato has to say explicitly about explanation is mainly to be found in the *Phaedo* 95–107,[1] and in some remarks at the end of the *Theaetetus* 201–8,[2] to which I shall turn at the end of this chapter. This chapter on Plato is, on balance, less well integrated into the main lines of argument of the book than are the other chapters. In the main, I use Plato's strictures against the explanation of and by opposites as a way in which to pose the question of (what is usually called in the literature) probabilistic explanation. This is not a concept that Plato would have been prepared to accept, but I do not think it has been generally appreciated how his explicit remarks on explanation depend on that non-acceptance. I do not find in Plato many other insights about explanation which I wish to export from his text for my own use.

In chapter I, I ascribed to Plato a non-argument determinative theory of explanation. My interim account of a determinative theory of explanation (to be revised in chapter VII) is that it is one which asserts that the explanation of a particular is always by way of the deterministic or necessitating cause of that particular. However, terms like 'necessitating' and 'cause' did not mean for the Greeks what they mean for us, and some account needs to be taken of this, in attributing such a view to Plato.

In spite of Vlastos's spirited attempt to read a distinction between logical and physical necessity back into Plato's text, I do not believe that the text will bear the distinction.[3] Vlastos rests his case on the *Phaedo* 97a, 2–5, but it does not seem to me to bear out the distinction that he wants. I agree with Evan Burge's judgement:[4] 'What is not made clear

45

[in Plato's *Phaedo*] is the difference between different kinds of necessity, in particular the difference between logical and physical necessity' (Burge 1971: 8). When I attribute a view about necessity or necessitation to Plato, I think it should be understood as an undifferentiated idea of necessity, covering (what we would call) logical or mathematical necessity, metaphysical necessity, and physical necessity.

The Greek term, *aitiai*, in spite of its being standardly translated as 'cause', had for the Greeks, and hence for Plato and Aristotle, a much wider sense than it has for us. For us, a cause is the efficient cause, that which moves something or puts into motion some event, process, or whatever. As Vlastos reminds us, all of the following are, for the ancient Greeks, statements giving something's *aitiai*: the Persians invaded Attica because the Athenians raided Sardis; this statue is heavy because it is made of bronze; he is taking an after-dinner walk because of his health; this angle at the semicircle is a right angle because it is equal to the half of two right angles (the examples are Aristotle's). When Plato uses '*aitiai*' in the *Phaedo*, what does he mean by it? I return to this question after sketching an outline of his discussion of explanation.

Finally, Plato introduces three ontological 'levels', as it were, into his discussion: things like physical objects and numbers, which I represent by 'x', 'y', 'z' . . . etc.; the Forms, by 'A', 'B', 'C' . . . (Tallness, Coldness); and the individual instances of properties in the object, by 'f', 'g', 'h' (*my* tallness, *the rock's* coldness). The distinction between things and their properties is clearly drawn at 103b–c:

> Then we were talking about the things which possess the opposites, calling them by the same name as the opposites themselves have, but now we are talking about those opposites themselves which, by their presence, give their names to the things called after them. . . .

At 102d–e (and elsewhere), Plato distinguishes between Tallness in itself and 'that tallness which is in us', that is, Tallness and Shortness from the tallness of Phaedo and the shortness of Socrates. Let's call these latter 'individual characteristics', as distinct from the Forms. '. . . not only is the Form itself entitled for ever to the name that is given to it, but also something else which, while not the same thing as the Form, nevertheless in every instance, presents the manifestation of it' (103e). Individual characteristics are that something else.

The Phaedo

The *Phaedo* takes the form of a dialogue between Socrates and Cebes, and in what follows I identify the ideas expressed by Socrates in that dialogue as those of Plato himself, although this identification might be controversial, or mistaken, in some dialogues.[5]

The discussion falls into three parts. In the first (95e–99d), Socrates tells of his earlier attraction to explanations in terms of the physical causes of things which were offered by various pre-Socratic philosophers, and for a variety of reasons, some of which I shall examine in detail later in the chapter, he found these in the end to be unacceptable. Let us say that he rejects *physical* explanation. Notice that he did not find them less than fully adequate, and in need of supplementation. Rather, he says they are entirely unacceptable; he knows that he doesn't want to follow this alleged method of explanation at all (97b–c).

He then tells Cebes that he turned with high hopes to the sorts of explanations offered by Anaxagoras, which were supposed to be in terms of the best. Although Socrates does not offer an example of such an explanation, one assumes that they would be *akin* to what Aristotle would call 'final explanations' or what we would call 'teleological explanations'. Indeed, we might think of them as 'superlative-final explanations', for they explain things not just by the *good* at which they aim, but in terms of the *best*.

Socrates makes clear that such final explanations remain for him the preferred type of explanation to which one should aspire, but he expresses disappointment at Anaxagoras' practice, which Socrates claims departed from his stated intention, since Anaxagoras reverted to the sorts of 'explanation' in terms of *physical* cause that Socrates had already rejected. Again, he *rejects* the sorts of physical 'explanations' which Anaxagoras in fact offers, as 'quite absurd' (99a). The sorts of things physical explainers cite are at best necessary conditions for what is being explained, but they are not *aitiai* in any sense of that term: 'Fancy not being able to see that the real cause is very different from the mere sine qua non. . . . Yet that is what most people . . . seem to call "cause", using a name that doesn't belong to it' (99b). On the other hand, Socrates is clear that explanation in terms of the best, if there is such a thing, is genuine explanation involving the citation of an *aitiai*.

In the second part (100b–103a), Socrates introduces his own, admittedly second-best, approach to explanation, in terms of the Forms.

I call these 'Formal explanations'. Socrates first gives an account of the 'safe' version of such explanations. As Plato has Socrates saying at 100c: 'It seems to me that if there is anything else beautiful beside the Beautiful Itself, it is so purely and simply because it partakes of that "Beautiful".' Notice that these explanations, since they employ all three levels mentioned above, although safe, are not as obviously trivial as one might fear. The explanations do *not* just have this form: x is F because it participates in F-ness. Rather, it is this: x is f because it participates in A-ness. An example might be: Why is this rock cold? It has its coldness (f) because of the Form of Coldness (A) in which it participates.

Forms can never become characterized by their opposites. The Form of Beauty can never become ugly; the Form of Tallness can never be short. Similarly for the individual characteristics in things. Individual tallnesses can no more admit the short, individual beautifulnesses no more admit the ugly, than can the Forms themselves. '. . .what is more . . . that tallness which is in us never admits the short and will not be overcome by it . . . either it flees and beats a retreat whenever its opposite, the short, approaches it, or else, when that comes, it has perished' (102e). A thing, x, which becomes short does so only by the departure of its individual tallness, which is forced to flee the arrival of its shortness.

> . . .not only do these opposites [the Forms, and the individual characteristics in us] refuse to admit each other, but also those things which are not opposite to each other, but always contain the opposites, will not admit that character which is opposite to the character that they contain – instead, when it attacks, they either perish or retreat.
>
> (*Phaedo* 104c)

In the third and last part of the discussion (103a–106a), Socrates introduces a more informative, less safe, version of this kind of Formal explanation. A thing which is f is so, not just because it participates in the Form, A-ness, but because it participates in some other Form, B-ness, and its being B *compels* it (Plato's term at 104d) to participate in A, and hence be f. Why is this rock hot? Because it participates in the Form of Fire, and in virtue of this, it is compelled to be hot (103c–d), and indeed also compelled not to be cold: 'fire [brings with it] the opposite of the cold' (105a). As Socrates says, Threeness will 'compel' (104d) anything which admits it to be Odd, prevent it from admitting the Even.

One way in which to capture some part (but I doubt that it is all) of what Plato intended by this metaphoric talk of Forms compelling and forcing others, retreating and perishing, is with the idea of necessity. The Form of Fire necessitates or determines something to be hot, necessitates or determines the thing not to be cold. Plato is in some sense committing himself to a determinative theory of explanation: the *aitiai* of a thing's being thus-and-so determines it to be as it is. Formal explanations include some element of necessitation.

Otherwise, though, the interpretation of this extended discussion that I have quoted is far from simple and uncontroversial. If we permit ourselves for the moment Aristotelian terminology, Plato has introduced three types of (at least purported) explanation: physical explanation (the rejected 'explanations' offered by the physicists and Anaxagoras), final explanation (explanations in terms of the best), and Formal explanation (explanations in terms of the Forms). Efficient causal explanation, that closest to our modern conception of causal explanation, is arguably a more general category than just physical explanation, for the former leaves open the possibility of non-physical efficient causes. But this wider notion of efficient causation has not been introduced by Socrates as a distinct type; all that we have been offered by him is physical explanation, which is perhaps a particular kind of efficient causal explanation. Physical explanations, let us say, are efficient causal explanations in which the efficient cause is something physical.

What kind of explanation is Formal explanation for Plato, and how does it relate to efficient and final explanation? What is clear is that Plato rejects physical explanation (explanation in terms of physical things) as any kind of genuine explanation. But if there is a notion of efficient explanation wider than that of explanation by physical causes, then perhaps Plato thought that the Forms were another type of efficient cause, in place of physical substances.

Vlastos argues against this.[6] That is, he claims that Plato draws a distinction between logical and causal explanation, and saw that explanation by Forms was a species of the former rather than the latter: 'What Socrates is telling us, put into modern language, is that the reason why the group of ten is more numerous than the group of eight is simply that it satisfies the logico-metaphysical conditions of greater numerousness' (Vlastos 1969: 314–15). '...Plato ... uses the "safe" *aitiai* to explode pseudo-problems which arise when the categorial difference between logical and physical *aitiai* is ignored' (ibid., 325).

It is a modern doctrine that abstract (non-spatiotemporal) items can play *no* efficient causal role. The argument for this is often in terms of change: whatever causes or is caused must undergo real change, and abstract objects are not capable of real change.[7] The question that then arises is this: did Plato think of the Forms in the same way as we think of abstract objects?

At several places in 102–5, Socrates speaks of Forms doing things to particulars.[8] He says that Forms approach and take hold of particulars and compel or force them to have certain qualities. They depart when other Forms approach: 'Not only do opposite Forms refuse to stand firm at each other's attack. . .'(104c). Unless these are mere metaphors (perhaps they are, but this too needs detailed argument), Forms do not seem to be much like abstract objects in the modern sense. In spite of what Vlastos says, I cannot see any clear evidence in the text that Plato is distinguishing between two kinds of explanation at all. Whether he ought to have done so is, of course, a different matter.

Another point in favour of minimizing the difference between Plato's Formal and his efficient causal explanation is that Socrates says that those who offer physical explanations (the physical explainers) were attempting to explain 'generation and destruction in general' (95e–96b). Plato regarded Formal explanations as answers to *the same questions* that the physical explainers were unsuccessfully trying to explain; if so, Formal explanations attempt to explain why things come into and pass out of existence in terms of the Forms, and this seems clearly to be a kind of efficient causal explanation.

Vlastos attempts to find a sharp distinction between two kinds of explanation, efficient causal and logical, in Plato's text. I agree with the judgement of Julia Annas to the contrary.[9] In offering Formal explanations, 'there is no recognition' by Plato that this 'is something totally distinct from offering causal explanations. . . . Plato has failed to see that he is confusedly treating together very different kinds of explanation. . . . Plato shows no sign of any such grasp' that there is a distinction between the two kinds of explanation (Annas 1983: 324–5). Given that Plato also wants Forms to be changeless, he should have grasped that Formal explanation was not a kind of efficient causal explanation, but there is no sign that he did fully appreciate this.

Are Formal explanations final or teleological? It would seem not, since Plato tells us that he is still 'deprived' of teleological explanations, and has taken Formal ones as second best. If it was a complaint against physical explanation that they lacked any teleological element, Formal explanations, in both the safe and the informative versions, would at first glance seem to fare no better on this score. However, it is not at all clear how different Formal explanations and explanations in terms of the best really are. Vlastos dismisses the possibility that Formal explanation is a type of final explanation, or contains an element of teleology. Taylor argues that all Platonic explanations are meant to trace back to the Form of the Good, and hence be final or teleological in that sense.[10] Cresswell, following R.S. Bluck, reminds us that Plato speaks of the particulars as wanting, striving, and desiring to be like the Form itself (74d–75b), which, if taken seriously, might indicate that Plato did see the relationship between particular and Form on the model of an agent and a goal.[11] Again, the point seems inconclusive; it is not obvious what relationship Plato's Formal explanation bears to final or teleological explanation.

These are, however, not matters that I wish to pursue further. I am much less interested in questions of pure scholarship concerning Plato's system than I am in finding whether there is anything in what he says that can be of value in producing a viable theory or account of explanation. What I wish to concentrate on, then, is what Plato says is inadequate about the physical explanations advanced by his predecessors. I do not discuss all of these purported difficulties, for there are some which, I think, need not detain us. What I do wish to look at are his remarks about opposites explaining the same thing, and the same thing explaining opposites.

Platonic explanantia and explananda

The purpose of my discussion in this chapter (unlike my purpose in the other two historical chapters of the book) is *not* to set out accurately in detail Plato's thoughts. I do think that there are interesting ideas contained in what he is saying, and hence the justification for this chapter. But, in order to get at these ideas, I must read Plato anachronistically, by importing into the discussion a number of contemporary distinctions and insights that were not available to him. I do so shamelessly. When I come to look at his examples of 'unacceptable' physical explanations below, I shall not be interested in the detailed examples themselves, but in the general message which he – perhaps wrongly – extracted from them.

What sorts of entities does Plato think of as being explanantia and explananda? In truth, I doubt whether Plato thought much about this question. Certainly, he thought of Forms, or The Best, as explanatory, and these seem to be particulars or individuals of some sort. Plato is 'predisposed by his most frequent syntactical usages to regard a request for an *aitiai* as a request for giving an explanation by naming some entity'.[12] On the other hand, as we shall see, he surely sometimes thinks of explanantia as occurrences or states of affairs: a division and a bringing of two things together. It is easy to fit the example below of 'the head' into this latter pattern; it isn't the head that explains, but there being a head difference between the two men, and this latter seems to be a state of affairs. It will suit me, in what follows, to foist onto Plato an ontology of explanation that *at least* includes states of affairs and occurrences. Although a criticism that Aristotle makes of Plato that we shall look at in chapter III seems to depend on taking the Forms as explanatory in themselves, one might insist that it is not the Forms themselves which are explanatory, but the particular or individual's *participating* in some Form which is what explains why the particular is the way it is.

In raising Plato's problems about physical explanation, two words will be essential: the 'same' and the 'opposite' (explanans or explanandum). In so far as we ask questions about the *opposite* of what actually happened, our questions can be usefully phrased as questions about what happens in other possible worlds that does not happen in the actual world.

There are two different ways in which one might raise Plato's problems about *sameness*. The first way, (a), uses token identity across possible worlds; the second way, (b), needs only sameness of type of two non-identical tokens.

Consider some token event e that actually occurs. We can ask: (a) in other possible worlds, what would explain that very same token event e, or what would that very same token event e have explained? If we raise Plato's problems in this first way, we must hold all other causally relevant circumstances constant as we move from possible world to possible world.[13] After all, it isn't really just the match's striking which fully explains its lighting, but only its striking-in-the-presence-of-oxygen-when-dry, etc. For ease of exposition, I speak as if it is simply a token event like e that explains or is explained, but the reader must understand these and similar claims in such a way that all other causally relevant circumstances are implicitly assumed to be co-present with the token event in other possible worlds in which it occurs.

Alternatively we can ask: (b) what would explain or be explained by *a different* token instance e′, which is of the relevantly (for the purposes of full causal explanation) same type as e? Since I use possible worlds in any case to get at Plato's idea of opposites, I also get at the idea of sameness in the first way, using possible worlds and a single token event. But for readers who are happy with possible worlds, but unhappy with token identity across them, everything I say about sameness using (a) could be translated into the second way of speaking, (b). (b) achieves what (a) does in terms of the sameness of fully explanatory type to which tokens belong, rather than by holding all causally relevant circumstances fixed as one moves from possible world to possible world in which the same token event (re)occurs. (I assume the idea of a full explanation here as a primitive notion; Plato's question is whether physical explanations could ever count as full explanations.)

Problems for the physical explainers

Let me begin by quoting from two passages. First, 96c–97b:

> I had formerly thought that it was clear to everyone that a [man] grew through eating and drinking . . . only then did the mass which was small become large, and in the same way the small man big. . . . I used to think that I was justified in my conclusion, whenever a big man standing by a short one appeared to be taller 'just by the head' – and a horse taller than a horse in the same way; and there are still clearer examples of this – ten seemed to me to be greater than eight because of the addition of two, and the two-cubit measure to be greater than the one-cubit because it exceeded it by half its own length. . . . I am very far . . . from thinking that I know the explanation of any of these things. . . . if you cut one thing in half, I can no longer be convinced that this, the division, has been the explanation of the generation of 'two'; for there is a cause of the generation of 'two' opposite to that of the former instance. First, it was because they were brought together alongside of each other, and one was added to another, and next it was because one was taken away and separated from another.

The second passage occurs at 100e–101b:

> So you too wouldn't accept the statement, if anyone were to say that one person was taller than another by a head, and that the shorter person was shorter by reason of the same thing. . . . You

53

would be afraid . . . you might come up against an opponent who would say that the taller is then taller and the shorter is shorter by reason of the same thing. . . . You would be afraid to say that ten is more than eight by two . . . and that the two-cubit length is greater than the cubit by a half. . . . Then you would beware of saying that when one is added to one the addition is the explanation of the two, or that when one is separated off from one, the division is the explanation. . . .

Plato regards these, and other, features of giving an explanation in terms of physical cause as grounds for rejecting this sort of explanation altogether. Let me try to state what some of these features are. The *purported* explanations (which in the end he will reject as being bona fide explanation at all) that Plato has in mind, with explanans and explanandum identified, are these:

    (1) Explanandum: an instance of two things having come into being, where previously there had been only one thing.
        Purported explanans: a dividing of that one thing in half.
    (2) Explanandum: one person, t, being taller than another, s.
        Purported explanans: by a head, or in virtue of a head.
    (3) Explanandum: ten's being more than eight.
        Purported explanans: on account of two.

(The cubit-measure example seems to repeat whatever point it is that (3) makes.)

The gist of Plato's objection to these three purported explanations is this. Let's take (1) first. If an explanation like (1) were acceptable, then since 'there is an explanation of the generation of two opposite to that of the former', then an explanation like (1') would, in the appropriate circumstances, be equally acceptable:

    (1') Explanandum: an instance of two things having come into being, where previously there had been only one thing.
        Purported explanans: an adding of a second thing to that first thing.

Plato's argument is that if we accepted (1), we might have to accept (1') as well. But we cannot accept both (1) and (1'), for there cannot be two 'opposite' explanations of the same thing. So it follows that we can accept as an explanation neither (1) nor (1'). The kind of explanation the physical explainers offer, which commits them to there being opposite explanations for the same thing, is not a kind of explanation that we should accept.

How could this really be a problem? Are the explananda of (1) and (1′) about one token instance, or two? Surely there can be 'opposite' explanations for two different tokens. But one can see what bothered Plato, if my remarks in the previous section are recalled. Either Plato is asking whether there could be an explanation of the same token instance, *the* two things coming into existence, in another world in which *it* occurs (and holding constant all the causally relevant circumstances), but an explanation in terms of an adding rather than the dividing, or he is asking whether there could be an explanation of another token instance of what he takes to be the relevantly same (for the purposes of full explanation) type, an example of two things having come into existence, where previously there had been only one, but an explanation in terms of an adding rather than a dividing.

We shall have to go along with Plato's example, and pretend. Either we shall have to pretend that types, such as an adding of two things together, or two things having come into existence where previously there had been only one, are types under which a particular fully explains or is explained, or we shall have to pretend that the only causally relevant information that has to be held constant across the worlds in which the token adding, dividing, and generating of two things occur, is, for instance, that previously there had only been one thing. Both are utterly implausible, but I ask the reader to make the pretence, in this and Plato's other two examples, for I think the lesson he draws from such admittedly awful examples is worthy of serious interest.

A similar pattern of argument concerns (2) and (2′), and (3) and (3′), with the difference that Plato extends his argument to cover the case of the same explanation for opposite occurrences as well as opposite explanations of the same thing. If we were to accept (2) and (3), we would also sometimes have to accept purported explanations such as:

(2′) Explanandum: a person, s, being shorter than another person, t.
Purported explanans: by a head, or in virtue of a head.

(3′) Explanandum: eight's being less than ten.
Purported explanans: on account of two.

But it cannot be the case that 'the taller is then taller and the shorter is then shorter by reason of the same thing' (101a). So neither (2) nor (2′) is acceptable (and similarly for (3) and (3′)).

Since I have chosen (a) rather than (b) as providing the vocabulary for the discussion of Plato, we can express Plato's Principles as:

(PP1) Two opposites cannot explain the same thing.
(PP2) The same thing cannot explain two opposites.

The two principles make claims about the explanations there *could* be for and by the same token thing. We have already said quite a bit about what counts as 'a thing' for the purposes of the principles. But which things are *opposites*? I now turn to the task of elucidating (PP1) and (PP2).

Some terminology

There are a few additional questions of terminology on which I should like to be clear, before I begin the discussion proper of the principles on which Plato is relying, in making these claims about the unacceptability of some (pairs of) explanations. Some of his terminology is merely a historical curiosity, as far as I am concerned; other points need developing before we can extract anything of interest from this.

(1) Although I will try to reconstruct Plato's arguments using modern notions of contrariety and contradictoriness, in fact the primary sense of opposition for Plato is the opposition between two Forms, like addition and subtraction, tallness and shortness, more and less. Other oppositions (between physical things, events, bits of language) can only be understood in virtue of their participation in Forms which are opposed.

Moreover, for the Greeks, there are Forms which are opposite which would not seem so to us; addition and division, for example, were opposites for them. For us, there is no opposition, in any interesting sense, between Tallness and Shortness as such, that is, between t's being taller (than s), and s's being shorter (than t). *For Plato, there is opposition here, simply because the two states of affairs include opposite Forms.* It is clear that for Plato opposite states of affairs can, indeed (sometimes) must, simultaneously exist. At one and the same time, t *can be* taller than s and shorter than r; if t is taller than s, it follows that s *must be* shorter than t.

I think we will make headway by imposing on Plato the distinction between contrary and contradictory statements, in the usual sense, whether or not so doing permits us to remain faithful to the full intention of his text. The terminology is not his, and indeed it is clear that the distinction does not capture all of his examples of opposites. But I think that the modern terminology will help us state perspicuously at least the salvageable core of what Plato's Principle is asserting. In what follows, I speak of events or states of affairs as being contrary or contradictory, but this can easily be cashed out as statements about them being contrary or contradictory.

If we do impose on Plato's text our ideas of contrariety and contradictoriness, the assumption which he made, that two 'opposite' things can exist at the same time, must be rejected. If an event occurs, it follows that its contrary or contradictory (in our sense) cannot have occurred. For example, if x is blue all over at t, x cannot be red at t and x cannot fail to be blue all over at t. But of course we can still ask about what the explanation of the contrary or contradictory (merely possible) event, x's being red at t or x's failing to be blue all over at t, *would have been* if counterfactually it had occurred. It is this terminology that I shall use in what follows.

Two events are contrary or contradictory only as described, or only relative to specific descriptions. Two events can be contradictory when described in one way, but display no sort of opposition or incompatibility when described in another. Further, two events can be contraries when described in one way; contradictories when described in another. Suppose a ball that is blue all over at t had not been blue all over at t. Consider the world in which it is red at t. Its being red at t is merely contrary to its being blue all over at t. It could also have been yellow at t. However, if it is red at t, it follows that it is not blue all over at t, but its not being blue all over at t is contradictory to its being blue all over at t.

In chapter V, I develop the idea that explanation of an event is only of an event as described or conceptualized; talk of contradictory or contrary events here should always be understood as being relativized to some specific description of them. A modern doctrine has it that if c causes e, then it is a truth whatever true descriptions of c or e are used in the statement of causality. Clearly, when I speak of one event causing and explaining another in this chapter, this is not the sense of 'cause' I am using. The reader may think of my use of 'cause' in this chapter as shorthand for 'causally explains'. One event could causally explain a second when described in one way but could fail to causally explain the second when described in another way.

(2) It would be an anachronism to enquire about Plato's views on the place of laws in explanation. He had, as far as I can see, no explicit view about this at all. To some extent, I have brought laws in by the back door, by including all of the information from the appropriate law as part of the constant context for the particular token (or, alternatively, by insisting that the relevantly similar type in fact be the type which would occur in the statement of the appropriate law). Later, I will introduce a further reference to laws. The historical Plato notwithstanding, we shall not get very far unless laws find *some* place in the statement of Plato's Principles (although it need not be the same place given them by other theories of explanation).

(3) The middle period Plato of the *Phaedo* had not, as yet, sorted out the distinction between relational and non-relational properties. It is only the Plato of the late dialogue, the *Sophist*, who is able to draw this distinction.[14] For us, a person, t, being taller than another person, s, and a person, s, being shorter than t, are two different descriptions for the same state of affairs. For Plato, who would read all this non-relationally, since being taller and being shorter are opposites, t's being taller (than s) and s's being shorter (than t) are not only not the same state of affairs, but are opposite states of affairs. Similarly, Plato regards 10's being more (than 8) and 8's being less (than 10) as two opposite states of affairs. It is not worth our while to follow Plato in this tangle; the examples I employ in developing Plato's Principles will be non-relational in our sense.

Plato's Principles

My interest in the ensuing discussion will be to see what might be said in favour of Plato's Principles. Plato, to be sure, used his principles to discredit physical explanation altogether. The logic of his argument was that if one accepted any such explanation, then one would have to accept the opposite explanation, and so, since one should not accept both, one should accept neither. For Plato, an acceptable explanation is one such that there is no possibility of there being the opposite explanation at all, and he thought that only explanations in terms of the Forms (and presumably final explanations as well), but never physical explanations, could meet this requirement. A more plausible use of (PP) might be to assume that some physical explanations are acceptable, but if they are, then the opposite physical explanations are unacceptable. It is the latter use of (PP) in which I shall be interested.

Plato himself can be construed as using (PP2) in this more plausible form in his discussion in *The Republic* of the tripartite nature of the soul (436a–441c). Plato begins the argument by obtaining Glaucon's agreement to the following principle: 'It is obvious that the same thing will never do or suffer opposites in the same respect, in relation to the same thing, and at the same time' (436c). If we were to replace 'do or suffer opposites' by 'explain opposites', we obtain something very much like (PP2), but with the idea of 'one thing', in 'one thing cannot explain opposites', more finely sharpened, to include a specification of time, respect, and relation.

The use that Plato then makes of the principle stated at 436c is indeed concerned with the requirements of explanation, in particular psychological explanation. He considers the case of a man acting in various contrary ways ('contrary' in his sense, but not in ours): the man who both desires and refuses to drink (439c); the man who desires to see corpses and at the same time is repelled by the idea (440a). Plato's moral is that one cannot explain both of the contrary desires in each pair by the same explanans: his soul moves him. Such an explanation, in terms simply of the Soul, would explain the opposites of desiring and refusing, desiring and being repelled, by the same thing. The solution is to refuse to treat the soul as simply *one* thing. One faculty of the soul, reason, is one thing; another faculty of the soul, high-spiritedness, is another thing. In each of the contrary pairs, one desire must be explained by one thing, one part of the soul; the other by a different thing, a different part of the soul.

Even if we take into account all the remarks about terminology that I made above, Plato's Principles are still not expressed very precisely. Let 'd' refer to a token dividing in half of something, and 'g' to a token generating of two things where previously there had been only one, and 'D' and 'G' to the appropriate (adequate for the purposes of full explanation) descriptions or types respectively. I let '~d', '~g', '~D', and '~G' refer to tokens and types of these actions or events failing to occur. If d is a token event, ~d is an event omission, d's failure to occur at a specific time and place. I assume that, at least sometimes, failures and omissions can both cause and explain. As I indicated before, I assume throughout that although both d and ~d occur in two different possible worlds, the worlds agree in respect of all other causally relevant circumstances.

We might think that we could represent Plato's Principle (PP1) as:

(4) If d and ~d are contradictories, and if d explains g, ~d does not explain g.

(5) If d and e are contraries, and if d explains g, e does not explain g.

(4) and (5) cannot be what we need, because they are trivially true. If d explains anything, then d occurs. If d occurs, it follows that neither ~d nor e occurred (if d and e are contraries, then at most only one of them can occur; if d and ~d are contradictories, one but only one must occur). But since what did not happen does not explain anything, it follows that if d explains g, then neither ~d nor e does explain g. If there being two things where there had been one is caused and explained by a dividing, that *same instance* of there being two things where there had been one is not also caused and explained by an adding. This surely cannot be all Plato is trying to tell us.

The above argument relies on the premiss that what does not happen does not explain anything. Is this really true? Can't we sometimes explain things on the bases of lacks, failures, and other sorts of absences? Of course we can, but the sense in which we can does not constitute a counterexample to my claim. For example, suppose my failure to come to the party explains why the party was a bore. The occurrent token event which has explanatory force is my failing to come to the party. My failure to come is what *did* happen. What does not occur, viz. my not failing to come to the party (viz. my coming to the party), is what has no explanatory force.

So we need a rendering of (PP1) which has its consequences in the subjunctive mood. If d and ~d are contradictories, or if d and e are contraries, then if d explains g, trivially neither ~d nor e *do* explain the same token g, nor indeed do they explain anything else for that matter, since it is impossible for either to occur if d does. The right question is not: do ~d or e explain?, but rather: *could* they have explained? As I claimed before, if we use the terminology of (a) in which to express the Platonic puzzle, the right question must be about an explanation there could or could not have been. The first of Plato's Principles is expressible in some form such as this (this is not the final and ultimately acceptable version):

(6) If d and ~d are contradictories, and if some token event d explains some token event g, then there is no possible world in which ~d occurs, and in which ~d explains g.

(7) If d and e are contraries and if d explains g, then there is no
possible world in which e occurs and in which e explains g.

Plato's point is this: if, in one world, d occurs and does explain g, then,
although there are many other worlds in which ~d or e occurs rather than
d, in none of them does either ~d explain g or e explain g.

I have laboured this point a bit, because I think that it is relatively
easy to miss this subjunctive consequence requirement in formulating a
claim like Plato's Principle. Indeed, I think that Hugh Mellor implicitly
misses the point in setting out his argument against a low dependency
theory of explanation.[15] Thus far, we have been trying to formulate a
version of (PP1), but Mellor, and the theories he is attacking, are
concerned with (PP2). In fact, Mellor is arguing in effect for (PP2).

Mellor argues by reductio against a low dependency theory of
explanation in the following way. Suppose d did explain g which is
improbable given d (let g's low probability be p). But if d did explain g,
it could just as well have explained ~g, since ~g will be highly probable
(1–p) given d, and hence has at least as good a claim to be explained by
d as g has. (Let us take for granted that a theory of explan- ation which
said that we could explain improbable but *not* probable events would be
implausible.) Low dependency theories are committed to the view that
some explanans d could explain both g and ~g, and since that is
impossible, Mellor argues that d cannot explain g which is improbable
given d. Mellor's argument here relies on the premiss that no explanans
could explain both g and ~g, and this is in substance (PP2).

But why should we accept that no explanans could explain both g and
~g? His argument for this (with 'g' and '~g' substituted for his 'q' and
'~q') is as follows:

(a) Explananda must be true.
(b) No theory of explanation is acceptable if the criteria it
    proposes for a successful explanation 'are indifferent to the
    explanandum's truth value.'
(c) An explanans that could relate as well to a false as to a true
    explanandum is no explanation at all.
(d) Therefore, nothing explains g that 'would by the same token'
    explain ~g.

(Mellor 1976: 237)

Mellor's argument, as set out above, relies on a crucial modal
ambiguity. What (b) rules out is d explaining ~g if d explains g, since it

61

is not possible to explain what does not happen any more than it is possible that what does not happen explains something. But if Mellor's argument is to cut against low dependency theories, it must establish something much stronger, modally speaking. It must show that if d does explain g, d *couldn't* have explained ~g, had ~g occurred instead of g.

We can make this point in possible worlds terminology. What (b) says is that if d explains g in a world, then it is not possible for d to explain ~g in that same world (because in that world '~g' is false). What Mellor needs in order to dismiss low dependency explanation is that if d explains g in a world, then there is no other possible world in which ~g rather than g occurs, and in which d explains ~g. Mellor's argument certainly cannot show this. Considerations about the truth of the explananda will surely rule out d's explaining g and ~g in the same world, but could not rule out d explaining g in a world in which g occurs, and d explaining ~g in some other world in which ~g occurs. After all, in the other world in which ~g occurs, '~g' will be true, rather than false, unlike in the first world. So low dependency theories do not 'relate' an explanans to a false explanandum in the sense that the explanandum can be false in the world in which it gets explained by the explanans.

In the argument above, if (d) is read in an indicative sense, it follows from the conjunction of (a), (b), and (c). Nothing explains both g and ~g in the same world. But in the indicative interpretation, (d) is consistent with low dependency theories of explanation. If (d) is read in the subjunctive sense, that nothing that explains g in one world explains ~g in any other world, it is inconsistent with low dependency theories, but the premisses Mellor adduces go no distance in showing that (d) is true. So Mellor's argument for (PP2) neglects the indicative/subjunctive mood distinction that we have found crucial in formulating both parts of (PP).

(6) and (7) do not provide a plausible formulation of (PP1), for the following reason. Even if token event d explains token event g, surely there must be some logically possible world in which ~d explains g, and another in which e, d's contrary, explains g. (And this is so, even when the worlds share all causally relevant circumstances.) If Plato's Principle denied this, it must be wrong. If we allow all the logically possible worlds, then some of them will differ from our world, namely, the one in which d explains g, in respect of their laws. In the actual world in which d explains g, there may be a law that Ds cause (and hence, let us suppose, explain) Gs. Even so, there is a logically possible world with the law that ~Ds (or, Es) cause (and explain) Gs, and in that world ~d (or, e) explains g. If we allow unlimited changes in natural laws, there is

no difficulty in allowing possible worlds in which ~d or e explains g, even when d explains g in the actual world.

In order to get Plato's Principles correctly formulated, we need to identify a subset of the logically possible worlds, namely those with the *same* laws that hold in the actual world. We need to select those worlds with the laws of nature fixed as they are in our world, and in this way yet another consideration of laws must enter into a formulation of (PP1). Let's call this subset of the logically possible worlds 'the nomos-identical possible worlds' (nomologically identical possible worlds), or the n-possible worlds for short. So (PP1) should be formulated as the conjunction of (8) and (9):

(8) If d explains g, and if d and ~d are contradictories, then there is no n-possible world in which ~d explains g.

(9) If d explains g, and if d and e are contraries, then there is no n-possible world in which e explains g.

(8) and (9) capture, I claim, what is *salvageable* in (PP1). (PP2) concerns itself with the explanation of contrary and contradictory explananda by the same thing. Taking our cue from (8) and (9), (PP2) should be formulated as the conjunction of (10) and (11):[16]

(10) If d explains g, and if g and ~g are contradictories, then there is no n-possible world in which d explains ~g.

(11) If d explains g and if f and g are contraries, then there is no n-possible world in which d explains f.

It is important to include this implicit reference to laws for another reason. Couldn't a pair of 'explanations' by opposites confer *high* probability on both g and ~g? Suppose in the actual world d explains g and g has a probability of p, given d. Suppose further, contrary to (10), that there is some other possible world, call that world 'w', in which d explains ~g. It is true that, in the actual world, ~g's probability of occurring (it never, of course, occurred) given d was 1–p. Are we entitled to assume that in w, ~g will still have a probability of 1–p, given d? As we switch possible worlds, couldn't the conditional probabilities of events change? Couldn't it be the case that g, given d, has the probability p in the actual world, but that it is ~g (rather than g), given d, that has probability p in w, the same probability that g, given d has in the actual world?

In general, of course, it is true that the conditional probabilities assignable to events will change across logically possible worlds. But recall that we are only interested in a subset of those possible worlds, namely the n-possible worlds. These are worlds which have the same laws. If worlds are deterministic, they will share deterministic laws; if worlds are nondeterministic, they will share stochastic laws. In virtue of stochastic nomos-identity, whatever g's probability conditional on d is in the actual world, *it* will have the same probability conditional on d in all n-possible worlds.

Consider then two possible worlds with the same laws, and suppose d occurs in both. In world w, the conditional probability of g, given d, is p. Is it true that the conditional probability of ~g, given d, in any other world with the same laws must be 1–p? There might after all be the following two laws which obtained in *both* of the nomosidentical worlds: (1) whenever a D but not an H, the probability of a token event of type G is p; (2) Whenever a D and an H, the probability of a token event of type ~G is p. There could, of course, be two such laws. But this will not provide a counterexample, because of the requirement of stability of causally relevant circumstances across worlds. It is not true that all the causally relevant circumstances are the same in both worlds. In one world, d occurs in H-ish circumstances; in the other, d occurs and there are no H-ish circumstances.

Plato's (PP2)

What might be said, whether by Plato or more generally, in favour of (8)–(11), as formulations of Plato's two principles? Let's take the second principle, as expressed by (10) and (11), first. Mellor, in the argument I cited earlier, was arguing for a high dependency theory of explanation, against a low dependency theory; in effect, he was arguing for (10).[17] It is (10) that has received the most attention in the contemporary literature.

What, for example, would be involved in the rejection of (10)? Suppose d does cause and explain g, and suppose further that there were some n-possible world (a world which shared all its laws with the actual world) in which d causes and explains ~g. In one of the worlds, suppose that bringing an atom to a certain level of 'excitement' causes and explains its decay, and that in another possible world bringing the atom to the same level of 'excitement' causes and explains its failure to decay (and of course holding all other causally relevant circumstances fixed in the two worlds).

A necessitating or determining cause is, let us say, sufficient[18] in the circumstances for its effect. One thing is clear: *it is inconsistent with the supposition above that d is a necessitating or determining full cause of g*. If d is the sufficient or determining cause of (and explained) g in one world, d must be the cause of (and explain) g in all n-possible worlds in which it occurs (and in which all other causally relevant circumstances are the same). This is just what 'sufficiency' means. In particular, d would have to cause g in that n-possible world in which it occurred and was also the necessitating or determining full cause of (and explained) ~g.

It is impossible that there be a world in which both g and ~g occur. Therefore, if d causes and explains g in one world, and causes and explains ~g in some other n-possible world (and all other relevant causal circumstances are the same in both worlds), such causation cannot be deterministic, and such explanation cannot be accounted for by a determinative theory of explanation. Such causes cannot be sufficient for their effects, except in the weak and uninteresting sense of material sufficiency.

So if we reject (10), we must accept explanations employing nondeterministic causation, and the n-possible worlds will include probabilistic or stochastic laws of causation. A rejection of (10) will commit the rejector to a non-determinative theory of explanation. Indeed, the rejector of (10) is committed to a *low dependency theory*, for d causes and explains (in different possible worlds) g and ~g, one of which must have a low objective probability given d. Contrapositively, acceptance of a determinative theory of explanation commits one to (10). It should come as no surprise that Plato's adherence to (10) is coupled with, and indeed underpinned by, his determinative theory of explanation.[19]

How do matters stand with (11)? Two statements are contraries if not both can be true (although they might both be false). Suppose that d explained g in the actual world, but could explain f in some other n-possible world, and that f and g were contraries. For example, suppose in one world the emission of a certain particle from a source causes and explains its landing at position p_1 on a photographic plate, and in another world the emission causes and explains its landing at position p_2 on the plate (and of course holding all other causally relevant circumstances fixed between the two worlds).

An application of the previous argument will show that a rejection of (11) also implies rejection of a determinative theory of explanation, for otherwise there would be a possible world in which both f and g occur. If (11) is surrendered, it is also the case that some explaining causes will not be sufficient for their effects. In this way, we can see why Plato would have been led to embrace (11) as well as (10), which I have jointly referred to as (PP2).

If we, unlike Plato, were willing to reject a determinative theory of explanation, would we then be free to accept that one explanans can explain two contrary explananda? If f and g are contraries, then ~(f&g). The probability calculus tells us that in this special case in which $p(f+g)=0$, $p(fvg)=p(f)+p(g)$. Since all probabilities are less than or equal to 1, $p(fvg)\leq1$. Substituting, $p(f)+p(g)\leq1$. Therefore, it follows that $p(f)\leq1-p(g)$.[20]

So if the probability of either one of f and g is high, the probability of the other is low. If d explains both, it must be able to explain an explanandum with a low probability. A high dependency theorist cannot accept the explanation of two contrary explananda by one explanans, just as such a theorist could not accept the explanation of two contradictory ones by one explanans. This is something only a low dependency theorist can accept. Only a low dependency theorist can reject (10) or (11).

Plato's (PP1)

What of (8) and (9), which I have jointly referred to as (PP1)? (8) and (9) cash out the idea of the unacceptability of opposite explanations of the same thing, rather than the idea of the unacceptability of the same thing explaining opposites. Unlike the same explanation for opposites, (10) and (11), there has been little or no discussion of Plato's (PP1) in the contemporary literature.

There are two lines of argument that might be tried, in order to argue for (8) and (9). The first focuses on the necessity of a cause for its effect; the second addresses the intuition that such explanations are empirically empty. Let's take (8) first. If (8) is rejected, then there could be two n-possible worlds, otherwise identical with regard to causally relevant circumstances, and in one of which d occurs and causes (and explains) g; in the other, ~d occurs and causes and explains g.

Just as the rejection of (10) commits the rejector to a form of non-deterministic causation in which a cause is not in the circumstances sufficient for its effect, rejection of (8) commits the rejector to causation in which a cause is not, in the circumstances, necessary[21] for its effect. After all, if d was necessary for g in the first world, and since the second world is just like the first in point of both laws and other causally relevant circumstances, g will not occur in the second world unless d does. But the supposition is that, in the second world, g occurs in spite of d's failing to occur (~d occurs). So if d is a cause of g in the first world and if ~d is a cause of g in the second, neither d nor ~d can be a cause which is *necessary* in the circumstances for its effect.

Can there be causes which are not necessary in the circumstances for their effects? There is disagreement about this, and I have no desire to take sides in the dispute, but only to point out how Plato's Principles link up with certain ideas about causation. In chapter I, I mentioned that John Mackie insists that a cause be strictly necessary in the circumstances for its effect, although it need not be sufficient.[22] A nondeterministic cause, according to Mackie, is not sufficient in the circumstances for its effect, but even a nondeterministic cause is necessary in the circumstances for its effect. David Lewis, on the other hand, speaks of chancy causation: if the cause had not been, then the effect would have been less likely to occur, but might still have occurred.[23] On the Lewis account, a cause is not even necessary in the circumstances for its effect. So, a rejector of (8) needs causes which are not necessary in the circumstances for their effects, if such there be; those unwilling to accept this (like Mackie) could not consistently reject (8).

We can also show that the rejection of (9) commits the rejector to causes which are not necessary in the circumstances for their effects. The two worlds are alike in all relevant respects (laws and circumstances) save this one: in one world, d occurs and causes and explains g, and in the second world, e, d's contrary, occurs and causes and explains g. In that second world, since e occurs, d cannot occur (they are contraries). So, in the first world, d cannot be necessary in the circumstances for g, because g can occur without d (as g does in the second world). If d causes and explains g in the first world but e does so in the second, neither d nor e can be a cause which is necessary in the circumstances for its effect.

The second argument for (8) concerns the apparent empirical 'emptiness' of an explanation for g in terms of d, if there could have been an explanation (in otherwise the same circumstances and with the same laws) of g in terms of ~d. In truth, the same intuition sometimes informs arguments in favour of retaining (10). John Watkins, for example, says this about explanations of 'opposite' results in terms of the same information:

> if d can 'explain' g given that g turned out to be true, then d could have explained ~g at least as well had ~g turned out to be true [according to a low dependency theory]. ... Thus, d, as well as 'explaining' the occurrence of the event depicted by g, could equally well have 'explained' its non-occurrence. I hold that such a dual purpose 'explanation' that will serve whichever way things go, does not provide a genuine explanation of the way things actually went.[24]

Suppose d causes and explains g, and, contrary to (8), suppose that there is an n-possible world in which all causally relevant circumstances are the same and in which ~d causes and explains g. It would be tempting to suppose that this supposition means that g would be 'caused' and 'explained' 'whichever way things go', and therefore that the 'explanation' would be empirically empty. Within these possible worlds which have the same laws and the same fixed causally relevant circumstances, g will be 'explained' whatever happens, so how can the explanation of g depend or be contingent upon *anything*? (This argument assumes the Law of the Excluded Middle, but we can take that as uncontroversial for the purposes of this argument.)

The above argument from empirical emptiness is more complicated than might at first seem to be the case. The empirical emptiness argument presupposes something that has not yet been made explicit. Let 's' be that subset of logically possible worlds which have the same laws and the same fixed causally relevant circumstances as does the world in which d causes and explains g. The argument from empirical emptiness presupposes that occurrences of d and ~d in s have *the same explanatory impact* on g, from which it is concluded that the causal or explanatory impact of either d or ~d on g in s-worlds must therefore be nil. Within worlds in s, *it cannot matter to g whether d or ~d*.

However, d and ~d are irrelevant to the explanation of g in the worlds in s, only if they both explain g to the same extent or with the same impact in all the worlds in s. On a determinative theory, this requirement of sameness of explanatory impact is automatically met. If d explains g in a world in s, then g's occurrence is *necessary* in any s-world given d (d is sufficient for g); if ~d explains g in a world in s, then g's occurrence is *necessary* in any s-world given ~d (~d is sufficient for g). But d and ~d between them exhaust the possibilities, so g's occurrence is unconditionally necessary in any world in s. The empirical emptiness of the purported explanations relates to the fact that neither d nor ~d seems really to make any difference to g's occurrence in s. Since Plato holds a determinative theory, we can also see why he would have held (8).

We can similarly show that, on a low or high dependency theory, if d and ~d confer the same likelihood on g's occurrence, then the 'explanation' is empirically empty, because d and ~d make no difference to the *likelihood* of g's occurrence in any s-world.

The argument for this last contention is as follows. Suppose that it is claimed that d explains g, since given d, g is probable to some degree (whether the probability is high or low) and also that ~d explains g, since given ~d, g is probable to some degree (whether high or low). In the special case in which the probability of g, given d, and the probability of g, given ~d, is *the same*, we can reject the supposition that both d and ~d explain g by means of the following argument. If the probability is the same, then d is statistically irrelevant to the probability of g. That is,

$$p(g/d)=p(g/\sim d) \rightarrow p(g/d)=p(g)=p(g/\sim d)$$

But since the two dependency theories of explanation conjoin explanatory power with dependency, d is explanatorily irrelevant to g as well. On the determinative account, the supposed explanation of g by d and ~d collapsed because of the determinative irrelevance of d and ~d to g; g was unconditionally necessary in s. In the case of a high and a low dependency account of explanation, in the special case in which d and ~d confer the same probability on g's occurrence, there is a parallel dependency irrelevance of d and ~d to g in any s-world. g has an unconditional probability p in s-worlds (not conditional at any rate on d or on ~d).

But there is no reason why any dependency theorist who wanted to argue for the explanation of g by d and by ~d within s would have to assume that the likelihood or chance of occurring conferred on g by d and by ~d was the same. As far as the requirements of the probability calculus go, if d confers probability n on g and ~d confers probability m on g, m and n might not be, and indeed it would be exceptional if they were, equal. Both m and n might have any value between 0 and 1. Both m and n might be high, or both might be low, or one might be high and the other low. There could be two stochastic laws, *both* of which held in the worlds in which d causes and explains g *and* in the worlds in which ~d causes and explains g: if a D-type event, then there is a probability *n* that a G-type event; if a D-type event fails to occur (~D), then there is a probability m that a G-type event ($m \neq n$). Intuitively, whether d or ~d is not irrelevant to g's occurrence.

If d explains g and ~d explains g, what do d and ~d do to g's unconditional or prior probability? We can show that if d raises the probability of g from whatever probability it had, then ~d must lower that probability. The argument runs as follows:

(1) $p(g)=p(g/d) \, p(d)+p(g/\sim d) \, p(\sim d)$ [follows from the probability calculus: the definition of conditional probability and additivity].

(2) Suppose that $p(g/d)>p(g)$ and that $p(g/\sim d) \geq p(g)$.

(3) Then $p(g)>p(g) \, p(d) + p(g) \, p(\sim d)$ [by substitution in (1)].

(4) $p(g) \, p(d) + p(g) \, p(\sim d) = p(g) \, (p(d) + p(\sim d))$ [by factoring].

(5) $p(d)+p(\sim d)=1$ [the probability calculus].

(6) $p(g) \, p(d)+p(g) \, p(\sim d) = p(g)$ [by substitution in (4)].

(7) $p(g)>p(g)$ [by substitution in (3)].

Whether we assume a high or a low dependency theory, this result is the same. If we assume that both ~d and d raise the probability of g from some unconditional or prior probability (or even that one raises that probability and the other keeps it the same), we can derive a contradiction. So if both d and ~d cause and explain g within s, then if one of them raises g's probability, the other must lower g's probability.

Imagine that g's unconditional probability is 0.97. Suppose d raises it to 0.98. ~d might only lower the probability of g to 0.96, so the probability of g, on both d and ~d, might be very high, both after the raising and after the lowering. The requirement that one of the contradictory pair lower the probability of the explanandum is consistent with g's probability being high or low, given d or given ~d. However, although the rejection of (8) is therefore consistent with both high and low dependency theory, assuming that d and ~d do not confer the *same* probability on g, explaining an explanandum by contradictories is consistent only with the forms of these doctrines which permit an explanation actually to lower the probability of what is being explained.

Finally, what of (9), the idea that contraries cannot explain the same explanandum? We cannot use the argument from empirical emptiness in the case of contraries, because contraries do not exhaust the possibilities in the way in which contradictories do. Suppose we have a machine that sorts through balls of three different colours, balls that are red all over, balls that are blue all over, and balls that are green all over, and either unfailingly or with a certain probability rejects balls if and only if they are either red or green. The machine unfailingly or with a certain probability accepts blue balls.

Suppose there is some specific ball, b, that is red and which the machine rejects. If asked to explain why the machine rejected ball b, I can reply that it is because b was red. But if a contrary state of affairs had obtained, b's being green, b's being green could have just as well explained b's rejection. So we could have explained the same explanandum, ball b is rejected, by a contrary explanans, b is green, if b had been green. b's being red and b's being green are only contraries, and do not jointly exhaust the relevant empirical possibilities, which, in the light of the machine's laws of working, explain the machine's behaviour. It is this fact that saves the explanation from emptiness or non-contingency. So the rejection of (9) is well-motivated, and is consistent with all theories of explanation, and we might therefore wonder why Plato subscribed to (9). We could explain the same explanandum by means of two contrary explanantia, whatever our theory of explanation might be.

There are, however, cases in which we dislike explanation by contraries. Suppose some psychological theory explains a piece of behaviour by citing the agent's inferiority complex. Suppose further that, had the agent had a superiority complex, the theory would have explained the same piece of behaviour by citing the superiority complex. (I assume that the two explanations will have *some* other differences in what they explain, for otherwise they will be empirically equivalent.) We intuitively feel that this sort of explanation is empty. Strictly speaking, 'Agent a has a superiority complex' and 'Agent a has an inferiority complex' are merely contraries, because both cannot be true but both might be false, and we have already seen that there is nothing intrinsically wrong with explanation by contraries.

The two statements are strictly contraries, because 'Agent a has neither an inferiority nor a superiority complex' is non-empty. It is empirically possible that both 'Agent a has a superiority complex' and 'Agent a has an inferiority complex' be false. Agent a could have had a lobotomy, or be dead, or be in a permanent catatonic trance. But although these are possibilities, they are not the sorts of possibilities up for consideration by the theory in the way in which the possibility of the ball's being blue, as well as red or green, was up for genuine consideration in the preceding example. This is to say, I think, that we often relativize the possibilities to the theory at hand, and what are in fact technically contraries often get thought of as *if* they were contradictories, as if (~d&~e) was empty for all the practical purposes the theory is intended to cover. For the purposes of the psychological theory being assessed, having a superiority complex and having an inferiority complex between them exhaust the relevant possibilities.

I conjecture, then, that in those cases in which we are uneasy about the possibility of explanation of the same explanandum by contraries, it is because we think of the contraries as if they were contradictories. (9) is false, but there are interesting special cases like the one from psychology in which a suitably restricted version of (9) would be true. In those cases in which we think of the contraries as genuine contraries, in which we think of (~d&~e) as non-empty, there is no reason to accept (9).

The Theaetetus

I now turn to some of Plato's remarks in the *Theaetetus* 201d–210b. In that dialogue, Plato is discussing knowledge, but given the close relationship between explanation and knowledge, both of which are epistemic or at least quasi-epistemic concepts (or so I shall argue in chapter V), it is hardly surprising that some of the things he says about knowledge are, or can be construed as being, relevant to explanation. On several occasions, Socrates speaks of explicability and inexplicability, as well as knowability and unknowability.

Towards the end of that dialogue, Theaetetus suggests to Socrates the following analysis of knowledge: knowledge is true belief with the addition of an account (*logos*) (201d). In the contemporary epistemological literature, it is sometimes said that Plato's suggestion amounts to the claim that knowledge is justified true belief, but it is clear, I think, that 'an account' means more than 'a justification'. I may have a justified true belief that p if I learn that p from a reliable authority, but Plato would never have allowed this as a case of having an account for p. Plato here means by 'account' something more like 'an explanation'.[25] Theaetetus' suggestion, then, is that knowledge that p is true belief that p, plus having an explanation for p's being so. Aristotle's analysis of scientific knowledge, as we shall see, includes a similar requirement.

Plato addresses two questions about explanation in these passages: first, the question of the regress of explanation, whether explanation ultimately comes to a stop with something itself inexplicable; second, what it is to have an explanation for something, the additional element required for knowledge of that thing.

Plato discusses the regress of explanation question with regard to a specific theory about the stopping of that regress. On that theory, giving an account is tantamount to resolving something into its ultimate constituents. Complex entities can be analysed into their simple constituents. The complexes are explicable by means of that analysis; the ultimate simples, for which no further analysis or decomposition is possible, are therefore inexplicable. So explanation stops at the inexplicable simples.

Plato presents the doctrine with a dilemma: either the complexes are just the sums of their elements, or they are 'emergent' new entities which are more than their parts and therefore strictly speaking have no parts (or so Plato says). If the former, then anyone who knows and can explain the whole entity necessarily knows the elements: 'the letters must be neither more nor less knowable and explicable than syllables, since we made out that all the parts are the same thing as the whole'. If the latter, then as having no parts and hence no analysis, the syllables are simples and as unknowable and inexplicable as the letters. 'But if, on the other hand, the syllable is a unity without parts, syllable and letter are equally incapable of explanation and unknowable' (205d–e).

Note that, on the first horn of the dilemma, Plato is tacitly relying on the following principle:

(12) If x is a whole and $p_1 \ldots p_n$ are all its parts, and if x is just $p_1 \ldots p_n$, then x is explicable iff each of $p_1 \ldots p_n$ is explicable.

The idea is that one cannot get an explicable something from inexplicable parts. On the first horn of the dilemma, the whole is just the sum of its parts, so the whole is explicable if and only if *each* part is explicable. Of course, if the whole is just the sum of its parts, then if the whole is explicable, the sum of the parts must be. That follows from the law of the indiscernibility of identicals, and is uncontentious. But Plato is not just arguing this. He is arguing that if the whole is explicable, then not only must the sum of the parts be explicable, but *each* part must be (and conversely).

If this is meant to follow from a general principle that says that a whole has a property iff each of its parts has the property, then this seems to be a clear case of the fallacy of composition (or decomposition). One can get a vanishing Indian tribe from braves and squaws, no one of whom is vanishing. Of course, Plato might argue for (12) not as an instance of a general principle, but on its own, in virtue of the meaning of explicability. In that case, Plato needs to supply the missing special case argument.

On the second horn of the dilemma that Plato offers, the wholes are more than just the sums of their parts and indeed, as he argues, therefore strictly speaking *qua* emergent entities, they have no parts. On this horn, they would in fact be new entities, unities. A consequence of this would be that, like the elements, they would be neither knowable nor explicable, for there would be no parts through which, by analysis, they might be explained or known. To repeat: 'if . . . the syllable is a unity without parts, syllable and letter likewise are equally incapable of explanation and unknowable' (205e). The doctrine under examination was that partless simples, from which explicable and knowable complexes are composed, are themselves inexplicable. But if the so-called complexes become partless, emergent entities, or 'unities', then they too become inexplicable. His conclusion, then, is that 'we must not accept this statement – that the syllable can be known and explained, the letter cannot' (205e). Plato accepts that *both* the basic constituent elements or parts and the composite entities formed from them which are studied by an ordinary science (his examples at 206a–b are music and grammar) are knowable and explicable.

Although there is no mention of the Forms in this passage from the *Theaetetus*, no doubt Plato would say that it is only with the Forms that the regress of knowability and explicability can come to an end, for the Forms are self-explanatory, the high point in the process of dialectic such that there is no vantage point still higher by which to explain or through which to know them. One way in which to construe the famous Third Man Argument in the *Parmenides* is that it shows that the Forms must be self-explanatory.[26] Alcibiades is certainly beautiful, and his participation in the Form of Beauty explains why he is beautiful; his participation in that Form compels his beauty. The Form of Beauty is beautiful too; in fact, supremely beautiful. How can we explain the beauty of the Form of Beauty? If in terms of another beautiful form, in virtue of which the Form of Beauty is beautiful, we shall clearly be involved in an infinite regress. The Form of Beauty must self-explain its own beauty. So, Plato does not deny that there is an end in the chain of explanation. Indeed, there must be. What Plato insists upon is that the regress of explicability does not come to an end at the level of the analysis of an entity in terms of its parts or constituents.

As for the second question, what is it to provide an explanation or give an account, Plato canvasses three attempts at answering it, none of which is found to be satisfactory, and only two of which are of any interest to us. First, 'giving an account of x' might mean 'enumerating x's elements' (207a). Second, 'giving an account of x' might mean 'being able to name some mark by which the thing one is asked about differs from everything else' (208c), rather, I suppose, like offering a thing's individual essence. The second suggestion is dismissed as being circular, for one not only would need to *have* a notion of some distinguishing mark of x, but also would need to *know* that the mark was distinctive of x. This shows, if Plato is right, not that 'explaining' cannot mean 'knowing what is distinctive about a thing', but rather that no member of such a tight little family of interrelated concepts can be illuminating in analysing any other member.

The first suggestion is dismissed as being insufficient for explanation (or knowledge). Plato argues that I might know all the elements that compose x, and still lack an explanation of x. Plato's argument is that I cannot be said to know the syllable 'The' if, when I write 'Theaetetus' I write 'The' but when I write 'Theodorus' I write 'Te'. If I am in this situation, then, concerning the 'The' in 'Theaetetus', I can give an account, i.e. the letters that compose the syllable, in addition to having true belief, but I do not yet know 'The'.

I find Plato's argument against this first suggestion difficult to reconstruct in detail. In a more general way, though, the interest of these passages at the end of the *Theaetetus* is that they further reflect the Platonic disinclination to take physical explanation or (what Aristotle would call) material explanation seriously. However the argument is to be reconstructed, it is clear that its conclusion is that giving an account of a thing can't be the same as enumerating the thing's elements. In both the *Theaetetus* and in the *Phaedo*, physical explanations or explanations in terms of a thing's matter have been canvassed by Plato and found lacking.

Summary

What have we learned about explanation from the discussion of this chapter? It is true that, in comparison with the remaining historical chapters, there is little in this chapter that I shall want to carry forward as a substantial contribution to the theory of explanation that I advance in chapters V, VI, and VII. The main point of the chapter seems to be of great interest none the less. Plato was opposed to 'physical explanations' for the reason, among others, that they licensed the explanation of opposites by the same thing. When unpacked into my terminology, what Plato is opposing is a low dependency theory of explanation. However, his own theory is a determinative theory of explanation, which would disallow both high and low dependency explanations. In chapter VII, I develop a theory of explanation which, unlike Plato's, is compatible with any of the three theories: determinative, high, and low dependency theories of explanation.

CHAPTER III

Aristotle on Explanation

Does Aristotle have a general account of explanation? Richard Sorabji denies that he has: 'Of course, it would have been satisfying if he [Aristotle] had been able to give a perfectly general account of what explanation is. Since he does not. . . .'[1] On the other hand, Julius Moravcsik takes Aristotle to be offering just such a general theory: 'The claim that Aristotle's theory of *aitiai* is a general theory about explanation is further strengthened. . . .'[2] Who is right? Perhaps a proper answer to this question depends on what one counts as a 'perfectly general account', and two of the questions I shall want to address, in discussing Aristotle, are: what is a general account of explanation?, and how is one to justify one account over another? This last question returns us to a theme begun in chapter I. Is Aristotle's method for justifying an explication of explanation based on language use, or is it a 'technical' account, in the sense that I gave to those expressions in chapter I? If the latter, what considerations would Aristotle offer to justify his account?

The doctrine of the four causes

If anything in Aristotle could count as a general account of explanation, it would be his discussion of the four causes (*aitiai*) of things. Almost every philosophy undergraduate knows that Aristotle held that there were four causes of or explanations for things: the matter, form, goal or end, and motion-originator of a thing. I follow Julius Moravcsik, Max Hocutt, Julia Annas, and many other contemporary scholars, and take this doctrine to be about explanation rather than simply about causation as we understand that latter idea.[3] I refer to the traditional doctrine as 'the doctrine of the four causes', but I sometimes reform quotations

77

from older translations that refer to the *aitiai* of a thing, by changing 'cause' to 'explanation'. The doctrine of the four causes *is* about four explanatory principles. The modern conception of efficient causation is closest to, but by no means identical with, Aristotle's idea of the motion-originator, which is only one of his four 'causes' or explanatory principles.

Is it possible to cite an efficient cause, or indeed any other of the four items, but in an *unexplanatory* way? Aristotle develops a terminology in which one can do just this. Later in the discussion, I shall also need a term for an Aristotelian cause in a non-explanatory sense (what Aristotle calls 'the incidental cause'). When there is any possibility of confusion, I refer to these Aristotelian incidental non-explanatory causes as 'causes' *simpliciter*, and the causes that do explain as 'explanatory causes'. It must be remembered that these causes, both explanatory and non-explanatory, include not only causes in (what is close to) our modern sense, but also matter, form, and end or goal.

The doctrine of the four causes is set out in at least two different places, which I quote below. First, there is the following long passage in *Physics* II, chapter 3 (compare also *Physics* II, chapter 7), which is repeated almost verbatim in *Metaphysics* V, chapter 2, 1013a25–1014a25:[4]

> Knowledge is the object of our inquiry, and men do not think that they know a thing till they have grasped the 'why' of it. . . . In one sense, then, (1) that out of which a thing comes to be and which persists, is called 'explanation' . . . . In another sense (2) the form or the archetype . . . and its genera are called 'explanations'. . . . Again (3) the primary source of the change or coming to rest. . . . Again (4) in the sense of end or 'that for the sake of which' a thing is done. . . .
>
> This then perhaps exhausts the number of ways in which the term 'explanation' is used . . . .
>
> As the word has several senses, it follows that there are several explanations of the same thing. . . . Further, the same thing is the explanation of contrary results. For that which by its presence brings about one result is sometimes blamed for bringing about the contrary by its absence. Thus, we ascribe the wreck of a ship to the absence of a pilot whose presence was the cause of its safety.
>
> (*Physics* II, chapter 3)

Aristotle holds that one does not have the fullest type of knowledge about a thing unless one possesses an explanation for it. In this, he follows Plato, who, as we saw, held that knowing something involves being able to give an account of it. I return to Aristotle's analysis of knowledge later in the chapter.

A second passage in which the doctrine of the four causes is set out is in the *Posterior Analytics*, Book B, chapter 11. Aristotle again refers to his doctrine of the four causes and asserts that 'there are four explanations'. Formal, final, and change-initiator explanations are clearly mentioned, but where we expect material explanation, Aristotle speaks instead of 'if certain things hold, it is necessary that this does'. Aristotle says elsewhere that the premisses of a deduction are the matter or material explanation of its conclusion. Jonathan Barnes argues, convincingly in my view, and *pace* Ross, that in fact this sort of explanation is material explanation 'under a non-canonical description'.[5]

As the opening sentence of the first quotation above makes clear, Aristotle is thinking of explanation as whatever appropriately occurs in response to a why-question. He repeats this in *Physics* II, chapter 7: there are as many kinds of explanation as there are things 'comprehended under the question "why"'. Aristotle appears to put considerable weight on this grammatical point. How seriously should we take this? In my view, not very seriously.

In the contemporary literature, there are other sorts of questions with which why-questions are contrasted, e.g. what something is or how something was done. What kind of explanation is it if I explain what is wrong with my car or how the fight started? Surely there might be no difference between asking what is wrong with my car and asking why my car won't operate normally, or between asking how the fight started and asking why the fight started. On the other hand, some what-questions and how-questions are not interchangeable in this way with why-questions. Neither: 'What are the rules of chess?', nor: 'How does one greet the Queen?', are convertible to: 'Why [anything]?'

Could we say that an explanation is an answer to a why-question or an answer to a question which can, without loss of sense, be transformed into a why-question? But even this won't do. First, some why-questions can be understood as requests for justification or defence rather than explanation: why did the framers of the American constitution insist on a system of checks and balances?[6] An appropriate answer might be a justification in terms of the arguments the framers might have given for such a system, whether or not it was those arguments which actually moved them to include such a system in the constitution. Not all answers to why-questions are explanations. We require a prior sense of what an *explanatory* request is, in order to distinguish between why-questions which are requests for justification and those which are requests for explanation.

Second, Aristotle understands the idea of a why-question in such a wide sense, that one already needs a concept of explanation to see which questions are why-questions. That Aristotle thought of why-questions in a much wider sense than we do is confirmed by looking at *Physics* II, chapter 7, 198a15–20. Aristotle says that, regarding things which do not involve motion, a why-question relates to the what of a thing, e.g. to the definition of a straight line, or of commensurability. But can the 'what of a thing' be converted into a question with the form, 'Why . . . ?'?

Aristotle does insist that an answer to a why-question *can* be given in terms of a thing's essence, and in the case of things which do not involve motion, this will be the *only* sort of appropriate answer to a why-question. It may be that Aristotle was thinking that the question, 'What is a straight line?', was transformable into the why-question, 'Why are these lines straight lines?' Whatever he was thinking, I do not think that one can pick out which questions he thought were why-questions in the wide sense he intended, unless one already had in mind his doctrine of the four explanatory principles. Aristotle's remarks on why-questions should be taken merely as a heuristic device for picking out the area in which he is interested, not as an adequate philosophical criterion offering necessary and sufficient conditions for when an answer to a question is an explanation.

Aristotle also asserts that, since the word 'explanation' can be used in more than one way, there can be more than one explanation of the same thing. Some translations have Aristotle speaking of ways in which 'explanation' can be used; others (like the one I quoted above) have him speaking of 'senses of explanation'. In his discussion of the *Physics* passage, Wieland says that, according to Aristotle, 'Cause has several meanings in ordinary usage. . . . Strictly speaking, therefore, we are dealing here not with four causes, but with the four senses in which we speak of causes.'[7]

Wieland is simply wrong about this. Nothing in the text would justify us in attributing to Aristotle a full-blown semantic point, to the effect that 'explanation' is equivocal and can bear four distinct senses. Aristotle is offering a classification of different kinds (the Greek word here is *topoi*) of explanation, and it does not follow that *aitiai* bears four different senses. One can classify animals into various species and genera; it does not follow from this that 'animal' is ambiguous as applied to humans, ducks, and slugs. I know of nothing in the text to suggest that Aristotle is doing anything more than offering such a classification (Wieland also notes that Aristotle is offering a classification of explanations, but does not distinguish with any care between that and holding that the word 'explanation' is equivocal). I therefore stick to the less semantic-involving formulations: that 'explanation' can be used in four ways or with regard to four different elements of things or that there are four different types of explanation.

What are these four different types of explanation? Sometimes referring to the material from which a thing is made, sometimes referring to its form, sometimes to that which initiates change, and sometimes to that for the sake of which it acts, will be an appropriate reply to a why-question. Individuals capable of coming into being (i.e. generable primary substances) have explanations in all four senses.

> When one inquires into the cause of something, one should, since 'causes' are spoken of in several senses, state all the possible causes, e.g., what is the material cause of man? Shall we say, 'the menstrual fluid? What is the moving cause? Shall we say, 'the seed'? The formal cause? His essence. The final cause? His end.
> (*Metaphysics* VIII, 4, 1044a33–7)

Aristotle is not committed, though, to the view that things of every type or category, or even every particular of the type, substance, has an explanation in each of the four senses. Both things that are not substances (like the examples of straight line and commensurability mentioned above), and substances which are eternal may fail to have a material explanation:

> Regarding the substances which are natural and generable, if the causes are really these, and of this number, and we have to learn the causes, we must inquire thus if we are to inquire rightly. But in the case of natural but eternal substances, another account must be given. For perhaps some have no matter. . . . Nor does matter belong to those things which exist by nature but are not substances; their substratum is the substance. E.g., what is the cause of eclipse? What is its matter? There is none; the moon is

that which suffers eclipse. What is the moving cause which extinguished the light? The earth. The final cause perhaps does not exist.

(Metaphysics 1044b3–14)

Also, at *Metaphysics*, Beta, 995b, 22–35:

For how can a principle of change or the nature of the good exist for unchangeable things. . . . So in the case of unchangeable things this principle could not exist, nor could there be a good-itself. This is why, in mathematics, nothing is proved by means of this kind of cause, nor is there any demonstration of this kind – 'because it is better or worse. . .'.

As the passage from the *Physics* (and its repetition in *Metaphysics*) quoted early in this section makes clear, Aristotle obviously believed that an important consequence of the doctrine of four causes was the rejection of Plato's view that we discussed in the previous chapter, namely that the same thing (the pilot) cannot explain contraries. Or so I interpret the passage. Aristotle asserts that the same thing can explain contrary results. Aristotle seems anxious to make the point; it does not follow naturally from the doctrine of the four different types of explanation, which immediately precedes it in the text. I conjecture that Aristotle has Plato in mind in the discussion. To repeat the relevant portion of the *Physics* passage:

As the word has several senses, it follows that there are several explanations of the same thing. . . . Further, the same thing is the explanation of contrary results. For that which by its presence brings about one result is sometimes blamed for bringing about the contrary by its absence. Thus, we ascribe the wreck of a ship to the absence of a pilot whose presence was the cause of its safety.

(Physics II, chapter 3)

His view is that even if the pilot explains why the ship reached port safely, the pilot could also have been the explanation of why the ship did not reach port safely if the ship had failed to reach port.

Of course, Aristotle sees that the explanation is not just 'the pilot', but rather in one case it will be the pilot's steering the ship, in the other case the failure of the pilot to steer the ship. Aristotle often speaks of a thing or substance as efficient cause or motion-originator: Polyclitus as the cause of the statue; the doctor, of health; sperm, of the man. These are, for him, formulations of potential causes only. He distinguishes between actual and potential motion-originators (*Physics* II, chapter 3, 195b15–25). A full formulation makes clear that an explanation is in terms of the actual cause, the substance-as-doing-something: this healing person and that housebuilding man.[8]

To what extent is Aristotle's criticism of Plato fair, if this is what Aristotle had in mind? Not very fair at all. Aristotle does not himself really think that the pilot could be the explanatory cause of both shipwreck and ship safety, because he does not think that the pilot could be the full actual cause of either. The pilot on his own is only a potential cause.

As I remarked in chapter II, Plato does not really address himself to the question of the ontology of explanation. Certainly, sometimes Plato speaks, at least as far as the Forms are concerned, as if they *tout court* explain. But it would not take a great leap of imagination to see that what is really explanatory for Plato is some event or process or whatever: the particular participating in the Form, or the Form compelling the particular. Paraphrasing Aristotle, Plato could say: the Forms are only a potential cause; it is only the Form-as-doing-something (or, the particular-as-participating-in-the-Form) which is an actual cause.

This is certainly his general strategy. In *The Republic*, in the case in which it seemed as if it was a single substance, the soul, that explained contraries, on reflection he held that there were further distinctions to be made. The soul at one time and in one respect and in one part might explain something, but the soul at another time or in another respect or in another part could explain its contrary. So Plato could easily say that the pilot in respect of his steering the ship explains its safe arrival; the pilot in respect of his failing to steer the ship could explain its being wrecked, if it had been wrecked.

Does Aristotle have a general account of explanation?

Let's return then to the question with which we began. Does Aristotle have a general theory of explanation? We might put Aristotle's view in this way:

> (E) Something can be explained only by either its matter, or its form, or its end, or its change-initiator.

Is (E) at least the kernel of a general theory? I said that this question is

83

important. There is a way to trivialize the answer so that it has no importance, and I want now to rule out this trivialization. What counts as *one* theory or analysis of something? Suppose we have an analysis of p by r and of q by s? If we allow unrestricted disjunction, can we not say that we have a single theory or analysis of pvq, namely by rvs? I rule out artificial analyses formed by the *ad hoc* technique of disjunction, although I do not say that there could be no genuine, non-artificial case of a disjunctive analysis.

Now, (E) is a disjunction of conditions for explanation, and as I have just argued, the existence of a disjunctive set of conditions might not by itself count as a single general theory. But is (E) *just* an *ad hoc* disjunction formed from unrelated disjuncts? Aristotle appeared to have some reason for thinking that these four modes of explanation were exhaustive of the sorts of explanation there are: 'It is evident, then, even from what we have said before, that all men seek the causes named in the *Physics*, and that we cannot name any beyond these' (*Metaphysics* I, 10, 993a12–15). If any theory of explanation is not to be *ad hoc*, it must be based on something. But on what? In chapter I, I distinguished two broad approaches: the language users' approach and the technical approach.

Does Aristotle take the language users' approach, and base his theory on how the term 'explanation' or 'scientific explanation' was used, either by everyone in classical Greece or by classical Greek scientists or perhaps even just by classical Greek philosophers? As we saw earlier, this was the view of Wieland, against which I have already argued: 'The doctrine of the four causes does not consist of a recondite theory of fundamental metaphysical principles . . . but of something much simpler. Here . . . we are in fact confronted with the results of an analysis of linguistic usage' (Wieland 1975: 147). It is also the view of Peter Achinstein. Peter Achinstein asserts that Aristotle's view that explanation must be in terms of either form, end, matter, or change-initiator was based on semantic considerations about the meaning of the term.[9] As far as I can see, Achinstein's view, like Wieland's, rests on a rendering of the Greek text at *Metaphysics* 1013a25, as 'means semantically', for which, as I have already said, there is no warrant.

In support of the Wieland–Achinstein view, one might point to Aristotle's remarks under the topic of final cause in *Physics* II, chapter 3, where he seems to justify the category by an appeal to ordinary usage: 'Why is he walking about? we say: "to be healthy", and having said that, we think we have assigned the cause.' Although it is true that Aristotle refers to what we commonly say in his remarks on final causation, the style of his discussion of the four causes seems overall to be noticeably different from his discussions of many other topics, where he demands that his exposition 'save the appearances', by being in line with common opinion on the subject.[10] This is a line of argument that he appears to avoid with explanation.

The alternative would be to interpret Aristotle as subscribing to the technical approach, and as introducing a special concept of explanation, whatever linguistic usage may or may not be like. If so, we still have to confront the question of how Aristotle would justify his analysis over other possible competing explications of explanation. According to Julius Moravcsik, the Aristotelian theory of explanation is ultimately grounded on and to be justified in terms of metaphysics.[11] I agree with him.

To see how this works, Moravcsik offers the following Aristotelian definition of substance: a set of elements with a fixed structure that moves itself towards self-determined goals. The four factors in this definition are: element, structure, motion originator, and goal. These correspond to, and justify, the four types of explanation. Since everything else that can be said to be is an aspect of substance, the four types of explanation are both non-arbitrary and exhaustive. If Moravcsik is right, Aristotle does have (at least the kernel) of a general theory of explanation, grounded on metaphysical considerations, and (E) tells us what that kernel of a theory is. Aristotle's technical approach introduces a very special and distinctive idea of explanation, and Aristotle's metaphysics provides the justification for so doing. It may be that this concept of explanation was, to a greater or lesser degree, reflected in ordinary or specialist Greek speech, but whether or not it was, is irrelevant. Its defence is metaphysical, not linguistic.

In some ways, the contrast between metaphysics and linguistic usage as an anchor for a view of explanation is not well-expressed as it stands. Suppose it turned out that what lay behind linguistic usage was itself a certain metaphysical view of things (indeed, how could this fail to be the case, although it might of course be several incompatible metaphysical views which informed that usage?). I take it that Wieland and Achinstein are arguing that linguistic usage is where Aristotle stops; that there are no further metaphysical principles which one could uncover that lie behind that usage, for otherwise the contrast explicitly drawn by Wieland would be pointless.

On the Wieland–Achinstein view, Aristotle really does not have what might be called a general theory of explanation at all. There is just this four-fold linguistic usage, with no more general principles by which to unify or explicate the classification. The disjunction in (E) would be simply that: a disjunction of the ways in which the term is actually used (by everyone or by some). On this view, since based on linguistic usage, (E) would not be exactly *ad hoc*, but it is no more than a disjunction of four separate elements. Wieland attempts to block this unacceptable consequence of his view: 'the formal unity of these distinct meanings is established through a functional element, namely through the question "Why?"' Is Wieland's attempt successful?

I have already expressed my reservations about the usefulness of the why-question approach, but in any case the approach offers no real solution to the ultimately *ad hoc* disjunctiveness of Aristotle's concept of explanation, on Wieland's account. If 'explanation' were four-way ambiguous for Aristotle, and if all explanations were answers to why-questions, then 'why' ought to be four-way ambiguous as well. To ask 'Why?' would not be to ask a question that was unequivocal. Suppose that Aristotle's four senses of 'explanation' not only differed in meaning, but also had no part of their meaning in common. Then the unity provided by 'why' could only be an uninteresting kind of unity; 'why' would be syntactically a *single* word which also bore four different, non-overlapping senses.[12]

Aristotle, at least as interpreted by Moravcsik as rejecting this language users' approach, has supplied an answer to the question of how we might ground or justify a technical approach to the explication of explanation. Although explanation, being an epistemic concept, must suit our epistemic needs and capacities, it can do so only by fitting what we think the world itself is like.[13]

It may be that the concept of explanation that we actually use is outmoded; it has evolved over a long period of time, and it may reflect erroneous, or even incompatible, beliefs about reality. It may no longer fit what we currently think the world is like. It may be so outdated that conceptual tidying-up is no longer sufficient. If so, concept replacement is the order of the day. If possible, a concept of explanation should be adopted that fits what we think the world is like.[14] How we conceive of what the world is like, what its constituents are and how it works, will justify (at least in large measure) choice of concept of explanation. We have seen how Aristotle's account of explanation fits his metaphysics. What I shall want to explore in chapter VII is what *our* conception of explanation should be like, given what we know or believe about reality.

I do not necessarily presume that the metaphysics relevant to an account of explanation will be composed only of a priori or metaphysically necessary truths. There is room in a conception of metaphysics for the most general and abstract truths of contemporary science, and these may be a posteriori and contingent. Aristotle may have thought of his metaphysics as (in some sense other than logically) necessary, but certainly it was for him a posteriori. I think that Aristotle would have been sympathetic to the methodology of Wesley Salmon:

> what constitutes adequate explanation depends crucially upon the mechanisms that operate in our world. In all of this there is . . . no logical necessity whatever.
> I have not been trying to lay down conditions that must be satisfied by all admissible scientific explanations in all possible worlds. . . . My aim has been to articulate contingent features of scientific explanations in this world as we presently conceive it.[15]

The nature of metaphysics is not an issue that need detain us here; clearly, what I have to say is compatible with any view concerning the epistemic and logical status of metaphysics the reader might wish to adopt.

Incidental and per se causes

Polyclitus is a (potential) cause (the efficient cause or motion-originator) of the statue. However, Aristotle distinguishes between a substance as described in an explanatory way (Polyclitus, *qua* sculptor) and as not so described (Polyclitus, *qua* pale man). Aristotle calls Polyclitus *qua* sculptor the *per se* cause of the statue, Polyclitus *qua* pale man the incidental cause of the statue. For Aristotle, *per se* causes are explanatory causes; incidental causes are non-explanatory causes. 'Again we may use a complex expression . . . and say, e.g., neither "Polyclitus" nor "sculptor", but "Polyclitus, sculptor"' (*Physics* II, chapter 3, 195b5–12). The same must be true for the material from which something is made and the end or goal for which something strives. It is not just the material that explains, but the material as described in one way rather than another. It is not just the thing that is in fact the goal that explains, but the thing described in the terms under which it is desirable to the agent.

Aristotle says that the same is true of the thing explained: 'Similar distinctions can be made in the things of which the causes are causes,

87

e.g., of this statue or of statue. . .' (*Physics* II, chapter 3, 195b7–9). What gets explained by Polyclitus *qua* sculptor is the statue, *qua* statue and not *qua* a bronze object. Under the latter conceptualization, it presumably is explained by Polyclitus *qua* brazier. To use modern terminology, explananda, as well as explanantia, are only such when conceptualized in an appropriate way.

Aristotle gives us a definition of the incidental or accidental in *Metaphysics*:[16]

> 'Accident' means (1) that which attaches to something and can be truly asserted, but neither of necessity nor usually . . . for neither does the one come of necessity from the other or after the other, nor . . . usually. . . . And a musical man might be pale; but since this does not happen of necessity nor usually, we call it an accident. Therefore, since there are attributes and they attach to subjects, and some of them attach only in a particular place and at a particular time, whatever attaches to a subject, but not because it was this subject, or the time this time, or the place this place, will be an accident.
>
> (*Metaphysics* V, 30, 20–5)

Aristotle is distinguishing two senses of *aitiai*, only one of which can properly be tied to explanation. It is true that nothing in the text commits Aristotle to the view that this distinction provides two different *senses* of 'cause'; there is no more textual evidence to ascribe a semantic point to him here than there was in his discussion of the four-fold typology of causes. But I think that, if what Aristotle says here is true, then there are two different senses of 'cause'.

In the first, 'accidental' or 'incidental' sense, the concept of causation is not logically tied to the concept of explanation. *Aitiai* do not necessarily explain that for which they are the *aitiai*. In the second, *per se* sense, explanation and causation are tied, and therefore a cause in this sense necessarily explains what it causes. That difference amounts to a difference in the meaning or sense of the two usages of the term *aitiai*.

Suppose the sculptor was a pale man. In the incidental and non-explanatory sense, it is true that the pale man caused the statue to come into existence. In the explanatory and *per se* sense (or, as some translations have it, the 'in virtue of itself' sense), it is true that the sculptor caused the statue to come into existence. *In this latter sense* of *aitiai*, although the sculptor caused the statue to come into being, and even if the sculptor was a pale man, it does not follow that the pale man caused the statue to come into being. This *per se* sense qualifies as *non-extensional* in at least one meaning of that term, because substitution of singular terms *salva veritate* fails for that sense. Things (causally) explain and are explained only as conceptualized or described in an appropriate way.

Aristotle, then, is marking what we would call an extensional and a non-extensional sense of *aitiai*, only the latter of which is explanatory. As I indicated at the beginning of this chapter, where there is any chance of confusion, I use 'causally explains' or 'explanatory cause' for Aristotle's *per se* sense of *aitiai*, and simply 'causes' or 'cause' for the incidental or accidental sense.

In the passage quoted above, Aristotle also tells us how we are to distinguish between accidental and *per se* descriptions of the cause. The criterion for a description of a cause being a *per se* description rests on the existence of suitable laws. Suppose we have an assertion with the form, the F caused the G. We want to know whether the F, as conceptualized, is an incidental or a *per se* cause of the G, as conceptualized. The text quoted above began: '"Accident" means (1) that which attaches to something and can be truly asserted, but neither of necessity nor usually. . .'. Aristotle in effect is telling us:

(A) The F is the *per se* or explanatory cause of the G iff the F causes the G and 'F' and 'G' occur as (at least part of) the antecedent and the consequent respectively in the statement of a deterministic or a stochastic law.

The deterministic law covers the case in which things like that happen necessarily or, anyway, always; the stochastic law, the case in which things like that happen usually or for the most part. In the simplest but unlikely case, the law will be: Fs cause Gs. The final clause, 'at least part of', is meant to cover the more complicated case, in which more descriptive content must be added to 'F' or 'G' or both to obtain a true universal law. For Aristotle, 'the F causally explains the G' can be true only if the F and the G are linked by a law under the same descriptions that occur in the explanatory singular assertion, namely 'the F' and 'the G'.

Is there an explanatory cause for everything that happens? Is there an incidental cause for everything that happens? Aristotle's answers to these two questions are complicated. In a related set of discussions at *Physics* II, chapters 4–6, *Metaphysics* V, 30, VI, 2–3, and XI, 8, Aristotle asks whether chance is a cause. The answer is tied in with the discussion of accidental or incidental causes. One example of his is this.

Consider those things which do not happen always in the same way or even for the most part in the same way. Some of these things are the results of choice and deliberation, and some are not (like the musical man being pale), but let us restrict our discussion to examples of the former sort. Notice that Aristotle in this passage need not be taken as asserting that *no* outcomes can be linked to choices by always-or-for-the-most-part laws, but only that *some* choices and outcomes cannot be joined by such laws.

Suppose a man, who is busy collecting subscriptions for a feast, goes to the market to buy food. While there, by chance he stumbles upon a man from whom he collects money for the feast. Had he known that the man was there, he would have gone to the market and collected the money, but that wasn't why he went there. He went there to buy food.

Does the collector's meeting the subscriber have a cause? Aristotle thinks it does, and that the cause is chance: 'Things of this kind, then, when they come to pass incidentally are said to be "by chance"' (*Physics* II, chapter 5, 196b24). In which of the two senses that we have indicated did Aristotle think that chance was a cause? 'Chance is an incidental cause. . .' (197a5). He adds: 'strictly it is not the cause – without qualification – of anything; for instance, a housebuilder is the cause of a house; incidentally, a flute-player may be so' (10–15). That is, in the incidental and non-explanatory sense, chance caused him to meet the subscriber and collect the money.

Is there any explanatory cause of his collecting the money, even if chance was not it? There can be *no* explanatory cause of his collecting the money, because there is no universal or for-the-most-part law that links wishing to buy food and collecting of subscriptions. Accidents do not have explanatory causes; in the explanatory sense, there was no cause of his collecting the money. Nothing causally explains his collecting the money. 'Evidently, there are not causes . . . of the accidental, of the same kind as there are of the essential. . .' (*Metaphysics* XI, 7, 1065a7–9).

Let's return again to the incidental cause. Which is the incidental cause of collecting the money: chance, or the collector's wanting to buy food? Aristotle seems clear that the correct reply is: chance. He seems loth to count the collector's desire to buy food as the incidental cause, since 'there is no definite cause of an accident, only a chance cause, i.e., an indefinite one' (*Metaphysics* V, 30, 1025a23). In the case of the collector of subscriptions, Aristotle argues:

90

And the causes of the man's coming and getting the money (when he did not come for the sake of that) are innumerable. He may have wished to see somebody or been following somebody, or may have gone to see a spectacle. . . . Hence, to conclude, since causes of this kind are indefinite, chance too is indefinite.

(Physics II, chapter 5, 197a15–20)

In a similar case in which a sailor finds himself in Aegina because he was carried away by a storm (*Metaphysics* V, 30), Aristotle asserts that since the storm was an accident, there was only an indefinite, chance cause of the man getting to Aegina, and also that the storm, a definite event if ever there was one, was the cause of his 'coming to a place for which he was not sailing'. Aristotle makes a clear distinction between two different descriptions of the same occurrence: 'coming to a place for which one was not sailing' and 'coming to Aegina'.

If we describe the effect incidentally, as a coming to Aegina (compare: collecting the subscription), the effect has *only* an incidental and indefinite cause, namely chance. After all, there is no law that joins storms and coming to Aegina (or wanting food and collecting subscriptions). The effect, *qua* a coming to Aegina, has no *per se* cause, and therefore nothing causally explains the sailor's coming to Aegina, as so described.

On the other hand, if we describe the *same* effect per se, as a coming to a place for which one was not sailing, then there is a definite *per se* cause of it, viz. the storm. The storm is the *per se* cause of coming to a place for which one was not sailing, and hence causally explains coming to a place for which one was not sailing, since there is presumably a law to the effect that storms often or for the most part cause sailors to arrive at places other than that for which they were sailing.

Note the further evidence here for the non-extensionality of the per se, explanatory causal context. On Aristotle's view, even though the storm was the *per se* cause of, and therefore causally explains his getting to a place for which he was not sailing, and his coming to a place for which he was not sailing=his coming to Aegina, it does not follow that the storm is *per se* cause of and hence causally explains his coming to Aegina.

For Aristotle, then, (a) 'chance is the incidental and indefinite cause of the sailor's coming to Aegina' and (b) 'getting blown off course by the storm is the *per se* cause of the sailor's coming to a place for which he was not sailing' are both acceptable assertions (compare: 'chance is the incidental cause of his collecting the subscription' and 'the wish to buy food is the *per se* cause of his buying food').

What is *not* acceptable is (c) 'getting blown off course by the storm is the cause of his coming to Aegina' (or, (d) 'the wish to buy food was the cause of his collecting the subscription'), in either sense of 'cause'. (c) and (d) cannot be true in the *per se* sense, because of the close connection that Aristotle draws between *per se* cause, explanation, and law. Nor can (c) and (d) be true in the incidental sense, since in that sense only chance is a cause.

Let's accept, for the sake of argument, that (c) and (d) cannot be true in the *per se* sense. But why can't they be true in the incidental sense of 'cause'? Why does Aristotle insist that only indefinite chance can be a cause in the incidental sense? Aristotle's argument, quoted above, is dreadful:

> And the causes of the man's coming and getting the money (when he did not come for the sake of that) are innumerable. He may have wished to see somebody or been following somebody, or may have gone to see a spectacle. . . . Hence, to conclude, since causes of this kind are indefinite, chance too is indefinite.
>
> (*Physics* II, chapter 5, 197a15–20)

From the fact that any one of a large and indefinite number of causes *might* have led to his coming and getting the money, it does not follow that there was anything indefinite about the cause that actually did operate on this occasion. If he came to buy food, there seems to be, despite what Aristotle claims, a definite incidental cause of his getting the money, namely his desire to buy food.

Aristotle is certainly ready to countenance definite incidental causes when he is not discussing specifically the nature of the accidental:

> Another mode of causation is the incidental and its genera, e.g., in one way 'Polyclitus', in another 'sculptor' is the cause of a statue, because 'being Polyclitus' and 'sculptor' are incidentally conjoined. Also the classes in which the incidental attribute is included. . . .
>
> (*Physics* II, chapter 3, 195a35–195b3)

At *Metaphysics* 198a5–7, he says that 'spontaneity and chance are causes of effects which, though they might result from intelligence or nature, have in fact been caused by something incidentally', which appears to say that chance, *qua* indefinite incidental cause, presupposes or supervenes upon some definite incidental cause. Why his insistence, at least in some passages, that accidents have no definite incidental cause?

Necessitation and laws in explanation

Aristotle treats incidental causes in the case of accidents differently, because of their implications for necessitation.[17] He is keen to avoid the view that all things happen by necessity, which he regards as obviously false (see *Metaphysics* VI, 3): '. . . all things will be of necessity, if there has to be a cause non-accidentally of what goes through a process of beginning or ceasing. . .' (Sorabji's translation of *Metaphysics* VI, 3, 1027a30). Definite causes necessitate their effects and explain them. Aristotle 'concedes that an effect is necessary, given its [definite – my addition, DHR] cause'.[18] Explanatory causes necessitate their effects. On this basis it is fair to ascribe to Aristotle a determinative theory of explanation (although I shall indicate some contrary evidence below).

On the other hand, a mere indefinite cause like chance neither necessitates nor explains its effect: since 'the cause of the [accidental] is indefinite' (*Metaphysics* VI, 3, 1028a), the accidental is not necessary, and the chain of necessitation is broken. In order to introduce contingency into his metaphysics, Aristotle introduced accidents which lack any definite cause. If there is no definite cause of an accident, then there is no possibility of its being necessitated. What follows the accident may then be necessary *given* the accident, but the non-necessitated occurrence of the accident has introduced a contingency in the subsequent necessary unfolding of events.

Given the close connection between *per se* or explanatory causation and law, one might wonder whether Aristotle is committed, in this *general* exposition of explanation (which is to be distinguished from his view of scientific explanation in the *Posterior Analytics*), to an account of explanation which requires the presence of a law in every full explanation. I think that he is *not* so committed. The concept of law figures here only as a criterion for *distinguishing* between *per se* and incidental descriptions of causes. As far as this account goes, 'the F caused the G' might be a full explanation of why the G, assuming that the conceptualizations therein are *per se*, and without the explicit *addition* of any laws to the explanation itself. The existence of the appropriate laws is what makes these conceptualizations *per se* rather than incidental, but it does not follow that those laws must be a part of the explanation. Explanations might work not because they include laws but because the descriptions they use are derived from laws. In such a case, let us say that explanations are *backed* by laws but do not include them.

What sorts of laws did Aristotle believe backed the explanations of non-accidental actions, i.e. ones done for the sake of something and also done in accordance with deliberate intention? Such laws must be the laws of practical science. Aristotle's remarks at *Metaphysics* VI, 2: 'no science – practical, productive, or theoretical – troubles itself' with this category of the accidental. It is only accidents for which there can be no science: 'That a science of the accidental is not even possible will be evident if we try to see what the accidental really is' (*Metaphysics* 1064b30). Practical science explains actions by means of practical syllogisms, e.g. why (C) a man who desired food went to the market: namely because (P1) he desired food, and (P2) he knew that the market was where the food was, and (P3) whoever desires something and believes that some action is the way to get what he desires, does that action.[19] So Aristotle holds that explanations of human actions are backed by laws like (P3), which we might call 'action laws', and which presumably have the same epistemic status as natural laws.

Aristotle's views on laws and necessitation are somewhat more complicated than the above account would so far suggest. Aristotle believed, as we saw, that there are some laws that hold only for the most part. He repeatedly informs us that often a predicate will belong to a specific kind only for the most part (*De Generatione Animalium*, 727b29, 770b9–13, 772a35, 777a19–21, *De Partibus Animalium* 663b28, *Prior Analytics* 25b14, 32b4–13, *Metaphysics* VI, 2, 1027a20–5). In the passage from *Metaphysics* listed above, Aristotle even argues that the proof of there being accidental occurrences rests on the fact that 'the majority of things are only for the most part'. In the *Posterior Analytics* itself, he says:

> Some occurrences are universal (for they are, or come to be what they are, always and in every case); others again are not always what they are, but only as a general rule: for instance, not every man can grow a beard, but it is a general rule.
>
> (*Posterior Analytics* II, 12, 96a8–19)

If he is to be taken at his word, that is, if there really are fundamentally for-the-most-part laws, and not just universal laws knowledge of which is sometimes incomplete, it would have been open to him, on this basis, to say that a man's reaching puberty (remember: this will be the 'wide' event which is the full cause, and so includes all of the causally relevant circumstances) caused him to grow a beard, or made his growing a beard more likely, without necessitating him to grow it. His growing a beard, when he did, could depend on his attaining puberty, without being determined by it. Aristotle could have thereby introduced contingency into his system without introducing accidents which fail to have definite causes, by denying that all (definite) causes determine or necessitate. But he does not seem to have seen this possibility. Aristotle seems to have had the materials available with which to deny that causes always necessitate, but not to have taken the additional step and deny that they do.

Aristotle on scientific explanation

The topic we have been discussing in this chapter has been Aristotle's general theory or account of explanation. Nothing so far has been said about *scientific* explanation. There is a lengthy discussion by Aristotle of explanation in the *Posterior Analytics*.[20] It is clear that this is his account of explanation in the sciences. How does that discussion fit into the exposition that I have already offered?

To begin with, the topic of the *Posterior Analytics* is *knowledge*. This is sometimes translated as 'scientific knowledge', but the Greek word is *episteme*, and is sometimes translated with the qualification 'scientific' and sometimes without. What prompts translators to add the qualification is clear enough. Aristotle's paradigm for knowledge, at least here, is scientific knowledge.

Aristotle accepted that there were kinds of knowledge other than theoretical or scientific knowledge, namely practical and productive knowledge. There is the productive knowledge of a craftsman, and more generally the productive knowledge, knowledge-how, pursued for the sake of making something. There is also practical knowledge, knowledge pursued for the sake of acting, and represented by the ability to engage in practical reasoning. In the *Nichomachean Ethics*, he talks of knowledge of, or a science of, the good, but it is evident that such a practical science would be very different epistemologically from the sciences he speaks of in the *Posterior Analytics* (Aristotle himself points this out in the *Nichomachean Ethics*, Book I, chapter 3).

Even though there are these other sorts of knowledge, scientific knowledge for Aristotle deserves special consideration. So Aristotle is restricting his discussion in the *Posterior Analytics* to the kind of knowledge found in the physical and biological sciences, and his remarks there on explanation are similarly so restricted.

Aristotle delimits a separate sphere of scientific explanation as distinct from explanation in general, and imposes special requirements or conditions on scientific explanation that may not be appropriate for explanation in other contexts or spheres. This contrasts with Plato's view, since for him ordinary explanation, if it is to withstand philosophical scrutiny, must pass the same requirements as explanation in science or anywhere else.

I have raised the problem of how a philosopher is supposed to justify the requirements he sets for explanation. Arbitrary stipulation, fidelity to linguistic usage, sensitivity to metaphysics? I followed Moravcsik in claiming that it was the latter that Aristotle used in his general exposition of explanation. But in his discussion of scientific explanation, new, additional requirements are imposed on explanation. From whence do they arise? *For Aristotle, special requirements for explanation in science arise from considerations about the nature of scientific knowledge and its objects.*

First, the link between scientific knowledge and explanation is made in *Posterior Analytics:*

> We suppose ourselves to possess unqualified scientific knowledge of a thing, as opposed to knowing it in the accidental way in which the sophist knows, when we think that we know the cause on which the fact depends, as the cause of that fact and of no other, and further, that the fact could not be other than it is. . . .
>
> (*PA* I, 2, 71b8ff.)

Aristotle distinguishes two kinds of knowledge: knowledge of the bare fact and knowledge of the reasoned fact. Knowledge of the bare fact is knowledge that. Knowledge of the reasoned fact is knowledge why, which Aristotle calls 'unqualified scientific knowledge'. We shall see this distinction at work later. Aristotle can account for knowledge of the reasoned fact in terms of knowledge of the bare fact, and explanation. The view in the above quotation then is this:

(A): x knows the reasoned fact that p (knows why p) iff,

(1)   for some q, x knows the bare fact that q is the explanation of
      p, and
(2)   (x knows that?) ~p is impossible.

It is ambiguous in Aristotle's text whether 'x knows that...' should
precede the '~p is impossible' in clause (A2). But since the point of
explanation is epistemic, it makes better sense of Aristotle's intentions
to include the additional requirement. An analysis of knowledge-why
(knowing the reasoned fact) presupposes a prior grasp of the idea of
knowledge that (knowing the bare fact).

Aristotle's view is that all scientific explanations are demonstrations.
I classify him, therefore, as holding an argument theory of explanation
(but only as far as *scientific* explanation goes, not in his general account,
discussed at length above). Aristotle's theory of the demonstration is a
sketch of what we must possess in order to have understanding in his
sense; demonstrations must be such that they permit us to meet the
conditions for understanding set out in the two clauses of (A). One can
see *why* Aristotle was led into thinking that explanations in science had
to be demonstrations, when one considers what he took to be the nature
and objects of scientific knowledge.

Aristotle's (A2) commits him to the view that one can only have
scientific knowledge of that whose contradictory is impossible ('the fact
could not be other than it is'). Aristotle believed that the laws of nature,
although (as we would say) a posteriori, were necessary, and hence that
their denials were impossible. (Aristotle's necessity and impossibility
are, of course, weaker than logical necessity and logical impossibility.)
'...the object of scientific knowledge cannot be other than it is' (*PA* I,
6, 74b5); 'Since the object of pure scientific knowledge cannot be other
than it is...' (*PA* I, 4, 73a21).

Laws are therefore the *only* suitable candidates for being the objects
of scientific knowledge. Normally, one would assume that there can be
scientific knowledge and explanation of both laws and particular facts,
but there is no attempt by Aristotle, in the *Posterior Analytics*, to extend
the discussion to include the latter. It is true that Aristotle's scientist is
sometimes interested in explaining particular facts (see for example *PA*
II, 11, 94a36–b8), but Aristotle shuns a discussion of such knowledge in
this treatise on scientific knowledge:

Scientific knowledge is not possible through the act of perception
... one must at any rate actually perceive a 'this somewhat', and

at a definite time and place: but that which is commensurately universal and true in all cases, one cannot perceive. . . . Seeing therefore that demonstrations are commensurately universal, and universals are imperceptible, we clearly cannot obtain scientific knowledge by the act of perception. . . . So if we were on the moon and saw the earth shutting out the sun's light, we should not know the cause of the eclipse: we should perceive the present fact of the eclipse, but not the reasoned fact at all, since the act of perception is not of the commensurate universal. . . .

(*PA* I, 31)

If we set out to understand and hence explain a law of science, the requirement that the explanation take a demonstrative form follows naturally from two of Aristotle's views: namely that the objects of scientific knowledge must be necessary, and must be *known* to be so (or so I interpreted the second clause of the definition of knowledge). Aristotle held that if the conclusion is to be known as necessary, it must follow necessarily from premisses themselves known to be necessary. First, each step in the inferential chain must be necessary, beginning with the initial premisses: 'the truth obtained by demonstrative knowledge will be necessary. And since demonstrative knowledge is only present when we have a demonstration, it follows that demonstration is inference from necessary premisses' (*PA* 73a22–4), and 'But when the middle term [of a demonstration] is from necessity, the conclusion too is from necessity, just as from truth, it is always true' (*PA* 75a4–6).

Moreover, the connections between each step in the chain must also be necessary connections; only deductively valid demonstrations are productive of knowledge. '. . .demonstrative knowledge must be knowledge of a necessary nexus . . . otherwise its possessor will not know . . . the fact that his conclusion is a necessary connexion. . .' (*PA* I, 75a12–18). 'Since it is impossible for that of which there is understanding simpliciter to be otherwise, what is understandable in virtue of demonstrative understanding will be necessary' (*PA*, A4, 73a22–5). Although Aristotle agrees that there may be some other kind of knowing, he concludes:

What I now assert is that at all events we do know by demonstration. By demonstration, I mean a syllogism productive of scientific knowledge, a syllogism, that is, the grasp of which is eo ipso such knowledge. Assuming then that my thesis as to the nature of scientific knowing is correct. . . .

(PA I, 2, 71b17–20)

Perhaps one can non-deductively infer a necessary truth from a necessary truth; Aristotle nowhere, as far as I know, explicitly rules this out. However, even if I know that the premiss in such a non-deductive inference is true and necessary, Aristotle would be, I think, loth to allow that I thereby could *know*, rather than just have reason to believe, that the conclusion is true and necessary, even if it is so. It is only deduction that ensures *knowledge* of necessity-preservation from premisses to conclusion. The deductive requirements of scientific explanation follow from the very high demands Aristotle makes on scientific laws (that they are necessary) and on scientific knowledge (to know the reasoned fact that p entails *being certain* that ~p is *impossible*). Aristotle holds a deductivist theory of explanation.

Since Aristotle held that some laws hold only for the most part, how could there be a demonstration of them? Aristotle discusses the form that a demonstration of such a stochastic generalization might take. In the *Posterior Analytics*, Book II, chapter 12, Aristotle says:

In the case of such connections, the middle term too must be a general rule [a rule-for-the-most-part]. . . . But we have assumed a connection which is a general rule; consequently the middle term B must also be a general rule. So connections which embody a general rule . . . will also derive from immediate basic premisses.

(PA II, 12)

In the *Posterior Analytics*, Book I, Aristotle explicitly tells us that we can have scientific knowledge of what happens for the most part:

There is no knowledge by demonstration of chance conjunctions; for chance conjunctions exist neither by necessity nor as general connections. . . . Now demonstration is concerned only with one or other of these two, for all reasoning proceeds from necessary or general premisses, the conclusion being necessary if the premisses are necessary and general if the premisses are general. Consequently, if chance conjunctions are neither general nor necessary, they are not demonstrable.

(PA I, 30)

He seems to be contemplating deductive syllogisms ('demonstrations') with 'for the most part' premises and a 'for the most part' conclusion, although he is not likely to be successful in constructing valid deductions with this form.[21]

Is there any evidence that he might be willing to contemplate a non-deductivist argument theory of explanation? Certainly, Aristotle has an account of induction (*epagoge*): 'Thus it is clear that we must get to know the primary premises by induction. . .' (*PA* II, 19, A100b 5–15).[22] But these particular instances cannot provide the explanation for the ultimate principles of a science; indeed, it would be closer to the truth to say that it is the ultimate principles which explain the particular cases.[23]

There is also no doubt that Aristotle recognized something which he was prepared to call 'inductive argument'. He mentions it in Book I, chapter 1, of the *Posterior Analytics*, where he discusses the Socratic idea that one must know something before one can learn it: 'the two forms of dialectical reasoning, syllogistic and inductive. . .'. He treats it again briefly in Book I, chapter 12, of the *Topics*. In the latter, he asserts that, of the two forms of dialectical argument, induction is even more convincing and clearer than deduction. All of this suggests, although doesn't quite say, that an inductive argument might constitute an explanation of its conclusion.

Also, since Aristotle does assert that there are generalizations which hold for the most part, then if he were to shift from his official view and consider the possibility of the scientific explanation of particular events, then any such explanation of a particular event which used a 'for the most part' generalization would have to be an inductive or probabilistic explanation, since no deductive inference could capture an explanation with those features. Aristotle toys with this thought in one place, *Poetics* 10: the actions 'should each of them arise out of the structure of the plot itself, so as to be the consequence, necessary or probable, of the antecedents'. In *Rhetoric* I, 2, 1357a25–38, and II, 25, 1402, 15–1403a15, Aristotle introduces something which he calls 'argument by example' which is a form of analogical and certainly non-deductive argument. Although in what follows, I count Aristotle as a deductivist, as he certainly was concerning the explanation of laws whether holding universally or for the most part, there is some textual evidence that suggests that Aristotle might have been willing to consider a different view.

Aristotle's demonstrations

The idea of a demonstration gives content to the two conditions Aristotle requires for knowledge of the reasoned fact. What is a demonstration? Not just any deductively sound argument is a demonstration. (A) states the two conditions required for knowledge of the reasoned fact that p: one concerns the impossibility of ~p; the other, knowledge of the explanation of p. So a demonstration must do at least two things: (A1) it must provide the explanation of what we know; (A2) it must lead to knowledge of the necessity of what we know. For Aristotle, therefore, a demonstration is a deduction that is able to accomplish these two things.

In order to meet (A2), Aristotle insists that a demonstration must be a syllogism with necessary premisses and hence a necessary conclusion. What further conditions does Aristotle lay down, to ensure that the syllogism accomplishes (A1)? What has to be the case, in order that, for some q, one knows that q is the explanation of p? Not just any necessary q that entails a necessary p will do (where, of course, p and q are both universal generalizations). Suppose p and q are logically equivalent. If so, then a necessary p will entail a necessary q, and a necessary q will entail a necessary p, yet surely at most only one of them explains the other. We assume that the explanation relation is asymmetrical (or anyway non-symmetrical, which is enough for the case at hand): for the cases in which we are here interested, if p explains q, q does not explain p. How shall we account for this asymmetry (or non-symmetry) of explanation?[24]

As far as I can see, all of the remaining six conditions that Aristotle imposes, save truth (which I take as implied in the necessity condition in any case), are intended to introduce the requisite asymmetry (or non-symmetry) of explanation. Here is his own summary, of the additional requirements, each of which is later developed by a fuller discussion:

> Assuming then that my thesis as to the nature of scientific knowing is correct, the premisses of demonstrated knowledge must be true, primary, immediate, better known than and prior to the conclusion, which is further related to them as effect to cause .... Syllogism there may be indeed without these conditions, but such syllogism, not being productive of scientific knowledge, will not be demonstration. ...
>
> (*PA* I, 2, 71b119–25)

A demonstration is not only a deductively valid syllogism from necessary premises to a necessary conclusion. Aristotle adds that a demonstration is a special sort of such a syllogism, viz. one that meets the following further six requirements: first, the premises must be true; second and third, they must be primitive and immediate. Fourth, they must be prior to the conclusion drawn from them. Fifth, they must be explanatory of the conclusion, which itself must be true. Sixth, they must be more familiar (in nature and to us) than the conclusion. Requirements (4)–(6) relate to features of the premises relative to the conclusion; requirements (1)–(3) concern the premises *per se*.

It is not worthwhile to move through these conditions one by one. They are not conceptually independent, and at least two are equivalent.[25] In what follows, I remark on some of the requirements that are of interest, in a rather *ad hoc* way. However, the fifth requirement is extremely important, and we shall pause to look at it in more detail than the others.

Of the six conditions placed on syllogisms that lead to knowledge of the conclusion, the first, Aristotle tells us, is that the premises of an explanatory demonstration must be true. 'Now they[26] must be true. . .' (*PA* A2, 71b26–7). Aristotle's argument seems to be that one can come to know the explanandum conclusion only on the basis of premises which one already knows. But a necessary condition for knowing the premises is that the premises be true. So, says Aristotle, the premises of an explanatory demonstration must be true.

Is Aristotle right to require the truth of (as we should say) the explanans? This is a requirement which almost every philosopher who has written on explanation has adopted. I will accept without argument this Aristotelian requirement. That easy acceptance requires only the distinction between an explanation and a potential explanation (or, the explanation that there would have been, if. . .). It is possible for false empirical statements to explain potentially . It is this sort of thing we have in mind when we say that some false astronomical theory explained, for example, the motion of the planets. What we mean is that the theory would have explained the motion, had it been true.

Second and third, Aristotle's remarks on the immediacy and primitiveness (the non-demonstrability) of the premises cannot, of course, apply as a requirement to every scientific explanatory demonstration. Primitiveness can only apply to the first principles in a scientific chain of such explanatory demonstrations, which constitutes the form that a finished science takes, in Aristotle's view. If, *contra suppositione*, such first principles were non-primitive, i.e. demonstrable, they could not be the first principles of a science. Quite apart from Aristotle's particular theory of science, this requirement is interesting.

There is the following trilemma about explanation (there is an analogous trilemma about epistemic justification): either explanations regress *ad infinitum*, or there is some circularity in explanation, so that something can be part of the explanation for itself, or there must be some ultimate explanans which is itself inexplicable or self-explanatory. We attributed to Plato the view that the Forms are ultimate and self-explanatory, the third lemma of the above trilemma. Aristotle has this to say:

> Now some think that because one must understand primitives there is no understanding; others that there is, but that there are demonstrations of everything. Neither of these [views] is either true or necessary. For the one party, supposing that one cannot understand in another way – they claim that we are led back indefinitely on the grounds that we would not understand what is posterior because of what is prior if there are no primitives; and they argue correctly, for it is impossible to go through indefinitely many things. And if it comes to a stop and there are principles, [they say] these are unknowable since there is no demonstration of them, which alone they say is understanding; but if one cannot know the primitives, neither can one understand what depends on them simpliciter or properly, but only on the supposition that they are the case. The other party agrees about understanding; for it, [they say], occurs only through demonstration. But [they argue that] nothing prevents there being demonstration of everything; for it is possible for the demonstration to come about circularly and reciprocally.
>
> But we say that neither is all understanding demonstrative but in the case of the immediates it is non-demonstrable. . . .
>
> (*PA*, A3, 72b5–20)

The first party Aristotle rejects is the party of sceptics, who accept the first horn of the trilemma and construe it as showing that understanding anything is impossible. Explanation, they say, requires an infinite regress of explanation, and since this is impossible, explanation is itself impossible. The second party accepts the second, circularity lemma of the trilemma.

Aristotle's theory, like Plato's, embraces the third lemma of the trilemma. There is such a thing, according to him, as 'non-demonstrable understanding'. Ultimate explanantia (there will be more ultimate explanantia than there are ultimate sciences, for every ultimate science will have to have several such ultimate explanantia) are self-explanatory. If Aristotle and Plato are right, explanation is not an irreflexive relation; there can be things that explain themselves.

It may be, as Aristotle suggests in the very last chapter of the *Posterior Analytics*, that we come to these first principles by means of a process of induction (*epagoge*) from particular instances (the precise interpretation that should be put on Aristotle's doctrine of *epagoge* is controversial). But there still will be no explanatory demonstration of them. As I said before, these particular instances cannot provide the explanation for the ultimate principles of a science; indeed, it would be closer to the truth to say that it is the ultimate principles which explain the particular cases.

Notice that the idea of the self-explanatory is different from the ideas of both the a priori and the self-evident (I suppose that whatever is self-evident is a priori, but not conversely). Whatever is self-evident is self-evidently *true*, but it does not follow that one knows any explanation for the truth one has thus grasped, not even that it is its own explanation. One might see that something is true merely by thinking about or attending to it, and this may provide only knowledge of the fact rather than knowledge of the reasoned fact. What is self-evident may not be self-explanatory.

The first principles of *science*, in spite of being self-explanatory (and necessary), certainly cannot be a priori. Indeed, if, as Aristotle says, we obtain them by means of the process of epagoge, they cannot be a priori. Aristotle's claim is that the first principles of a science must be self-explanatory; *once* we have them, they explain themselves. But he does *not* assert that they are a priori, that we could come to know them, in some way other than via their instances.

The third condition, immediacy, is a relation that holds between two terms, A and B, iff there is no middle term C such that all A are C and all C are B. For Aristotle, in the finished setting out of a science, each generalization should be immediate; each generalization should follow immediately from its predecessor in the inferential chain. If it does not, then there are some further premisses on which its truth depends, or through which its truth is mediated, such that those premisses have not yet been incorporated into the science.

Fifth and sixth, the premises in an explanatory syllogism must be more familiar than and prior to that which they explain. Barnes takes these two requirements, priority and familiarity, to be equivalent.

Let me return to the fourth condition, which I omitted. The fourth condition is stated by Aristotle in the following way: 'the premises must be the explanatory causes of the conclusion' (*PA* I, 2, 29); 'Demonstration is syllogism that proves the cause. . .' (*PA*, 85b24). Aristotle introduces the need for this fourth condition at *PA*, A13, 78a23–78b15. The passage is lengthy, but I reproduce it in full, because a great deal of my discussion in chapters VI and VII will depend on the insights it contains:

> Understanding the fact and the reason why differ, first in the same science, – and in that in two ways: in one fashion, if the deduction does not come through immediates (for the primitive explanation is not assumed, but understanding of the reason why occurs in virtue of the primitive explanation); in another, if it is through immediates but not through the explanation but through the more familiar of the converting terms. For nothing prevents the non-explanatory one of the counterpredicated terms from sometimes being more familiar, so that the demonstration will occur through this.
>
> E.g., that the planets are near, through their not twinkling: let C be the planets, B not twinkling, A being near. Thus it is true to say B of C; for the planets do not twinkle. But also [to say] A of B; for what does not twinkle is near. . . . So it is necessary that A belongs to C; so that it has been demonstrated that the planets are near. Now this deduction is not of the reason why but of the fact; for it is not because they do not twinkle that they are near, but because they are near that they do not twinkle.
>
> But it is also possible for the latter to be proved through the former, and the demonstration will be of the reason why – e.g., let C be the planets, B being near, A not twinkling. Thus B belongs to C and A to B; so that A belongs to C. And the deduction is of the reason why; for the primitive explanation has been assumed.
>
> Again, [take] the way they prove that the moon is spherical through its increases – for if what increases in this way is spherical and the moon increases, it is evident that it is spherical. Now in this way the deduction of the fact comes about; but if the middle term is posited the other way about, [we get the deduction] of the

reason why; for it is not because of the increases that it is spherical, but because it is spherical it gets increases of this sort. Moon C; spherical B; increase A.

But in cases in which the middle terms do not convert and the non-explanatory term is more familiar, the fact is proved but the reason why is not.

(*PA*, A13, 78a23–78b15)

The same point is made at *PA* II, 16, 98b4–24. A plant is deciduous iff it has broad leaves, but it is deciduous because it is broad-leaved and not vice versa. (Jonathan Barnes tells me that poor Aristotle didn't know about the larch, which is deciduous but not broad-leaved.) If we know that all vines are broad-leaved, we can infer that vines are deciduous; if we know that vines are deciduous, we can infer that they are broad-leaved. Since 'demonstration through the cause is of the reasoned fact and demonstration not through the cause is of the bare fact', one who knows the broad-leavedness of vines through the deciduousness 'knows the fact . . . but not the reasoned fact'. Such a person does not know why the vine is broad-leaved; he only knows that it is.

The lesson of these examples is this. To use Aristotle's second example from the long quotation above, assuming that things increase in a certain way if and only if they are spherical, compare the following two deductions:

(1) Things increase in a certain way iff they are spherical.
(2) The moon increases in just that way.
∴ (3) The moon is spherical.

(4) Things increase in a certain way iff they are spherical.
(5) The moon is spherical.
∴ (6) The moon increases in just that way.

Aristotle claims that (4) and (5) explain (6), whereas (1) and (2) do *not* explain (3). If we have two convertible terms ('A' and 'B' are convertible terms iff all As are Bs *and* all Bs are As), we can often construct deductions that meet all of his other conditions for a demonstration, yet fail to be productive of 'knowing the reason why'. The premisses might be immediate, more familiar (to us, at least), necessary, universal, true, and deductively imply the conclusion. So Aristotle feels compelled to impose a further requirement on the syllogism, in virtue of which it can count as productive of understanding why – namely the premises must be 'explanatory of the conclusion'. 'And the deduction is of the reason why; for the primitive explanation has been assumed' (from the long quotation above).

Aristotle's example of the moon's shape and increase does not employ only laws in both premises and conclusion, which is what he is officially meant to be discussing, but the example of the vines does, and in any case it is not difficult to construct many similar examples having the following form, using only generalizations: let '(x) (Px⊃Qx)', and '(x) (Qx≡Rx)' be the premises and '(x) (Px⊃Rx)' be the conclusion in a deduction. It follows that this will also be a deduction: let '(x) (Px⊃Rx)', and '(x) (Qx≡Rx)' be the premises and '(x) (Px⊃Qx)' be the conclusion. One of the deductions may be explanatory; if so, typically, the other would not be.

Let's recall the explication of knowledge with which we began:

(A): x knows the reasoned fact that p (knows why p) iff
(1) for some q, x knows the bare fact that q is the explanation of p, and
(2) (x knows that?) ~p is impossible.

In explicating (A1), Aristotle tells us that we require a demonstration that meets six conditions. It might seem that Aristotle is going to offer us a 'reductive' explication of knowledge of the reasoned fact (understanding), in terms that refer to ideas such as demonstration, necessity, and so on. However, one of the crucial conditions for an argument's being a demonstration is that the premises must be *explanatory* of the conclusion.

We have not, then, in any sense 'eliminated' the idea of explanation, for Aristotle has used the idea of explanation in accounting for the first clause of (A). Can we further eliminate this final reference to explanation, or is it simply to be taken as a primitive?

Baruch Brody,[27] sketching what he calls 'an Aristotelian theory of explanation', claims that the point of the above discussion by Aristotle is that a certain disjunctive condition, typically omitted in modern theories of explanation, must obtain in order for a deduction to count as an explanation:

a deductive-nomological explanation of a particular event is a satisfactory explanation of the event when (beside meeting all of

Hempel's requirements) its explanans contains essentially a description of the event which is the [efficient] cause of the event described in the explanandum.... [Further,] we can set down another requirement for explanation as follows: a deductive-nomological explanation of a particular event is a satisfactory explanation of that event when (beside meeting all of Hempel's requirements) its explanans contains essentially a statement attributing to a certain class of objects a property had essentially by that class of objects (even if the statement does not say that they have it essentially) and when at least one object involved in the event described in the explanandum is a member of that class of objects.

(Brody 1972: 26)

On Brody's account of Aristotle's theory of scientific explanation, one knows why only if, *inter alia*, one knows the efficient cause or the essence of what it is that one is trying to explain. But there is no reason to think that Aristotle himself is limiting 'cause' to efficient causes (or, motion-originator, as I have preferred to put it) and essences. Aristotle, in the long passage I quoted, has in mind the *aitiai* in any of his four permitted senses. Further, he says:

We think we have scientific knowledge when we know the cause, and there are four causes: (1) the definable form, (2) an antecedent which necessitates a consequent, (3) the efficient cause, (4) the final cause. Hence each of these can be a middle term of a proof....

(*PA* II, 11)

Aristotle's theory of scientific knowledge (understanding) presupposes and makes use of (E), his account of explanation in general, but adds further requirements to it. His account of scientific knowledge requires (E), his general account, to spell out what is involved in explanation in a non-circular way.[28]

Summary

What lessons has Aristotle taught us about explanation that we should carry forward to later chapters? I think there are at least four. First, the connection he sees between a theory of explanation and metaphysics provides a methodological alternative to what I called 'the language users' approach'. I return to this theme in chapter VII. Second, his insight into *per se* causation offers the beginnings of a theory of how our conceptualization or view of things makes a difference to explanation. This forms the basis of my discussion in chapter V. Third, Aristotle believes that all explanations are arguments, and that laws have an especially central role to play in explanation. Chapter VI returns to these themes. Finally, Aristotle's requirement that no argument can be an explanation, unless it mentions the cause of what is to be explained in the premisses, suggests that any acceptable theory of explanation must be, in some sense, a causal theory of explanation. I examine this question as well in chapter VII.

CHAPTER IV

Mill and Hempel on Explanation

Carl Hempel, in his 1948 article, 'Studies in the Logic of Explanation', claims that at least part of the account of explanation that he develops has been defended by several previous writers: 'The account given above of the general characteristics of explanation and prediction in science is by no means novel; it merely summarizes and states explicitly some fundamental points which have been recognized by many scientists and methodologists.'[1] Among those precursors, Hempel lists John Stuart Mill, and offers the following two quotations in support of this claim: 'An individual fact is said to be explained, by pointing out its cause, that is by stating the law or laws of causation, of which its production is an instance', and 'a law or uniformity of nature is said to be explained, when another law or laws are pointed out, of which that law is but a case, and from which it could be deduced'.[2] It would seem that Mill subscribed to a deductivist account of explanation; for Mill, all explanations are a subset of the set of deductively valid arguments, namely those which meet additional requirements to be specified. Hempel agrees that some (although not all) explanations conform to the deductive model of explanation that John Stuart Mill outlines.

On the other hand, Mill holds a peculiar account of deduction: 'It must be granted that in every syllogism, considered as an argument to prove the conclusion, there is a petitio principii' (II, III, 2). Deductive inference, according to Mill, is in some sense circular, and is in fact founded upon some sort of non-deductive inference.

Now, there is certainly no formal contradiction in Mill's holding both a deductivist theory of explanation, and a 'reductivist' account of deduction as founded on a special kind of non-deductive inference. However, even if formally consistent, the conjunction of the two views seems odd and suspiciously unmotivated. The thought behind Mill's

110

rather murky doctrine about deduction is that one cannot learn something new via a deduction. Deduction cannot advance knowledge. One would have imagined that this epistemic down-grading of deduction would have carried over to Mill's views on explanation, which would have provided a natural extension of the doctrine. After reading Mill on deduction, one might reasonably expect a non-deductive view of explanation.

But Mill remained a deductivist about explanation. In none of his remarks about explanation does Mill return to his view of deduction, or remark upon how his deductivist account of explanation fits with that view. The oddity in this conjunction of views is noted by Alan Ryan, in his book on Mill, but he does little to dispel the worry that the views do not fit together well.[3] One thing that I shall do in this chapter is to discuss Mill's views, first on explanation, and then on deductive inference, to see if we can find better clues for why he might have held these views in tandem. In fact, I think that there is a natural explanation for why Mill thought that these two views fit together harmoniously.

This chapter offers an account of Mill's and Hempel's views on explanation, which are, at any rate, superficially very similar. Mill's views on explanation will be taken from his remarks in *A System of Logic*. Hempel has written extensively on explanation, but I will limit myself to two of his articles: 'Studies in the Logic of Explanation' (first published in 1948), which I sometimes refer to as 'the early article', and 'Aspects of Scientific Explanation' (1965), which I sometimes refer to as 'the later article'.[4] These two articles contain the essentials of his views, and are the starting points for any contemporary discussion of the nature of explanation.

Mill is part of the empiricist tradition in philosophy. From Hobbes and Bacon, through Locke, to Berkeley and Hume, there is an increasingly critical philosophical rejection of concepts or ideas which cannot be traced directly to experience. Substance, matter, essence or form, the self, and causation, are just some of the concepts about which various empiricist philosophers expressed doubts and reservations. None, as far as I know, had much if anything to say directly about the concept of explanation. But it is easy to see why the Aristotelian, or Aristotelian oriented, scholastic traditions of explanation would have made them suspect explanation had they turned their attention to it.

As we saw in the last chapter, explanation for Aristotle had been tied to such ideas as form or essence, matter, goal or end, and efficient cause. Each of these ideas is challenged or found perplexing in some way by at

111

least one of Mill's empiricist predecessors. Substance and matter are criticized by Berkeley; efficient cause, by Hume; both essence and final cause by Hobbes. All of these ideas *seem* to transcend all possible experience, and hence to present a problem for the empiricist. Either they must be rejected, or it must be shown that, despite appearances, they do not transcend experience after all.

In many ways, it is surprising that no empiricist philosopher before Mill turned in an explicit way to the scrutiny of the concept of explanation, which had – given its connections with these other suspect notions – every appearance of being experience-transcendent. Of course, many empiricist philosophers held views which have consequences for a theory of explanation. For example, much of what Bacon says is pertinent to a theory of explanation.[5] Locke's belief in the external world can be construed, indeed has been construed, as an example of inference to the best explanation. Berkeley's philosophy of science, Hume's various scepticisms, all of these topics will have important implications for explanation. But Mill is, as far as I know, the first empiricist philosopher to have *explicitly* addressed himself to the question of the nature of explanation, and it is this fact that I find surprising.

As I suggested above, there are two reactions possible for an empiricist to any concept that appears experience-transcendent. First, the philosopher can confirm that the concept not only appears but is experience-transcendent and therefore that he wishes to reject or eliminate the notion. Examples of this strategy include Berkeley on material substance, Hobbes on immaterial substance, and final cause, and Hume on the continuing and independent existence of objects. Second, the philosopher can hold that the appearance of experience-transcendence is misleading, that a reconstruction of the concept or notion can be offered, such that, on that reconstruction, the concept can be shown to be directly tied to experience. Examples of this second strategy include Hume on causation, Berkeley on objects like tables, chairs, and trees (including the one in the quad), and Hobbes's linguistic construal of essence.

The same choice of strategies is available to an empiricist in a discussion of explanation. If explanation invokes experience-transcending elements, it can be eliminated or rejected from sound philosophy and science. An example of this strategy is adopted by Pierre Duhem, in his *The Aim and Structure of Physical Theory*.[6] Duhem defines 'to explain' as 'to strip reality of the appearances covering it like a veil, in order to see the bare reality itself'. Since 'The observation of physical phenomena does not put us into relation with the reality hidden under the sensible appearances', Duhem has little difficulty in showing that explanation, as he understands it, is a 'metaphysical' (i.e. experience-transcendent) idea. If the purpose of physical theory were to explain, physical theory would be subordinate to metaphysics.

There is for Duhem an alternative way to understand the purpose of physical theory, namely that the aim of physical theory is merely to summarize and classify logically a group of experimental laws 'without claiming to explain these laws'. Having rejected explanation as a legitimate aim of science, Duhem claims that 'A physical theory is not an explanation. It is a system of mathematical propositions, deduced from a small number of principles, which aim to represent as simply, as completely, and as exactly as possible a set of experimental laws' (Duhem 1977: 19). Since explanation is connected for Duhem with a non-empirical conception of reality, it has no place in science.

Duhem, then, represents one empirically minded strategy for dealing with explanation, that of rejecting explanation as an experience-transcendent and hence illegitimate (at least for science) notion or idea. John Stuart Mill represents the other empirically minded strategy, the attempt to reconstruct or reconstrue explanation as an empirically acceptable idea. Mill goes out of his way to stress that his theory of explanation is a case of making explanation acceptable to the empiricist; he eschews any idea of explanation as unravelling the deeper mysteries of nature.

> The word explanation is here used in its philosophical sense. What is called explaining one law of nature by another, is but substituting one mystery for another, and does nothing to render the general course of nature other than mysterious: we can no more assign a why for the most extensive laws than for the partial ones.
>
> (Mill 1970: 310)

For Mill, explanation has none of the mystery attributed to it by Duhem or other philosophers. We need only the ideas of a law of nature, cause and causal law, and deduction, in order to explicate the idea of explanation. We do not need Plato's Forms, or Aristotle's final causes and essences, or Duhem's non-sensible reality.

Mill thinks that the ideas of a law of nature and a causal law are safe for empiricists. He has previously explained a law of nature as a generalization to the effect that 'a certain fact invariably occurs whenever certain circumstances are present, and does not occur when they are absent' (Mill 1970: 206). Such uniformities are among either simultaneous or successive phenomena, and causal laws are of the latter kind: 'The law of causation . . . is but the familiar truth that invariability of succession is found by observation to obtain between every fact in nature and some other fact which has preceded it. . .' (p.213). A particular causal law is merely a specific invariability of succession between facts of two kinds.

Mill explicitly rejects any non-empirical idea of causation as metaphysical:

> The notion of causation is deemed by the schools of metaphysics most in vogue at the present moment to imply a mysterious and most powerful tie, such as cannot, or at least does not, exist between any physical fact and that other physical fact on which it is invariably consequent . . . and thence is deduced the supposed necessity of ascending higher, into the essences and constitutions of things. . . .
>
> (Mill 1970: 213)

Mill has thereby rendered both 'law of nature', 'cause', and 'causal law' acceptable for an empiricist. And since explanation is built out of these concepts (and deduction), it is acceptable as well.

Mill admits that 'explanation' has an ordinary meaning as well as the 'scientific' one that he proposes to give it. In 'common parlance', an explanation often replaces the unfamiliar by the familiar, but Mill notes that in science, just the reverse is usually the case:

> it resolves a phenomenon with which we are familiar into one of which we previously knew little or nothing. . . . It must be kept constantly in view, therefore, that in science, those who speak of explaining any phenomenon mean (or should mean) pointing out not some more familiar, but merely some more general phenomenon, of which it is a partial exemplification. . . .
>
> (Mill 1970: 310–11)

Mill *contrasts* the meaning of 'explanation' in ordinary parlance and the meaning he will attach to it (and what those who use it in science '*should* mean' by it). In science, typically the unfamiliar explains the familiar; in the ordinary sense, the familiar explains the unfamiliar.

Hempel is part of the tradition that we can trace back to Mill, of making explanation metaphysically safe for the empiricist philosopher. As far as I know, Hempel does not say this explicitly, but I claim that it is implicit in the way in which he executes the project of explicating explanation. As we shall see, explanation for Hempel can be explicated via the concepts of deductive and statistical inference, truth, empirical content, and lawlike generalizations. All of these concepts are, for Hempel, comprehensible within the terms of empiricist philosophy, although he notes that the idea of lawlikeness presents difficulties which have 'proved to be highly recalcitrant' (Hempel 1965: 338).[7]

Mill's account of explanation: laws of coexistence and succession

In one sense, an explanans and an explanandum are sentences. But, as I have claimed, sentence explanation is parasitic on the idea of non-sentence explanation. In the non-sentence sense, for Mill, what sorts of entities are explanantia (do the explaining) and explananda (are explained)?

Mill sometimes says that facts explain facts: 'An individual fact is said to be explained by pointing out its cause' (Mill 1970: 305). In the very next sentence, Mill says 'a conflagration is explained. . .', and presumably a conflagration is an event. Events are not, I assume, facts.

Explanations need laws, on Mill's theory. Laws are uniformities, and uniformities are patterns of events, or some such. However, on one occasion, Mill calls a uniformity 'a fact'. If we distinguish between singular facts, like the fact that some particular conflagration has some feature or property, and universally general facts, like the fact that, for all objects, if they have property P, then they have property Q, we could think of uniformities or laws as universally general facts. Mill also tells us that laws are explained by laws from which the former can be deduced. But it is sentences which are deduced from sentences. Mill must be thinking of laws, in this last context, as sentences that express or state such uniformities of nature.

Mill switches freely between talk of events and facts as what explain and are explained, without much attention to the matter. This is the first we have seen of facts, other than the brief mention of them by Salmon in chapter I; facts did not figure in either Plato's or Aristotle's ontology of explanation. Whatever facts are, they are not events or even patterns of events, although there is the fact that some event occurred, or the fact that some law or pattern of events obtains. I return to these questions about the ontology of explanation in the next chapter.

Mill's definition of explanation, which I quoted on page 110 and repeat more fully here, is put rather simply and baldly. It is intended to cover both the case of the explanation of particular matters of fact and the explanation of general laws:

> The word 'explanation' occurs so continually and holds so important a place in philosophy, that a little time spent in fixing the meaning of it will be profitably employed.
>
> An individual fact is said to be explained by pointing out its cause, that is, by stating the law or laws of causation of which its production is an instance. Thus a conflagration is explained when it is proved to have arisen from a spark falling into the midst of a heap of combustibles; and in a similar manner, a law of uniformity of nature is said to be explained when another law or laws are pointed out, of which that law itself is but a case, and from which it could be deduced.
>
> (Mill 1970: 305)

Let me enlarge on my earlier remarks about these 'empirically safe' ideas of law and causal law. Mill distinguishes between uniformities of coexistent phenomena and uniformities of successive phenomena: 'The order of the occurrence of phenomena in time is either successive or simultaneous; the uniformities, therefore, which obtain in their occurrence, are either uniformities of succession or of co-existence' (Mill 1970: 377). As the names imply, the first kind of uniformity is of two sorts of things or events that happen at the same time; the latter, of two types that occur at successive times.

Uniformities of succession which are causal are *invariable* and *unconditional* regularities of experience. The regularity of night and day is a good example of a uniformity of succession. However much the night-day sequence might be a uniformity of succession, it is not an *unconditional* uniformity of succession, and hence not a causal uniformity. We can see that this uniformity is conditional on other things. Should these other things (e.g. the rotation of the earth) cease, there might be perpetual day, unsucceeded by night, or perpetual night, unsucceeded by day. The uniformity is a causal uniformity if and only if it is a uniformity of succession which is unconditional and invariable.

Mill's causation is what I have called deterministic causation. To repeat: 'The law of causation . . . is but the familiar truth that invariability of succession is found by observation to obtain between every fact in nature and some other fact which has preceded it. . .' (Mill 1970:

116

213). Mill argues that (1) there is a cause for everything that happens; (2) that every such cause is a determining cause. That is, he denies both nondeterminism and indeterminism.

Given a cause, an effect of the appropriate sort invariably follows. As I claimed in chapter I, this commitment to deterministic causation will lead Mill to hold some form of an epistemic certainty model of explanation. And this is indeed what he does hold, since he believes that an explanation is always a deductive argument, whose conclusion is the statement of the fact to be explained.

Mill holds that explanation of a particular fact or event is always by way of citing the invariable law of succession (i.e. the causal law) on which the 'production' of that fact or event depends. Presumably, although he does not say it, we can take it that he means that the full explanation involves both the law of invariable succession and an occurrence of a token of the type mentioned in the antecedent clause of that law. Explanation of a universally general fact (a uniformity) is by way of pointing to the more general law or uniformity of which it is a special case ('from which it could be deduced'). Explanation of both kinds, of singular facts and of uniformities, requires only invariability of succession[8] of kinds or types[9] and deduction.

Mill draws a contrast between ultimate and derivative laws. 'From a limited number of ultimate laws of causation, there are necessarily generated a vast number of derivative uniformities, both of succession and co-existence' (Mill 1970: 339). There can be both uniformities of co-existence and non-causal uniformities of succession (like that of night and day) at the level of derived laws. Sometimes we know on which laws derived laws depend; in other cases, we presume that these uniformities are derived, but we have not actually been able to discover on which more fundamental laws they depend. These latter are what Mill calls 'empirical laws':

> It is implied, therefore, in the notion of an empirical law, that it is not an ultimate law; that if true at all, its truth is capable of being, and requires to be accounted for. It is a derivative law, the derivation of which is not yet known.
>
> (Mill 1970: 338)

Mill says that 'From a limited number of ultimate laws of causation, there are necessarily generated a vast number of derivative uniformities, both of succession and of co-existence' (Mill 1970: 339). In some cases, we can explain the derivative uniformities on the basis of fundamental laws alone. But in other cases, we need also initial *particular* information about 'the collocation of some of the primeval causes or natural agents' or the 'mode of co-existence of some of the component elements of the universe'. This information is anomic; it is a brute fact that there is just this distribution of things in the universe, or that particular causes exist in just the number or distribution that they do. We can explain derivative uniformities of both kinds (coexistence and non-causal succession) by ultimate laws of causation, sometimes in conjunction with ultimate facts about the distribution of natural causal agents. But, so far, Mill seems to say that, for whatever is explainable, *ultimately* a causal law is part of the explanation for it.

Do laws of coexistence, as well as laws of succession, have any ultimate explanatory value for Mill? That they can, at least sometimes, *be explained*, is not open to doubt; the question is whether they can be used to explain anything, either ultimately or 'in the interim'. If the answer to the above question is 'no', then there is a sense in which, for Mill, all explanation is causal explanation. If the answer is 'yes', then there is room in science for ultimately non-causal explanations of things, explanations which do not rely upon causal laws. For the sake of convenience, I adopted, in chapter I, the assumption that all explanation of particulars is causal explanation. Perhaps Mill's treatment of this question will help us see whether this assumption is at all plausible.

Mill generally down-grades uniformities of coexistence. He explicitly considers two sorts of cases. First, some of these will be the result of the operation of a single law of causation, as when a single cause invariably has two effects. 'In the same manner with these deriv-ative uniformities of succession, a great variety of uniformities of coexistence also take their rise' (Mill 1970: 378). Suppose that As cause Bs and As cause Cs, and that, as a consequence, there is a derivative regularity of coexistence to the effect that Bs iff Cs. Such a regularity is nomic, and Mill is quite happy to call the statement of it a law: 'The only independent and unconditional co-existences which are sufficiently invariable to have any claim to the character of laws, are between different and mutually independent effects of the same cause...' (p.227).

However, even though the regularity is nomic, it is not explanatory. One cannot explain the occurrence of a B by the occurrence of a C, or vice versa. So nomic uniformities of coexistence that owe their origin to the fact that some single cause has more than one effect will not themselves have any explanatory value.

The second case of a law of coexistence that he considers is this. Suppose there is a uniformity of coexistence that arises from the fact that different 'primeval' causes happen to coexist, there being no further causal explanation why this should be so. As a matter of brute fact about the distribution and number of causal agents in the universe, there is a B iff there is a C. As we would put it, it is only an accidental generalization that Bs iff Cs. Mill himself makes the point by denying that the universal generalization is 'unconditional' (he even sometimes denies that it is 'universal', but he must mean by this only that it is not 'unconditional'). Such an accidental generalization is not nomic or lawlike at all, and one cannot therefore explain the occurrence of a B by the occurrence of a C, or vice versa.[10]

Such accidental generalizations could arise in either of two ways: Bs and Cs might themselves be primeval causes or natural agents; or Bs might be the effects of one such type of agents, and C's the effect of a *different* type. If there is a uniformity of coexistence between two 'primeval causes', or if the uniformity of coexistence is the effect of two different 'primeval causes', then the uniformity of coexistence is about two types of occurrence which coexist 'casually' and not universally, as Mill misleadingly puts it.

> Since everything which occurs is determined by laws of causation and collocations of the original causes, it follows that the co-existences which are observable among the effects cannot be themselves the subject of any similar set of laws, distinct from the laws of causation. Uniformities there are, as well of co-existence as of succession, among effects; but these must in all cases be a mere result either of the identity or of the co-existence of their causes . . . it follows that (except in the case of effects which can be traced immediately or remotely to the same cause) the co-existence of phenomena can in no case be universal, unless the co-existences of the primeval causes to which the effects are ultimately traceable, can be reduced to a universal law: but we have seen that they cannot. There are, accordingly, no original and independent, in other words no unconditional, uniformities of co-existence, between effects of different causes. . .
>
> (Mill 1970: 227)

Such a co-existence of two primeval causes, or the effects of two independent primeval causes, cannot be unconditional; it is merely a 'casual' (i.e. accidental or non-nomic) collocation: 'there is . . . no uniformity, no *norma*, principle, or rule, perceivable in the distribution of the primeval natural agents through the universe' (Mill 1970: 340). Uniformities of coexistence not resulting from the operation of a single cause are not unconditional, and hence do not deserve the title of 'law' at all. *A fortiori*, they are not explanatory.

Thus far, the only genuine laws available to play any part in explanation would seem to be causal laws. *This is, however, not the position that Mill finally adopts.* In his discussion of kinds and empirical laws (pp.377–81), he admits *ultimate* laws or uniformities of coexistence not dependent on causation: 'there must be one class of co-existences which cannot depend on causation; the co-existences between the ultimate properties of things. . . . Yet among these ultimate properties there are not only co-existences, but uniformities of co-existence' (p.379). These ultimate uniformities of coexistence are lawlike, and hence not to be confused with the brute and inexplicable coexistence of primeval causes or collocations, or the derivative effects of them.

Mill's ultimate laws of coexistence presuppose the idea of natural kinds: 'laws of this type assert that there is an invariable concomitance of determinate properties in every object that is of a certain kind'. Mill's examples include blackness and being a crow; woolly-hairness and being a negro.[11] He is thinking of these claims, viz. all crows are black, as claims about denotation and not about connotation; they are not verbal but real truths, if they are true. He warns us that it is hard to be sure that these coexistences are not just joint effects of a single cause, but he is willing to admit that there *must* be some uniformities of coexistence which are genuinely uniformities of coexistence between the ultimate properties of kinds, and 'it is of these only that the co-existences can be classed as a peculiar sort of laws of nature' (Mill 1970: 380):

> Uniformities of co-existence, then, not only when they are consequences of laws of succession, but also when they are ultimate truths, must be ranked, for the purposes of logic, among empirical laws, and are amenable in every respect to the same rules with those unresolved uniformities which are known to be dependent on causation.
>
> (Mill 1970: 386)

Ultimate uniformities of coexistence are laws, but 'must be ranked among empirical laws'; they are 'amenable in every respect to the same

120

rules' as empirical laws. But he does not quite say that they are empirical laws. But if they are not empirical laws, why are they 'amenable in every respect to the same rules'?

Mill does not place great reliance on these ultimate laws of coexistence, which do not depend on causation, mainly because he holds that, concerning any uniformity that we hold to be such an ultimate uniformity of coexistence, it can be overturned by the finding of a single counterexample:

> Universal propositions, therefore, respecting the properties of superior kinds, unless grounded on proved or presumed connection by causation, ought not to be hazarded except after separately examining every known sub-kind included in the larger kind. . . . Thus all the universal propositions which it has been attempted to lay down respecting simple substances . . . have, with the progress of experience, either faded into inanity, or been proven to be erroneous. . . .
>
> (Mill 1970: 385–6)

It is this feature of them which makes them comparable to merely empirical laws.

But he did not deny that there were such laws, whatever epistemic problems there may be in knowing what they are, and indeed his theory of natural kinds presupposes that there must be, for whatever ultimate constituents of things that there are, such laws of coexistence which do not depend on causation. Mill is only wary of being able to identify correctly the coexistences which are the unconditional, ultimate ones. So ultimate laws of coexistence are not empirical laws, because they are not derived laws. But epistemologically, the warrant we have for ultimate laws of coexistence is like the warrant we have for empirical laws, and therefore he draws the comparison between them.

Non-accidental laws of coexistence were also allowed by Ernest Nagel, and for reasons similar to Mill's.[12] Nagel says that this type of law rests on the assumption that there are natural kinds of substances. It is not clear, from Nagel's discussion, precisely what such a law would assert, but something like this is what is suggested by his remarks: 'Rock salt has a melting point of 804 degrees Centigrade, and a density of 2.163.' Nagel includes this in his list of laws 'that are used as explanatory premises in various sciences. . . '. Mill does not assert, like Nagel, that we can use these laws of coexistence in explanation. But equally he does not say that we cannot use them in order to explain something (of course, we cannot explain them, for they are, for Mill, ultimate laws).

This, then, raises an interesting question for Mill, although not one to which he addressed himself clearly and explicitly. Mill stresses the importance of causal explanation (explanation by causes, or by subsumption under causal laws). Is there any reason why we cannot use these ultimate coexistences between the properties of kinds, or any coexistences of properties dependent on them, as the explanans in some explanation? These laws of coexistence might have explanatory power in two ways. First, ultimate non-causal uniformities of coexistence might explain derivative non-causal uniformities of coexistence. Second, it is not clear why Mill should limit, as he does, explanation of singular facts to their causes. Suppose that it is an ultimate law of the uniformity of coexistences for the kind, crow, that all crows are black. It would seem entirely in keeping with the general thrust of his empiricist philosophy of explanation to argue that, in such a case, we could explain why a particular bird is black on the grounds that it is a crow and that it is an ultimate law that all crows are black. This is certainly the spirit, as we shall see, in which Hempel develops the theory. If we did develop Mill's theory of explanation in this way, we could produce examples of the explanation of a feature of a thing by one of its coexistent features, and hence, on Mill's account of causation, examples of non-causal explanation.

To whatever extent these ultimate laws of uniformity of coexistence may have explanatory power, it would be only a most reluctant admission by Mill, dragged from him unwillingly and tentatively. There is no doubt that he is happiest with causal laws. Mill, therefore, turns his attention to the discussion of explanation of and by causal laws, laws of the invariable and unconditional succession of phenomena, rather than to the possibility of explanation by laws of the simultaneity or coexistence of phenomena.

Mill spends some time in discussing the explanation of causal laws and delineates three subspecies of such explanations. 'There are, then, three modes of explaining laws of causation, or, which is the same thing, resolving them into other laws' (Mill 1970: 310). First, there is the case of 'an intermixture of laws, producing a joint effect equal to the sum of the effects of the causes taken separately. The law of the complex effect is explained by being resolved into the separate laws of the causes which contribute to it' (p.305). Second, there is the case in which a uniformity between two kinds of facts is shown to be the result of two uniformities, one linking the first kind of facts with a new, third kind, and another uniformity linking the third kind with the second: 'between what seemed the cause and what was supposed to be its effect, further observation detects an intermediate link' (p.306). The third is the subsumption of a law by another law: 'This third mode is the *subsumption* . . . of one law under another, or (what comes to the same thing) the gathering up of several laws into one more general law which includes them all' (p.309). Mill remarks that in all three cases, the explaining laws are always more general than the laws to be explained, so all three cases are examples of the explanation of the less general by the more general: 'It is of importance to remark that when a sequence of phenomena is thus resolved into other laws, they are always laws more general than itself' (p.307).

Mill repeatedly uses the language of 'resolution' in all three cases. In at least one passage, Mill speaks of the 'elimination' of the less general law by the more general (Mill 1970: 309). In more modern terminology, we might say that this type of explanation, of a law by other laws, is one form of reduction. The resolved or reduced law can be seen to be nothing more than a particular instance or application of more general resolving or reducing laws.

Mill's account of explanation: the symmetry thesis

Mill asserts what has come to be called 'the symmetry thesis' – that is, the claim that there is a symmetry of sorts between explanation and prediction. This symmetry thesis should be distinguished from a second and different question of symmetry that we shall be discussing later: the (controversial) claim that explanation is itself asymmetric, that if p explains q, it follows that q does not explain p. When I speak of the symmetry *thesis*, I shall mean the question of the symmetry between explanation and prediction. When I want to speak of the second question, I shall speak of the symmetry (or, asymmetry or non-symmetry) of the explanation relation. Mill does not address himself explicitly to this second question at all.

Mill says: 'As already remarked, the same deductive process which proves a law or fact of causation if unknown, serves to explain it when known' (Mill 1970: 310). One and the same deduction can answer either of two questions: 'Given a certain combination of causes, what effect will follow? and, What combination of causes, if it existed, would produce a given effect?' (p. 303) In the first case, we predict what will happen (Mill speaks of proving what will happen, rather than in terms of predicting); in the second, we explain what we know to have happened. The symmetry thesis holds that there is only a pragmatic, or epistemic, but no logical, difference between explaining and predicting. Explaining and predicting are human activities, both of which involve the producing of a deduction. The difference between these activities is only a difference in what the producer of the deduction knows just before the time at which the deduction is produced. Whether I fully explain why e occurred, or fully predict that e will occur, the deduction produced will be the same.

Recall the distinction I drew in the first chapter, between explanation as a process (or activity) and explanation as the product of such an activity. Such a product is, according to Mill, a deductive argument. Mill's symmetry thesis can be expressed by making use of this distinction. In the product sense, explanations and predictions are identical. One and the same deduction is both an explanation (product) and a prediction (product). The difference between explanation and prediction is only between acts of explaining and acts of predicting.

The symmetry thesis, more generally, is this: (a) the information produced in a (successful) explanatory act could have been the information produced in a (successful) act of prediction; (b) the information produced in a (successful) act of prediction could have been the information produced in a (successful) act of explanation. In the process or activity sense, explanations and predictions differ. Consider a case of explaining that p and a case of predicting that p. I will know or believe crucially different things in the two cases, and this will mean that *what* activity I am engaged in, in the two cases, is different. But in the product sense, according to the symmetry thesis, explanations and predictions of the same thing do not differ at all.

The plausibility of the symmetry thesis is closely tied to construing both explanations and predictions as arguments. If explanations and predictions are both arguments, it is perhaps not a large leap of faith to hold that the argument produced in an act of the one type of activity will be identical to the argument that would have been produced in an act of the second type. But suppose that explanations or predictions are not arguments. Whether the symmetry thesis is held to be true will depend on the details of the non-argument view. But it would be open to such a view to claim that the information content of explanations and predictions differ, and therefore that the symmetry thesis is false.

Mill on ultimate explanations

We have already mentioned both Plato's and Aristotle's views on ultimate explanations. Both agree that the regress of explanation must come to some end. Mill agrees with that view. It is now time to look at this question in some more detail. First, though, I want to develop a terminology in which to discuss this. Using Mill's own terminology of facts, let me introduce the idea of an explanatory tree. Explanatory trees look like this:

Each of the facts e, h, k, n, q, t on this tree is explained by those facts to the left of it to which it is connected by an arrow ('the arrow of explanation'). The facts that explain might be universally general facts (Mill's uniformities, like the fact that everything which is F, is G), or singular facts (like the fact that a is F), or existentially general facts (like the fact that there is something which is an F), or stochastic facts (like the fact that many or most Fs are Gs), facts of identity (like the fact that a=b), and conjunctions and combinations thereof (this list is meant to be indicative, but not necessarily exhaustive, of the kinds of facts that there are). Hempel calls singular facts 'particular facts', and I sometimes follow him in this. I use 'singular' and 'particular' interchangeably, and mark no distinction by the two expressions. In general, however, I prefer 'singular', because in classical logic a particular judgement has the form, 'Some A is B', and the fact that this expresses is an existentially general fact rather than a singular one.

There are parallels between causal trees and explanatory trees, but even for Mill they are not the same thing. Moreover, whatever our views about causation, different columns cannot be taken to represent successive times. Nor is the arrow of explanation the same as the arrow of causation. General laws or universally general facts at earlier times do not cause less general facts or laws at later times. More general laws explain less general laws without causing them; and if they explain them, they *atemporally* do so. So the tree employs the arrow of explanation, not the arrows of time or of causation, although of course both time and causation will figure in the tree where appropriate.

This tree is only a portion of a much larger and more extensive tree, since it goes back only to the explanation of e, in terms of a, b, and c. The more extensive tree branches at each point as we travel backwards (to the left) on it. Presumably, a, b, c, d, f, g, i, and all the other facts above whose explanation is not accounted for in the tree fragment there presented, themselves have explanations.

Our question is this: do such trees necessarily have initial starting points on the left? To put it another way: are there any ultimately inexplicable facts? Mill's reply is that there must be such facts, which have no possible explanation. According to Mill, there must be some inexplicable universally general facts:

> Derivative laws are such as are deducible from . . . and may . . . be resolved into other and more general ones. Ultimate laws are those which cannot. We are not sure that any of the uniformities with which we are yet acquainted are ultimate laws; but we know that there must be ultimate laws, and that every resolution of a derivative law into more general laws brings us nearer to them.
>
> (Mill 1970: 318)

Mill's view is that there must be an ultimate plurality of laws which have no further explanation, even though we may be unsure whether, concerning any particular law, it be ultimate or derived. We attributed to Plato and Aristotle the idea of self-explaining entities. They did not see how an ultimate inexplicable could in turn explain something else, so the ultimate points in the regress of explanation had, for them, to be self-explaining. Since, for Mill, explanation is *only* by way of derivation from something more general (unlike for Aristotle, for Mill there is no such thing as 'non-demonstrable understanding'), it follows that for him these ultimate starting points of explanation must be inexplicable rather than self-explaining.

I do not claim that *I* can see the difference between inexplicability and self-explicability, but only that the philosophers under discussion seem to see a difference. The real difference between ultimate inexplicability and self-explicability may be verbal rather than real. It is certainly not obvious what of interest follows from one that does not follow from the other.[13]

So far, we have seen that Mill subscribes to the thesis that there are ultimate, inexplicable laws. He also thinks that there are ultimate, inexplicable singular facts concerning the number and distribution of the primeval causal agents in the universe, a topic we have already touched on.

> Derivative laws, therefore, do not depend solely on the ultimate laws into which they are resolvable: they mostly depend on those ultimate laws and an ultimate fact, namely the mode of co-existence of some of the component elements of the universe. The ultimate laws of causation might be the same as at present, and yet the derivative laws completely different, if the causes co-existed in any different proportions....there is ... no uniformity, no *norma*, principle, or rule, perceivable in the distribution of the primeval natural agents through the universe.
>
> (Mill 1970: 339–40)

So Mill is committed to a double ultimacy of inexplicables: (1) there are laws for which there is in principle no explanation; (2) there are particular brute facts for which there is in principle no explanation.

In the last chapter, Aristotle presented us with the obvious alternatives to the doctrine of ultimate inexplicability or self-explanation. There are, at first sight, two. First, the trees might just extend indefinitely or infinitely backwards, with no stopping point. We might refer to this as the doctrine of the infinite (or, indefinite) regress of explanation. Aristotle, Plato, and Mill certainly assumed that such a regress, if it existed, would be vicious. But would it? A regress is said to be vicious if, for example, in order to have something, there is always an additional something one is first required to have. In general, in a vicious infinite regress, one could never be in a position to have any-thing at all, for the requirements for having the first or any additional thing could never be met.

For example, suppose that there is a tree of belief justification, analogous to my explanation tree. Each belief I hold can be justified in terms of other beliefs which I do or could hold, which themselves can be justified in terms of still other beliefs which I do or could hold, and so on, *ad infinitum*. Suppose *further* that, for any one of my beliefs to be justified, I must actually possess a justification for all the beliefs which justify it. This requirement sets in motion a vicious infinite regress, since the consequence would be that no belief could ever be justified.

However, it isn't just the fact that there is an infinity of justified and justifying beliefs that makes this regress vicious. The viciousness arises from that additional further supposition that no justification of some belief is possible until one *actually has* a justification for each of the beliefs which justify it. That there could be an infinitely long chain of beliefs, each of which 'objectively' could justify its successor, seems acceptable. What is unacceptable is the repeated application of the thesis that, for some belief of mine to be justified, I must actually be in possession of a justification for each of the beliefs which justify it.

Compare these two theses:

(1) All beliefs can be justified in terms of other beliefs, *ad infinitum* (or indefinitely).
(2) For any belief of a person's to be justified, he must actually be in possession of a justification for each of the beliefs which justify it.

with the following two theses about explanation:

(3) All facts can be explained in terms of other facts *ad infinitum* (or indefinitely).
(4) For any fact to be able to explain another, one must actually have an explanation for it.

(3 & 4) – like (1 & 2) – involves a vicious infinite regress. If everything has an explanation, and I couldn't actually have an explanation for anything until I had an explanation of everything that I used in the explanation, then I could never have an explanation of anything at all. But (3) by itself does not require this. I may be able to explain f by g, even though I have no explanation of g itself. There may be, objectively as it were, such an explanation of g, in the sense that there is some h such that h would or could explain g if I knew about h; (3) asserts that this is so. But I am not prevented from explaining f by g just because I fail to know the h that explains g.

Perhaps it is different with justification. It might be plausible to hold this: I cannot justify f by g if I do not actually have a justification for g; an unjustified belief cannot itself justify another belief. This is controversial. But, as far as explanation is concerned, unexplained (by me) g can still explain f. A fact itself unexplained can still explain another. (3) by itself requires an entirely non-vicious infinite regress of explanation. Plato, Aristotle, and Mill were wrong.

The second possibility is that such trees are not really trees at all, but in fact are loops. If one travels far enough to the left of some (particular or universally general) fact, one ends by being on that fact's right. No fact is inexplicable, but sometimes facts are explained by facts which are far to the right of them on the circular tree.

In a tree of explanation as I have imagined it, each fact is (part of) the explanation of the fact immediately to its right, to which it is joined by an arrow. For example, b is part of the explanation of e. If e is part of the explanation of h, does it follow that b is part of the explanation of h? Is the explanation relation transitive, as Robert Nozick asserts (he also says that the explanation relation is irreflexive and asymmetric)?[14] Intuitions differ here, and so I introduce the terms 'explanatory ancestor' and 'explanatory descendant'. If b is part of the explanation of e and e is part of the explanation of h, then b is an explanatory ancestor of h; h, an explanatory descendant of b. The relation of being an explanatory ancestor of is uncontroversially transitive, whether or not the explanation relation is.

Now, if b and t figure in an explanatory loop, then, even though b is an explanatory ancestor of t, t may also be a explanatory ancestor of b. In such a case, b will occur at least twice over as we journey in the explanatory loop: once as an explanatory ancestor of t, and once as an explanatory descendant of t. This would mean that the relation of being an explanatory ancestor of is not an asymmetric relation (it might be either symmetric or non-symmetric, depending on further details about the construction of these trees). Finally, if being an explanatory ancestor of is transitive and symmetric (or, non-symmetric), and if there are these loops, the relation will also be reflexive (or, non-reflexive); a fact must (or, can) be an explanatory ancestor of itself.

The idea of an explanatory relation, being the explanatory ancestor of, that is transitive, but fails to be asymmetric and irreflexive, departs drastically from the way in which we normally think of explanatory relations. (I return to the question of the asymmetry versus non-symmetry of the explanation relation in chapters VI and VII.) We may perhaps dismiss the idea of such explanatory loops altogether. However, even discounting explanatory loops and Aristotle and Plato's thesis of self-explanation, there seems to be the very plausible idea of a non-vicious infinite regress of explanation. Mill's conclusion that there must be ultimate inexplicable laws and singular facts is too swift.

Mill on deduction and explanation

I raised right at the beginning of the chapter the question of how well Mill's theory of explanation and his views on deduction cohere. His views on deduction are not unambiguously clear; in fact, several different theses seem to be conflated into what Mill regarded as a single thesis. I summarize his view below, to the extent that is required for my discussion, and without paying attention to the other strands that make up this ambiguous doctrine.[15] Nor am I much interested in stating whatever, if anything, is plausible in his views. My main aim is to see how one essential epistemic strand in his claims about deduction could fit with his views on explanation.

I stated the general point at the beginning of the chapter: if deduction cannot advance knowledge, it would have been natural for Mill's epistemic down-grading of deduction to have carried over to his views on explanation, since explanation is surely, or so anyway one might suppose, a way of advancing our knowledge. But in none of his remarks about explanation does Mill take any account of his general views about deduction, or explain how his epistemic down-grading of deduction fits with his holding a deductivist theory of explanation.

To infer, Mill tells us, is to reason in the widest sense. Mill means by an inference 'a means of coming to a knowledge of something which we did not know before' (Mill 1970: 120). That something, knowledge of which we acquire in making the inference, is the inference's conclusion. It is crucial to see that his conception of an inference ('a real inference'), unlike ours, is partly epistemic. Mill's concept of a real inference cannot be explicated just by syntactic or semantic concepts. A real inference moves the inferer *from* a state of not-knowing the truth of the conclusion of an inference, *to* knowledge of the truth of that conclusion.

Reasoning in the wide sense is *commonly* (but, as we shall see, not truly) said to be of two kinds: 'reasoning from particulars to generals, and reasoning from generals to particulars; the former being called Induction, the latter Ratiocination or Syllogism' (Mill 1970: 107). Reason in the narrow sense is ratiocination, of which syllogism is the general type. Mill identifies, in these passages, deductive reasoning with syllogistic reasoning, so that he speaks of all deductive inference as involving a passage from general to particular propositions. I will follow him in this, and direct my remarks to syllogistic reasoning.

Not all things taken to be inferences on the commonly accepted view are real inferences, and not all real inferences are taken to be such on the commonly accepted view. Mill has no doubt that induction, reasoning from particulars to the general, is a process of real inference, in his sense:

the conclusion in an induction embraces more than is contained in the premisses. . . . In every induction we proceed from truths which we knew to truths which we did not know; from facts certified by observation to facts which we have not observed. . . . Induction, then, is a real process of Reasoning or Inference.

(Mill 1970: 108)

Mill's assertion is that, in inductive inference, we move from known truths to truths hitherto unknown. And the same will be true for what Mill calls 'the third species of reasoning', unrecognized by the common view, in which we move from particular truth to particular truth, without the aid of general propositions at all.

Mill does not think that syllogistic reasoning can be a process of real inference in this same sense, whatever the common view of the matter might be:

we have now to inquire whether the syllogistic process, that of reasoning from generals to particulars, is, or is not, a process of inference; a process from the known to the unknown; a means of coming to a knowledge of something which we did not know before.

(Mill 1970: 120)

Mill argues that, since a syllogistic inference would be invalid if there were anything more in the conclusion than what was in the premisses, 'nothing ever was, or can be, proved by syllogism which was not known, or assumed to be known, before' (Mill 1970: 120). For Mill, every syllogism, if considered as an attempt to *gain* knowledge that the conclusion is true, on the basis of knowledge of the premisses, must be a *petitio principii*. No one could know that the premisses of a syllogistic inference were true unless they already knew that the conclusion was true. The idea of a syllogistic argument advancing knowledge about the truth of the conclusion is, according to him, epistemologically circular.

I abbreviate 'knows that p' as 'K(p)', and use the '→' sign for logical entailment. In what follows, 'x' is an unbound variable; 'a' is not a variable, but a name or definite description of an object. The principle on which Mill relies, stated for one type of syllogistic inference only, seems to be:

(1) [('All F are G' & 'a is F'→'a is G') & K(all F are G & a is F)]→K(a is G).

131

In ordinary language, someone who does *not* know that a is G, could not come to know that a is G by deducing it from his knowledge that all F are G and that a is F, because if he fails to know that a is G, and if there is this entailment, then he must also fail to know either that all F are G, or that a is F.

There is not much to be said in favour of Mill's principle, (1); on his principle, there could be no such thing as a surprising conclusion of a syllogistic inference, yet it is clear that some such inferences are informative (even if it is difficult to see this in my specific example). One might try to defend (1) by arguing that if one does know that all F are G and that a is an F, one does know willy-nilly that a is G, despite protests to the contrary on the part of the person. It's just that a person might not be aware of the fact that he knows that a is G, and it may indeed come as a surprise to him that this is what he knows. He knows, but he doesn't know that he knows. I shall not pursue the possibility of defending Mill with this sort of 'externalist' account. There is a sense in which the defence would not be of any help to him. Deduction would, on that defence, be a sort of real inference after all; by deduction, one could advance from a state of not knowing that one knew that a is G, to a state of knowing that one knew that a is G.

How could one know that all F are G, and that a is F, and not know that a is G? If one does not know that a, which (as one knows) is F, is G, how is it possible to know that everything which is F is G? The answer is that one could know the generalization via some other route than via the one which goes through a, which is F, being G. One might know 'All F are G' by deduction from a higher level principle, or by induction from many other cases of F-ish things being G, but not including the case of a. As John Skorupski says:

the conclusion [that syllogistic inference is epistemically circular] only follows if one assumes that any process of reasoning which can raise my confidence in the proposition that all men are mortal, has to include a specific and separate assessment of the probability that Socrates [my 'a'] is mortal. Suppose, on the other hand, that there is a sound method of reasoning which can rationally raise my confidence that all men are mortal, without requiring me to consider the particular case of Socrates. Then from the general proposition, together with my knowledge that Socrates is a man, I can infer that Socrates is mortal: and thus without circularity, I become more confident of Socrates' mortality. There obviously is such a method of reasoning – induction. I can argue inductively from cases other than that of Socrates to 'All men are mortal', and hence from 'Socrates is a man' to 'Socrates is mortal'.[16]

Skorupski's argument against Mill is expressed in terms of degree of rational confidence; mine (like Mill's), in terms of knowledge. Perhaps one might try to reply, on Mill's behalf, by taking advantage of this distinction. One can have, it might be said, a high degree of rational confidence in all F being G, based on lots of Fs being G, but without having considered the case of a (I may know that a is F, but simply have not considered whether a is G). But how, the Millian might continue, could I *know* that all F are G and know that a is F without having considered the case of a's G-ness?

The answer to this question surely is that the criteria even for *knowing* that a generalization is true cannot be set this high. I can *know* that a generalization is true, without having, *per impossibile*, separately and specifically assessed each instance of it. If I could not know a generalization in this way, all generalizations, except those grounded in a perfect induction, would be unknowable.

There is a principle worth considering that is more plausible than the one to which Mill actually commits himself:

(2) [K('All F are G' & 'a is F'→'a is G') &K(all F are G & a is F)]→K(a is G)

Suppose one knows, as before, that all F are G and that a is F, but now also *knows* that these two beliefs entail that a is G. It isn't *just* that one knows that sentences with the form, 'x is G' follow from 'All F are G' and a sentence with the form, 'x is F'. Rather, one knows, concerning *a*, that 'a is G' follows from 'All F are G' and 'a is F'. One is not in the dark about the fact that a's G-ness follows from a's F-ness. In a sense, one has considered a's status (the fact that a's G-ness follows from a's F-ness), although not whether in fact a is G.

Does it then follow that one knows that a is G? One might try arguing that it does, on the grounds that knowledge is closed under *known* logical entailment. One could, then, try to reconstruct Mill's view on syllogistic inference, using this more plausible principle. Robert Nozick rejects the principle that knowledge is closed under known logical entailment, so any defence of (2) would have to take account of his argument.[17]

Mill had a deep appreciation of the triumphs of natural science. How, one might wonder, could his view of deductive inference be compatible with his knowledge of scientific advance? His answer must be that science *advances* by induction and inference from particular-to-particular. It is possible to summarize or describe the advance in a general way, by use of deductive inference. But the advance of science itself cannot be via deductive inference at all.

How, if at all, is Mill's deductivist account of explanation consistent with his view of deduction? The answer is contained in the above: explaining is not advancing. Recall that Mill said: 'As already remarked, the same deductive process which proves a law or fact of causation if unknown, serves to explain it when known' (Mill 1970: 310). Prediction and explanation are to be distinguished by the fact that they ask the following distinct questions: 'Given a certain combination of causes, what effect will follow? and, What combination of causes, if it existed, would produce a given effect?' (p. 303) That the conclusion of an explanatory argument is true is what one already knows, *before* the explanation is produced. So there is no question of *coming to know*, on the basis of the explanatory deduction, that the conclusion is true. On Mill's view, explanation does not involve gaining new knowledge about the truth of the conclusion of an explanatory argument.

Explanations are surprising. Whence comes the surprise in an explanation? An explanation must teach something new, that was not known before. Of course, the premisses of a deduction typically contain more information than what the conclusion by itself asserts. In explaining an explanandum, I might learn a great deal of this new information. I might be surprised to learn that the major premiss (all F are G) or the minor premiss (a is F) of the explanatory argument is true. (On Mill's view, knowing that all F are G is just to know that there is a *real* inference from any sentence with the form, 'x is F' to a sentence with the form, 'x is G'.[18])

But somehow that can't be all there is to the surprise. I *might* explain the fact that a is G, already knowing that a is F and all Fs are Gs. After all, I can actually set out the explanation as a deductive argument only when I already know all the premisses and the conclusion. What, then, does putting the explanation in the form of a deductive argument do, when it does not surprise me about the truth of any premiss or conclusion? Why (to put the same question differently) must the law that all Fs are Gs be included in the explanation at all? What motive could Mill have had for being a deductivist about explanation? Mill does discuss the rationale for setting out sciences in a deductive form (Mill 1970: 141–7), but the considerations he there adduces will not help us to understand what is gained by insisting that explanations are deductive arguments with at least one law premiss.

The problem here runs very deep. One can sense how deep, by considering Mill's views on the third species of reasoning, which he says is the ground for both deduction and induction: immediate inference from a particular proposition, to a particular proposition, without the aid of any generalization at all:

> If from our experience of John, Thomas, etc., who once were living, but are now dead, we are entitled to conclude that all human beings are mortal, we might surely without any logical inconsequence have concluded at once from these instances that the Duke of Wellington is mortal. The mortality of John, Thomas, and others, is, after all, the whole evidence we have for the mortality of the Duke of Wellington. Not one iota is added to the proof by interpolating a general proposition. Since the individual cases are all the evidence we can possess, evidence which no logical form into which we choose to throw it can make greater than it is; and since that evidence is either sufficient in itself, or if insufficient for the one purpose, cannot be sufficient for the other; I am unable to see why we should be forbidden to take the shortest cut from these sufficient premisses to the conclusion, and constrained to travel the 'high priori road', by the arbitrary fiat of logicians.
>
> (Mill 1970: 122–3)

If we take seriously Mill's remarks on the conceptual priority of this type of reasoning that goes from particulars to a further particular, we might again wonder why he holds a deductivist account of explanation. Why, to paraphrase his remarks above on inference, can't we explain a's being a G, on the basis of a's being an F, and the fact that b, c, d, etc., which were F, were also G? What does a generalization do in a deductive explanation that could not just as well be done by a non-deductive 'explanation' from particular propositions to a particular proposition, without 'interpolating a general proposition'? Does it just serve as a reminder about other explanations we would be prepared to offer, in the way in which Mill says that a deduction serves as a register or reminder about other real inferences we are prepared to make? If that were the answer, then although we could sometimes give deductive explanations, there ought to be a category of real explanation from particulars to particulars, to parallel the category of real inference from particulars to particulars. But Mill offers no such doctrine.

I think there is a good answer to the question of why Mill retained deductive explanation, and did not espouse a view of real explanation, parallel to real inference. It is true that in setting out an explanation in deductive form, one might learn nothing new about the truth of any premiss or of the conclusion. The conclusion, 'a is G', I already knew was true; the premisses I either knew already or learned, in order to be in a position to set out the argument. But there is something else that one learns about the fact that a is G in setting out the deduction, other than its truth; namely, how a's being G fits into the overall pattern of nature. An analogy here might be with a jigsaw puzzle. One already has all the pieces; what one lacks is the ability to fit them all together. An explanatory deduction is rather like a set of directions that show how those pieces of the jigsaw fit together. The directions do not give one any new pieces to the puzzle; only new information about how they mesh into a whole picture. Putting the pieces together can be surprising. One had all the pieces, but was surprised to learn that that is the picture that results when they are assembled.

And so it is with deductive explanation. No new particular piece of knowledge of the sort one is likely to find in a premiss or a conclusion of a syllogism must be gained; all that typically will be gained in deductive explanation is new information about how all the same old pieces of knowledge fit together in an overall grasp of what nature is like. It isn't necessary that, in explaining why a is G, I learn *that* a is F or *that* all F are G (although I might learn one or both of these). What I may do is to bring all the information I already possess together, to assemble it, as it were, to form an overall view of how my existing stock of information interrelates; how some pieces of it bear on other pieces. And the new knowledge I acquire about this pattern, about these interrelations, typically will itself be surprising information.

Mill's view of what explanation does for us, quoted earlier, bears out these remarks:

> The word explanation is here used in its philosophical sense. What is called explaining one law of nature by another, is but substituting one mystery for another, and does nothing to render the general course of nature other than mysterious: we can no

more assign a why for the most extensive laws than for the partial ones.

(Mill 1970: 310)

Mill seems to be distinguishing in this passage between 'explaining' on the one hand, and providing an answer to 'why?' on the other. If Mill had thought of explanation as providing some sort of deep answer to a 'why-question', he might have accepted a Duhemian scepticism about explanation. But he does not think of explanation in this way; we never really ever know (in the 'deep' and demystifying sense) why, according to him. All that we can do, in explaining, is to embed the particular fact or law to be explained in this wider or more general pattern, without ever lessening the deeper mystery of the universe. We represent this fitting of facts into wider patterns by means of deductive arguments. In so doing, we can gain new knowledge of the patterns in nature itself. As Mill said: 'those who speak of explaining any phenomenon mean (or should mean) pointing out not some more familiar, but merely some more general phenomenon, of which it is a partial exemplification' (Mill 1970: 310–11). Mill's epistemic down-grading of deductive inference fits well with his deductivist account of explanation, because he thought of his theory of explanation as a similar epistemic down-grading of explanation, from its non-empiricist pretensions.

Mill's doctrines of explanation and deductive inference are both part of his overall project of making certain concepts 'safe' for an empiricist. An empiricist can surely accept explanation as merely registering the increasingly general patterns or structures into which all the particular substantive pieces of our knowledge are to be fitted. Deeper insight than that, if there be such, is a mystery, happily beyond the reach of sound empiricist philosophy and its acceptable doctrine of what explanation is all about.

How could Mill make his view of deduction consistent with making surprising *predictions*? This seems to me more difficult. Unlike explanations, predictions seem clearly to *advance* the predictor to new knowledge about the conclusion. Had Mill been willing to accept real predictions, analogous to real inferences, he could have explained how science advances by means of such predictions from particulars to particulars, while retaining his doctrines of the epistemic circularity of deductive inference, and of the deductive argument form of explanation. But he no more considers real prediction as a possibility, than he does real explanation. In any event, such a move, on its own, would have been inconsistent with the thesis of the symmetry between explanation and prediction.

Hempel's account of scientific explanation

We dealt at some length in chapter I with some of the features of Hempel's methodology. In this section of chapter IV, I will introduce and describe some of the substantive features of his account of explanation. In many ways, Hempel's account is a development and sophistication of what can already be found in Mill's theory of explanation.

Hempel holds that there are 'two basic types of scientific explanation: deductive-nomological [D-N] and inductive-statistical [I-S]. . .'.[19] (In some passages, there is a third, deductive-statistical, but I ignore that here.) In this chapter, and in chapter VI, I will take Hempel to be offering a disjunctive list of conditions that cover the two cases, the disjuncts being jointly necessary and individually sufficient for the concept of the (scientific) explanation of particular events.[20] Hempel mentions the need for a further condition which would rule out self-explanation.[21] This is a problem that I shall not discuss, and none of my criticisms turns on its omission.

Hempel's requirements for a deductive-nomological explanation of a particular event are these. Let '$c_1, c_2, c_3 \ldots c_n$' be sentences describing singular facts; let '$L_1, L_2 \ldots L_m$' be universally quantified sentences asserting certain lawlike regularities (these together constitute the explanans). Let 'e' be a sentence describing whatever fact is to be explained (the explanandum). The laws and singular facts described by the explanans sentences explain the fact described by the explanandum sentence iff: (1) e is a logical consequence of the conjunction of the explanans sentences; (2) e does not follow from any proper subset of the explanans sentences; (3) the explanans sentences must have empirical content; (4) the explanans sentences must all be true. Little or nothing in the analysis of D-N explanation goes beyond what can be found in Mill's position, although of course Hempel's presentation, unlike Mill's, is detailed, careful, and technically sophisticated.

As Hempel and Oppenheim (with whom Hempel co-authored the early article) point out, (3) is redundant. Since the explanandum fact is an empirical fact, and if, as (1) requires, the explanandum sentence that states that fact is derivable from the conjunction of explanans sentences, (3) is automatically fulfilled. The explanans sentences are bound to have *some* empirical content, in virtue of implying the empirical explanandum sentence itself. (1) is trivially true, since the kind of explanation being analysed by this disjunct of the analysis has been *restricted* to D-N explanations; the analysis of non-deductive explanation is to be covered by the other disjunct of the analysis of scientific explanation. It is not an amazing truth that the explanandum sentence is entailed by the conjunction of the explanans sentences *in a (full) D-N explanation.*

The history of (4), discussed by Lyon, is rather strange.[22] In the early article, and again in the later article, the notion of a potential explanation is introduced, similar to the one I used in my discussion of Aristotle, who like them required that the premises of an explanatory argument be true. But in a postscript to the early article added in 1964, Hempel says that the fourth requirement characterizes what might be called a correct or true explanation. In an analysis of the logical structure of explanatory arguments, he says, (4) may be disregarded (Hempel 1965: 249).

For Hempel, what sorts of entities are explanantia and explananda, in the non-sentence sense? What is the ontology of explanation? Mill, as we saw, was less than clear about this. Hempel speaks of 'explaining a phenomenon' (Hempel 1965: 246), or 'why the phenomenon occurred' (p.246 and p.337), but elsewhere he tells us that an explanation explains 'in virtue of certain explanatory facts', which facts include 'singular facts' and uniformities (p.336). But then he also says that 'the object of . . . explanation in every branch of empirical science is always the occurrence of an event of a certain kind . . . at a given place and time' (p.233).

Hempel gives an extended discussion of this question in his later article, and it is this which I take to be his considered view:

. . .only when understood in this sense, as fully describable by means of sentences, can particular facts or events be amenable to scientific explanation. . . .

But the notion of an individual or particular event is often construed in quite a different manner. An event in this second sense is specified, not by means of a sentence describing it, but by means of a noun phrase such as an individual name or definite description, as for example, 'the first solar eclipse of the twentieth century', 'the eruption of Mt. Vesuvius in A.D. 79', 'the assassination of Leon Trotsky', 'the stock market crash of 1929'. For want of a better terminology, individual events thus understood will be referred to as concrete events, and facts and events in the first sense here considered will be called sententially characterizable, or briefly, sentential facts and events. . . .

In sum, a request for an explanation can be significantly made only concerning what we have called sentential facts and events; only with respect to them can we raise a question of the form 'why is it the case that p?' As for concrete events, let us note that what we have called their aspects or characteristics are all of them describable by means of sentences; each of these aspects, then, is a sentential fact or event (that the eruption of Mt. Vesuvius in A.D.79 lasted for so many hours. . .).

It would be incorrect to summarize this point by saying that the object of explanation is always a kind of event rather than an individual event. . .What might in fact be explained is rather the occurrence of a particular instance of a given kind of event. . .And what is thus explained is definitely an individual event; indeed, it is one that is unique and unrepeatable in view of the temporal location assigned to it. But it is an individual sentential event, of course. . . .

(Hempel 1965: 421–3)

So, in sum, I think we should read Hempel's previous more random remarks in the light of this long quotation. Hempel's theory of explanation is only a theory of explanation for 'sentential facts and events', never for singular or concrete events. To simplify, I shall attribute to Hempel an ontology of explanation that utilizes facts, but I shall not discuss the rationale for so doing until the next chapter.

Mill, as we saw, generally down-graded uniformities of coexistence. Hempel, in the early article, asserted that D-N explanation was 'causal explanation' (Hempel 1965: 250), and he does make it clear, especially in the later article (pp.347–52), that he takes a causal law to be a law of the succession of phenomena. Hence (although he does not say so explicitly) it is a notion available to an empiricist philosophy of explanation. But although he, like Mill, believes that causation is safe for an empiricist account of explanation, he is clear on what Mill seemed to waver about; there are for Hempel non-causal explanations of particular events. On his theory, non-causal laws of coexistence also have an explanatory role to play.

In a footnote to the 1964 postscript to the early article, he reminds us that causal explanation is but 'one variety of the deductive type of explanation'. The matter is more fully discussed in the later article. There, he qualifies the claim that explanation of the D-N type is causal explanation in two ways (Hempel 1965: 352–3). First, Hempel reminds us that we explain general laws by subsumption under more general laws, and such explanation is not explanation by causes. Hempel echoes Mill in this:

> The laws, thus explained or resolved, are sometimes said to be accounted for . . . there is often a confused notion that the general laws are the causes of the partial ones. . . . But to assert this would be a misuse of the word cause: terrestrial gravity is not an effect of general gravitation, but a case of it. . . .
>
> (Mill 1970: 311)

Second, Hempel, like Mill, distinguishes between laws of coexistence and laws of succession. For Hempel, as for Mill, a hallmark of causation is succession in time; if a law is about coexistent phenomena, the law cannot be a causal law. But Hempel holds that we can sometimes explain a particular occurrence by adducing a law of coexistence, and in so far as we do this, our explanations of particular events cannot all be causal explanations. The examples he offers are the explanation of the period of a pendulum by its length, and explanations which utilize the Boyle–Charles gas laws, and Ohm's law. Hempel holds that we can, for example, explain the period of a particular pendulum at time t by its length at t. Since this is a case of explanation by laws of coexistence, Hempel allows non-causal explanations, i.e. ones making use of non-causal laws, in the explanation of both singular facts and laws.

Hempel's methodology

Many who read Hempel's writings on explanation for the first time are struck by the apparent arbitrariness of the conditions he lays down in his analysis of explanation. On the view we have just described, one type of full explanation, deductive-nomological explanation, has the form of a deductively valid argument, one of whose premises being a true lawlike generalization. But there seems to be very little argument in Hempel for this, and most other requirements that he mentions. How could we show that this is a reasonable requirement for explanation of any type? Why should we accept it? In terms of the terminology of chapter I, does Hempel use the language users' approach, or the technical approach, in justifying his analysis of explanation?

With the exception of some remarks on the I-S model of explanation (Hempel 1965: 391) and an argument against treating laws as rules of inference (p.356), Hempel nowhere appeals even to a vague and ambiguous language use as a support for any of his requirements for explanation. Hempel explicitly denies that he is writing a dictionary entry: 'Explicating the concept of scientific explanation is not the same as writing an entry on the word "explain" for the Oxford English Dictionary' (pp.412–13). The point of this remark may not be entirely clear, since it is hard to think of any philosopher who thought of philosophical explication as just the same thing as dictionary definition. But whatever precisely the remark means, its thrust seems to be a rejection of the language users' approach.

Hempel asks that his explication be judged by the following constraints:

> Like any other explication, the construal here put forward has to be justified by appropriate arguments. In our case, these have to show that the proposed construal does justice to such accounts as are generally agreed to be instances of scientific explanation, and that it affords a basis for systematically fruitful logical and methodological analysis of the explanatory procedures used in empirical science. It is hoped that the arguments presented in this essay have achieved that objective.
>
> (Hempel 1965: 488–9)

There seem to be two constraints on scientific explanation mentioned in the above quote: (1) doing justice to generally agreed instances of scientific explanation; (2) affording a basis for systematically fruitful logical and methodological analysis of the explanatory procedures of science. As for (1), it is not clear what doing 'justice to' such accounts means, since he asserts elsewhere that

> these models are not meant to describe how working scientists actually formulate their explanatory accounts. Their purpose is rather to indicate in reasonably precise terms the logical structure and the rationale of various ways in which empirical science answers explanation-seeking-why-questions.
>
> (Hempel 1965: 412)

So doing justice to agreed instances of scientific explanation doesn't mean doing justice to them as they actually occur, but rather doing justice to something that can in some way be elicited from them, 'their logical structure and rationale.' But Hempel gives no clue as to how we are meant to determine what the logical structure or rationale of an agreed instance of scientific explanation is independently of his own account.

As for (2), Hempel never tells us what is meant by 'systematically fruitful logical and methodological analysis of the explanatory procedures used in empirical science.' What makes one explication or analysis of a concept like that of scientific explanation more fruitful than another?

I find Hempel's explicit remarks on the methodology of what he is doing infuriatingly vague and difficult to pin down. But his frequent use of terms like 'ideal', 'abstraction', 'schematization' (see Hempel 1965: 412, for example, and my remarks on this topic in chapter I), offers the real clue to what he is doing. His methodology, like his distinction between scientific and ordinary explanation that I discussed in chapter I, depends essentially on the distinction between complete and partial explanation, and is logically dependent on it. It does not matter whether anything *we* call an explanation (even those which 'are generally agreed to be instances of scientific explanation') is a complete explanation, or whether any genuinely complete explanation has ever been given.

However, explanations when ordinarily given and generally agreed to be such must have a certain relation to complete explanations as these are specified in Hempel's models. The relevant relation is the relation of being partially like (in ways described by Hempel); actual explanations, in science and in ordinary affairs, are any kind of explanation at all, only because they are partially like the ideal ones Hempel describes. Real, ordinary explanations, just about everywhere and always, turn out to be incomplete in some way, mere explanatory sketches, partial explanations, elliptical formulations, enthymemes, or whatever, which fall short of the criteria for adequate explanation that Hempel lays down.[23]

> We have found, then, that the explanatory accounts actually formulated in science and in everyday contexts vary greatly in the explicitness, completeness, and precision with which they specify the explanans and explanandum; accordingly, they diverge more or less markedly from the idealized and schematized covering-law models. But, granting this, I think that all adequate scientific explanations and their everyday counterparts claim or presuppose

143

at least implicitly the deductive or inductive subsumability of whatever is to be explained. . .

(Hempel 1965: 424–5)

His position is, I think, to be placed somewhere between a purely technical and a purely language users' approach.[24]

Would this be a helpful analogy? Just as ideal English grammar is implicit in spoken English grammar, and the rules of deductive and inductive logic are implicit in the deductive and inductive inferences we do actually make, so too Hempel supposes that complete explanations (as specified by his models) are implicit in the ones we actually give.

This purported analogy would be misleading. There *must* be a widespread overlap between how English is actually spoken and how we do infer on the one hand and how it should ideally be spoken and how we should ideally infer on the other. Methodologically, the idea of ideal practice and the idea of actual practice must intersect.

And this is an overlap or intersection that Hempel need not assume in the case of actual explanations and ideally complete ones. The purported analogy, as applied to explanation, would give us a language users' approach (with room for 'tidying up the discourse') rather than an approach to the analysis of explanation somewhere between the two approaches. Hempel's method assumes, unlike the analogy, that the set of actual explanations and the set of ideal explanations, could be (and indeed probably are close to being) wholly disjoint, non-overlapping. As I said above, it is logically possible that no one has ever actually given an ideal, complete explanation.

(In truth, surely *some* actual explanations have been complete, ideal explanations, in Hempel's sense, without any relevant information being omitted. But it must not be forgotten just how hard it is to give a complete explanation. Since its premisses must all be true, an ideal explanation must make use of strict, exceptionless laws, and we are able to state precious few of them, except at the highest and most abstract level of scientific theory. Additionally, in singular explanations at any rate, it is necessary to assume that one is dealing with a closed system, and these closure assumptions, although they have great heuristic value, are rarely true.[25] And so on.)

But how do we know that actual explanations are only partial? How do we know that the ideals Hempel proposes, in the light of which actual explanations are seen to be only partial, are appropriate for judging them? In order to answer these sorts of questions, I must be in a position to decide what belongs in a complete explanation, and what is merely presupposed by a complete explanation, or is the support or ground for the complete explanation. How do I decide whether actual explanations are partial, because they lack whatever an ideal explanation would have, or whether actual explanations are complete, the extra information in the so-called ideal being merely presupposed by complete explanations but no proper part of them?

Hempel's view (and the same could be said for any argument theory of explanation, like Mill's) builds what might be thought of as the support or grounds for the explanation into the complete explanation itself. Consider the analogous question for prediction. Suppose I predict that e will occur, on the basis of the occurrence of c, and the law that whenever a C, an E. What is my complete prediction? There are two views one might hold, with the content of the predictions put into parenthesis, to make the views unambiguously clear and distinct: (1) my complete prediction is that (e will occur), and the basis on which I make the prediction, although no part of the complete prediction itself, is that c has occurred and whenever a C, an E; (2) my complete prediction is that (e will occur since c has and whenever a C, an E).

Which view would be more plausible? In general, one cannot include in the content of one's warnings, criticisms, predictions, and so on, all of the bases on which they are made. How can we decide what to include, and what not? In the case of prediction, it seems to me that a complete prediction has the form specified by (1), rather than (2). If complete predictions were like this, and if complete explanations were valid arguments, we would have sufficient reason to deny Hempel's thesis of the structural symmetry between predictions and explanations. But perhaps explanations are not typically arguments, but rather, like predictions, can be singular sentences. I return to this question more fully in chapter VI.

Hempel on the symmetry thesis

Does Hempel, like Mill, subscribe to the symmetry thesis (or the thesis of the structural identity of explanation and prediction, as Hempel also calls it)? On this question, there is a shift in his views. In the early article, he says that the difference between explanation and prediction 'is of a pragmatic character':

If E is given, i.e., if we know that the phenomenon described by E has occurred, and a suitable set of statements [of laws and initial conditions]. . . is provided afterwards, we speak of an explanation of the phenomenon in question. If the latter statements are given and E is derived prior to the occurrence of the phenomenon it describes, we speak of a prediction. It may be said, therefore, that an explanation of a particular event is not fully adequate unless its explanans, if taken account of in time, could have served as a basis for predicting the event in question.

(Hempel 1965: 249)

Hempel's position here is identical to Mill's, save for the fact that, unlike Mill, Hempel confuses the definition by including as a requirement for prediction that E be derived *prior to the occurrence* it describes, and not just prior to our gaining knowledge of its occurrence. Hempel thereby excludes the case of retrodiction from his analysis. The symmetry thesis as stated has two distinct parts: (a) every successful explanation is a potential prediction; (b) every successful prediction is a potential explanation. In the early article, Hempel subscribes to both (a) and (b).

Hempel returned to the symmetry thesis in the later article. His position there is that the first portion of the symmetry thesis, (a), is sound, but that the second portion, (b), 'is indeed open to question' (Hempel 1965: 367), or is 'an open question' (p.376). The official discussion of this, as it relates to the D-N model, occurs on pp. 374–5. The case is that of Koplik spots, small, whitish spots on the mucous linings of the cheeks, which are an early symptom of measles. From the law that the appearance of Koplik spots is always followed by the manifestation of measles and the information that a specific patient has Koplik spots, one can predict that the patient will develop measles, but one cannot explain the subsequent measles on the basis of the appearance of the Koplik spots.

One might wonder why Hempel says only that (b) is an open question. Doesn't the Koplik spots case simply refute (b)? Hempel says about this case that it

does not constitute a decisive objection against the second sub-thesis. For the reluctance to regard the appearance of Koplik spots as explanatory may well reflect doubts as to whether, as a matter of universal law, those spots are always followed by the later manifestations of measles. Perhaps a local inoculation with a small amount of measles virus would produce the spots without

146

leading to a full-blown case of the measles. If this were so, the appearance of the spots would still afford a usually reliable basis for predicting the occurrence of further symptoms, since exceptional conditions of the kind just mentioned would be extremely rare; but the generalization that Koplik spots are always followed by later symptoms of the measles would not express a law and thus could not properly support a corresponding D-N explanation.

(Hempel 1965: 375)

Hempel's reply to this objection to (b) seems unacceptable. First, even if the generalization linking Koplik spots and measles fails to be an exceptionless law, Hempel should accept that Koplik spots can I-S explain measles, which they most certainly do not. Second, 'perhaps' the generalization fails to be a law. But perhaps it does *not* fail to be a law. In any case, surely there must be some cases in which a symptom for a phenomenon and the phenomenon itself are connected in an exceptionless, lawlike manner. And even if there were none, it is perfectly coherent to imagine a (physically, and not just a logically) possible case in which this is so. For example, *suppose*, whatever may in fact be the case, that no local inoculation with a small amount of the measles virus would produce spots but no measles. Finally, it simply is not true that a reluctance to regard Koplik spots as explanatory of measles reflects one's doubts about the exceptionless nature of the Koplik spots–measles connection. Even if I were psychologically certain that the connection is exceptionless, I would not believe that the spots explain the measles.

In general, in any case in which there is a necessary condition n for some phenomenon p (measles is a necessary condition for Koplik spots; syphilis is a necessary condition for paresis), one will be able to predict n on the basis of p, because p will be sufficient for n (one can predict measles from Koplik spots, predict syphilis from the presence of paresis), but often, as in these two cases, p will not explain n.

There are other types of counterexample to (b), the second part of the symmetry thesis, and Hempel deals with some of them in the context of a different discussion, the discussion of non-causal D-N explanations that I mentioned above. These are cases of 'reversibility', in which either the relevant law asserts a biconditional relationship (e.g. Aristotle's law that a planet twinkles iff it is not near) or is a functional law (an equation) that equates the values of two variables. (Both of these sorts of examples can employ laws either of successive or of coexistent phenomena.)

There are many such examples. One well-known one is Sylvain Bromberger's example of the height of the flagpole, the length of its shadow, and the angle of elevation of the sun.[26] We can both predict and explain the length of the shadow on the basis of the other two factors, and the theory that light travels in straight lines; we could predict the angle of elevation from the other information, but hardly explain it.

Recall the case in which we explain a pendulum's period by its length. Hempel notes:

> The law of the simple pendulum makes it possible not only to infer the period of a pendulum from its length, but also conversely to infer its length from its period; in either case, the inference is of the form (D-N). Yet a sentence stating the length of a given pendulum, in conjunction with the law, will be much more readily regarded as explaining the pendulum's period than a sentence stating the period, in conjunction with the law, would be considered as explaining the pendulum's length. . . . In cases such as this, the common-sense conception of explanation appears to provide no clear grounds on which to decide whether a given argument that deductively subsumes an occurrence under laws is to qualify as an explanation.

Hempel's remark about the failure of the common-sense conception of explanation to provide grounds for deciding which of the two (length of pendulum by its period; period of the pendulum by its length) is really an explanation is wide of the mark, for Hempel's 'technical' concept of scientific explanation does not do this either. One can predict the period of a pendulum on the basis of its length and predict its length on the basis of its period. If (b) of the symmetry thesis were correct, both would also be (potential) explanations. However, although one can successfully predict length on the basis of period, that prediction is not a potential explanation. So one of the predictions is not a potential explanation, and hence (b) must be wrong.

Ohm's law asserts that the intensity of a constant electrical current in a circuit is directly proportional to the electromotive force and inversely proportional to the resistance; Boyle's law says that the pressure of a fixed mass of gas at a constant temperature is inversely proportional to its volume; Hook's law claims that the force required to produce a distortion in an elastic object is directly proportional to the amount of distortion. These and similar laws assert a numerical equivalence; hence, they allow prediction in both directions. But in many of these examples of functional laws, we would not allow that explanation can go in both directions. We can explain the amount of distortion (elongation) to a steel spring by the quantity of force applied to the spring, but not vice versa.

So some successful cases of prediction via functional laws and laws containing biconditionals are not potential explanations. The second part of the symmetry thesis, (b), is false.

Hempel on inductive-statistical explanation

Hempel's thesis that some explanations have the form of an inductive argument is, as far as I am aware, an important addition to the empiricist philosophy of explanation. Even in the early article, 'Studies in the Logic of Explanation', Hempel and Oppenheim had indicated the existence of another, non-deductive, type of explanation (Hempel 1965: 251, 278, and pointed out by Hempel in the 1964 postscript, 291). For Hempel, *these are two models of complete explanation*: 'under a reasonable extension of the idea of explanatory completeness, any explanation conforming to our statistical model should qualify as formally complete. . .' (p. 418).

The I-S model is introduced thus:

> Explanations of particular facts or events by means of statistic-probabilistic laws thus present themselves as arguments that are inductive or probabilistic in the sense that the explanans confers upon the explanandum a more or less high degree of inductive support or of logical (inductive) probability; they will therefore be called inductive-statistical explanations, or I-S explanations.
>
> (Hempel 1965: 385–6)

Hempel's first example of an I-S explanation is this: we explain why John Jones recovered from a streptococcus infection, on the grounds that he had been given penicillin, and that it is highly probable that a person with such an infection who is given penicillin will recover. For Hempel, the basic form of an I-S explanation is this:

$$p\,(G,F) = r$$
$$\frac{Fb}{Gb}\,[r]$$

The first premiss says that the probability of something's being G, given that it is F, is r. The second premiss asserts that b is F. The double line under the second premiss shows that we are dealing with a non-deductive argument. The conclusion that b is G is not made certain by the premisses, but only probable to degree r (less than 1). Hempel never says how high r must be, in order for the premisses to explain the conclusion. He says only 'very high', and that, given the premisses, the conclusion is 'practically certain'.

Hempel is a probabilist. But we saw that a deductivist can accept a non-deductive relation between explanans and an explanandum in a partial explanation ('partial' here means 'part of a full explanation', not necessarily restricted to the more limited sense of 'partial' that Hempel uses). In a simple case, we may omit information which we assume that the audience is aware of, or information which we do not as yet possess. So why aren't all I-S explanations just incomplete D-N explanations?

Perhaps this is the answer: in an incomplete D-N explanation, I omit 'mention of certain laws or particular facts that are tacitly taken for granted [or, unknown] and whose explicit inclusion. . .would yield a complete D-N argument' (Hempel 1965: 415). But in a complete I-S explanation, I omit mention neither of relevant singular facts nor of a law; rather, what makes an explanation a complete I-S explanation, as opposed to an incomplete D-N explanation, is the presence of a statistical or stochastic law, like the law that only a high proportion of those who take penicillin recover from a streptococcus infection. An I-S explanation 'makes essential use of at least one law or theoretical principle of statistical form' (p. 380).

It is not clear why this reply would yield two different models of explanation, in the way intended by Hempel. There is, of course, the distinction that the above paragraph draws, but what is not clear is why anything of importance hangs on it. Why should it matter if the information omitted from the explanation, from ignorance or from other pragmatic concerns, is reflected in the omission of particular matters of fact or in total omission of a law, rather than in an incomplete statement of a law? Why should that distinction be important enough to ground a distinction between two types of explanation? Why not these two types of explanation instead: ones that omit some relevant particular fact and those which include all relevant particular facts?

If we lived in a deterministic world, stochastic laws would be merely incomplete statements of deterministic laws. In that case, it is hard to see why the distinction mentioned above would matter. The same ignorance, or voluntary omission of pragmatically-irrelevant features, that might manifest itself in the omission of the law, or of particular facts, from an explanation, might just as well manifest itself in an incomplete statement of the law. In a deterministic world, there does not seem to me to be any important difference between an incomplete D-N explanation and an I-S explanation, for *every* I-S explanation is really only a partial D-N explanation.[27]

But of course we do not, or might not, live in a deterministic world with strictly universal laws. In that case, statistical laws are not just incomplete statements of deterministic laws. Hempel ultimately, and I believe correctly, ties the distinction between incomplete D-N explanations and complete I-S explanations to the question of nondeterminism:

> It seems inadvisable to construct an extended concept of explanatory completeness in such a way as to qualify all statistical explanations as incomplete. For this qualification carries with it connotations of deficiency....the early explanatory uses of statistical laws and theories...were often propounded in the belief that the microphenomena...were all subject to strictly universal laws...But this idea has gradually been abandoned...
>
> (Hempel 1965: 417–18)

Hempel's later I-S examples, of the explanation by means of Mendelian genetic principles of the distribution of red and white pea plants resulting from a cross of pure whites and pure reds, of the explanation of the radioactive decay of radon, and the explanation of certain aspects of the Brownian movement of small particles suspended in a liquid, all offer what are perhaps more serious examples of I-S explanation, because they are, or may well be, explanations of genuinely nondeterministic phenomena.

Hempel says that 'statistical explanation is quite independent of the assumption of strictly universal laws' (Hempel 1965: 418).[28] I would go further, in keeping with claims I made in chapter I. Even in a deterministic world, there will be statistical explanations, but they will only be a rather special and interesting kind of *incomplete* D-N explanation. But the idea of a complete I-S explanation is not independent of the assumption of strictly universal laws; such an idea presupposes that some laws are *not* strictly universal. The concept of a complete I-S explanation (or its non-argument analogues) needs a metaphysical backing, and only some form of nondeterminism, and hence a high or a low dependency theory of explanation, can supply the rationale for it.

Hempel on epistemic ambiguity

Hempel spends some time discussing the problem of the epistemic ambiguity of I-S explanations (Hempel 1965: 394–405). My remarks in the preceding section bear closely on this difficulty in Hempel's account.

It is not possible to have a deductive argument such that, if the premisses are all true and imply some conclusion c, those same premisses, with the addition of any further true premiss, imply –c. But with inductive argument, this is possible. Suppose I know that John has a streptococcal infection and has been given penicillin (F), so I conclude, with a probability of r (which makes me practically certain), that John will recover (G). If, later, I learn that John is an octogenarian with a weak heart (H=has streptococcal infection and has been given penicillin *and* is an octogenarian with a weak heart), I may revise my probability estimate, and indeed may conclude that it is practically certain that he will not recover (–G). The above argument could be represented as follows:

$$\frac{p(-G,H)=r_2}{-Gb} \quad [r_2]$$

$$Hb$$

The difficulty is that two different inductive arguments, both with true premisses, can inductively support to a high degree, and (if we had no further way to rule this out) therefore explain, two contradictory conclusions.

As Hempel says, 'The preceding considerations show that the concept of statistical explanation for particular events is essentially relative to a given knowledge situation. . .' (Hempel 1965: 402). Relative to the knowledge of John's infection and receipt of penicillin, we are entitled to draw one conclusion; if the knowledge situation changes and we acquire additional relevant information, about his age and heart condition, it may be that we are entitled to draw the opposite conclusion.

Hempel therefore imposes what he calls the 'requirement of maximal specificity'.[29] Put informally,

> The general idea . . . comes to this: In formulating or appraising an I-S explanation, we should take into account all that information . . . which is of potential explanatory relevance to the

152

explanandum event; i.e., all pertinent statistical laws, and such particular facts as might be connected, by the statistical laws, with the explanandum event.

(Hempel 1965: 400–1)

Hempel also repeats what he takes to be a different formulation of the *same* idea, that the individual must be referred 'to the narrowest reference class of which, according to our total information, the particular occurrence under consideration is a member' (Hempel 1965: 398). Of course many of the reference classes to which John can be assigned are irrelevant: he might be a member of the class, octogenarian with a weak heart, with streptococcal infection, given penicillin, and wears a straw hat. That class is narrower still than the class of Hs, but the additional information that accounts for its being narrower is statistically irrelevant to the question of John's recovery. What Hempel wants is something like 'the reference class, no partition of which is known to be statistically relevant'. Hempel claims that this solution 'disposes of the problem of epistemic ambiguity', since, of two rival inductive arguments, both of which confer high probability on their conclusion, at least one must violate the requirement of maximum specificity.

In any probability argument, appropriate choice of reference class constitutes a problem, and on this there is a vast literature. What is surprising in this, and here I follow Coffa,[30] is that Hempel has chosen to put the resolution of this difficulty in the way he does. The distance between D-N arguments and I-S arguments is made very great by this manoeuvre. For Hempel, the notion of an objective I-S explanation, apart from the knowledge situation in which we find ourselves, makes no sense. Wesley Salmon, and others, have stressed that there is an alternative way to select the appropriate reference class for an I-S explanation: the correct reference class is one that is objectively homogeneous, no further statistically relevant partition of the class being objectively, and not just epistemically, possible. In a deterministic world, explanations which use objectively homogeneous reference classes will be D-N explanations; explanations which use unhomogeneous reference classes will be I-S explanations which are merely the epistemically available parts of complete D-N explanations. It is only in a nondeterministic world in which there will be I-S explanations which use objectively homogeneous reference classes.

Hempel's thoughts on this subject are a matter of some speculation, for he is not very forthcoming. In this speculation, I follow Coffa. If *every* I-S explanation must be relativized to an epistemic context, then for some reason Hempel must be asserting that no reference class mentioned in an I-S explanation could be objectively homogeneous.[31] If such reference classes are not objectively homogeneous, then there must be in principle some further partition possible that is statistically relevant in explaining the explanandum. The suggestion would then be that only reference classes mentioned in D-N explanations are objectively homogeneous; all I-S explanations, employing as they do only unhomogeneous reference classes, must be the epistemically available parts of D-N explanations. I-S explanations reflect a gap in our knowledge, but not the objective gappiness of the world. Although admitting I-S explanations as a model and his remarks on pp. 417–18 notwithstanding, in which he accepts the idea of indeterminism (or, nondeterminism), Hempel has not fully taken on board the thought that the world might be objectively nondeterministic, and that in such a world I-S explanations will have a role that cannot be played by D-N explanations, however much we may know and be prepared to say about what goes on in that world.

Summary

I have, in this chapter, in the main raised questions rather than answered them. In particular, I have asked questions about the form of, and the metaphysical 'backing' for, explanations. Hempel is clearest about these matters: all complete or full explanations are deductively sound or inductively good arguments; some singular explanations are non-causal explanations. Mill was less decisive about both of these matters. Given his remarks on real inference, it is not at all obvious why he did not introduce a category of real explanation, of particulars by particulars, which would not require the inclusion of laws or generalizations in the explanans. Are all singular explanations causal? Are explanations always, or typically, arguments? Do all full or complete explanations include laws? I return to these questions in chapters VI and VII.

CHAPTER V

The Ontology of Explanation

Explanation and epistemology

Epistemology and metaphysics come together, to give us our conception of explanation. I have tried, in the previous chapters, to show how metaphysical commitments make a difference to a view of explanation, and in the next chapter I return to these metaphysical issues. In this chapter, despite its apparently 'metaphysical' title, I bring out some of the ways in which epistemological (in the broadest sense) considerations play their part. This chapter returns to a theme that arose in the discussion of Aristotle's distinction between the *per se* and the incidental cause of something: Polyclitus might be explanatory of the statue when described in one way (as the sculptor), but not when described in another (as the musical or the pale man).

Peter Strawson, following Hume, draws a similar distinction when he speaks of natural and non-natural relations:

> . . . causality is a natural relation that holds in the world between particular events or circumstances, just as the relation of temporal succession does or that of spatial proximity. We also, and rightly, associate causality with explanation. But if causality is a relation which holds in the natural world, explanation is a different matter . . . it is not a natural relation in the sense in which we perhaps think of causality as a natural relation. It is an intellectual or rational or intensional relation. It does not hold between things in the natural world, things to which we can assign places and times. It holds between facts or truths.[1]

I think of natural relations as falling within the province of metaphysics; intensional relations, as falling at least in part within the province of epistemology.[2] The purpose of this chapter is to work through the issues raised so succinctly in the quotation from Strawson.

Extensionality and the slingshot

What sorts of entities stand in the explanation relation? Of course, we sometimes explain laws, and sometimes, or perhaps even always, use laws when we (fully) explain. I ignore, until chapter VI, the place of laws in explanation. But what other entities stand in this relation, other than laws? It is people who explain explananda by explanantia, but I shall simplify by treating 'explains' as expressing a dyadic relation, even if it is really a triadic one, since we are here uninterested in the ontology of persons.

Recall from chapter I that I, following Hempel, have limited the scope of explanation for which an analysis is being sought to cases of explanation *that*. None of the theories about the relata of the explanation relation that I shall discuss have anything whatever to say about such cases as: explaining how to ride a bike, explaining how the two men shook hands, explaining where the Wash is. The cases to which the ontological alternatives I shall discuss address themselves arise most readily in cases of explaining why, although, as I also have made clear, we cannot distinguish the cases we want simply by that grammatical feature alone.

Our discussions of Plato, Aristotle, Mill, and Hempel, have thrown up numerous candidates as the relata of the explanation relation: Forms, causes *per se*, facts, phenomena, concrete events, sentential events, an ordered pair consisting of an event and a particular description of it, are some of the most obvious. To this list, we might add statements and propositions (these are not the same as sentences). Nor should we assume that only one of the contenders can win the contest; perhaps all of them can be the relata of the explanation relation. The choice should not be assumed, without further argument, to be exclusive.

In the course of this chapter, I must say certain things about (token) events. What are events, and in particular what is the criterion for individuating and identifying events? On this topic, I should here like to say as little as possible. In chapter II, I have already dodged the issue of whether events were to be taken as wide or narrow. In this chapter, I assume, without argument, that token event identity does not require the identity of the properties used in the definite descriptions of the event. That is, I accept the view that the event e, say, o's being P at t, can be identical with event f, say, o's being Q at t, even though the property P ≠ the property Q. I note that this view is controversial, and that what I have to say in what follows depends on this view of event identity. I call this 'the rough-grained criterion of event identity'.

In what follows, questions of extensionality will arise. Let me start by introducing some terminology with which to discuss questions of extensionality. Extensionality is a single idea, but the question of extensionality arises for different expressions of a language. As Haack puts it,

> A context is extensional if co-referential expressions – singular terms with the same denotation, predicates with the same extension, or sentences with the same truth-value – are substitutable within it without changing the truth-value of the whole, 'salva veritate', i.e., if Leibniz' law holds for it; otherwise it is intensional.[3]

In what follows, I use 'intensional' and 'non-extensional' synonymously.

Let's call the first sort of truth-preserving substitutability of singular terms with the same denotation 'transparency'; the second sort, substitutability of predicates with the same extension, 'predicate extensionality'; the third sort, substitutability of sentences with the same truth-value, 'sentence extensionality' (or, 'truth-functionality').

John listens to his favourite nature programme, and on it there is an animal which, as John is told, has a heart. John does not know that that animal is the Queen's oldest corgi, and, being a biological ignoramus, does not know that all and only animals with hearts have kidneys. Consider the true sentence, 'John believes that the animal on his favourite nature programme has a heart.' The context following 'John believes that. . . ' is not transparent, because 'the Queen's oldest corgi' cannot be substituted for 'the animal on his favourite nature programme' *salva veritate*. Nor is that context predicate or sentence extensional, since the coextensive predicate, 'has a kidney', cannot be substituted *salva veritate* for 'has a heart', and a sentence with the same truth-value, e.g. 'John is ignorant about biology', cannot be substituted *salva veritate* for 'the animal on his favourite nature programme has a heart'.

There is a fourth sort of extensionality that we shall need. Consider two predicates, 'P' and 'Q', which express or stand for the same property (*whatever* the criterion of property identity the reader prefers, no doubt weaker than synonymy but surely stronger than coextensionality). Call any pair of such predicates 'co-typical predicates'. A context is co-typical predicate extensional iff there is substitutability *salva veritate* of predicates which are co-typical. The idea is that 'P' and 'Q' are co-typical if (and only if) they stand for the same property, and if there is any plausible criterion of property identity weaker than synonymy, this will *not* be the same as 'P' and 'Q' having the same meaning or intension.

The property of being a triangle=the property of being a three-sided closed plane figure. Consider the sentence, 'John believes that the figure before him is a triangle.' The context following 'John believes that. . . ' is co-typical predicate extensional iff it follows that John believes that the figure before him is a three-sided closed plane figure (views about whether or not this is so may differ).

It is important to see that as far as my argument is concerned, 'P' and 'Q' may stand for the same property, whether or not 'P=Q' is necessary or contingent, a priori or a posteriori. The reader is free to plug in his favourite views here. Although the specific example I offered above is one that is a priori and necessary, I do not mean to suggest that other examples must have the same epistemic status. Perhaps if 'P' and 'Q' are co-typical predicates, they have the same extensions in all possible worlds, but perhaps not. I see no reason to become involved in disputes about the epistemic status of statements of property identity. I do assume, later in the chapter, that there are *some* examples which are a posteriori, but whatever else the reader is inclined to believe about these matters is, as far as I can see, consistent with what I wish to say.

There is a well-known argument, sometimes called 'the slingshot', which purports to show that if a context is transparent (and if there is substitutability of logical equivalents *salva veritate*), then it is truth-functional.[4] Here is one version of that argument, which I repeat almost verbatim from the account by John Mackie. Let 'p' represent a sentence, and 'F(p)' a sentence containing the sentence represented by 'p'. Further, we suppose (a) that logical equivalents are interchangeable in 'F(. . .)' *salva veritate*, (b) and that 'F(. . .)' is transparent, if 'p' is.

Now consider the class of x's such that both (x=x) & p. If p is true, this class will be the universal class; if p is false, it will be the empty class. Further consider this statement: the class of x's such that both x=x & p is identical with the class of x's such that x=x. That statement will be logically equivalent to 'p', because whatever 'p' may be, it is true when 'p' is true and false when 'p' is false. Finally, if 'q' has the same truth-value as 'p', then the class of x's such that x=x & p will be the same class as the class of x's such that x=x & q, since when 'p' and 'q' are both true, each will be the universal class, and when 'p' and 'q' are both false, each will be the empty class.

The argument now goes as follows:

(1) p≡q	(by assumption)
(2) F(p)	(by assumption)
(3) F(the class of x's such that x=x & p is identical to the class of x's such that x=x).	(by substitution of logical equivalents in 'F(...)')
(4) F(the class of x's such that x=x & q is identical to the class of x's such that x=x).	(from (3), by substitution of co-referring terms)
(5) F(q)	(from (4), by substitution of logical equivalents)
(6) F(p)→F(q)	(from (2) & (5) by conditional proof)
(7) F(q)→F(p)	(by a similar series of steps)
(8) F(p)≡F(q)	(from (6) & (7))
(9) p≡q→F(p)≡F(q)	(from (1) & (8) by conditional proof)

As Mackie says,

> ... (9) says that the context 'F(...)' is truth-functional, and this has been proved from the suppositions that 'F(...)' is such as to allow substitution within it of logical equivalents and of co-referring expressions. That is, if 'F(...)' is both transparent and allows substitution of logical equivalents, it is truth-functional.

> (Mackie 1974: 250–1)

Although there are various possible objections to this argument to be found in the literature, I shall not pursue them here. I shall accept the argument without discussion. In particular, I accept, without argument, that the principle of the substitutability *salva veritate* of logical equivalents holds for the contexts under discussion, although this must be the Achilles' heel of the slingshot, if there is one at all. I do assume, though, that the argument only shows that if a context is transparent with reference to definite descriptions, then it is truth-functional; the argument does not go through for names.[5]

The relata of the explanation relation

There are three serious 'candidates' for being the relata of the explanation relation.[6] The first is events; the second, facts. I have little to say about the third candidate, statements (and propositions, no distinction between the two being required for the purposes of this discussion). Facts and events are the only two candidates whose case I consider in some detail. Sentences are *not* such a candidate, for they do not explain and are not explained in the conceptually primary sense. But statements remain as a candidate, even if sentences do not, so that I shall have to say something about them. (But remember that even if it were statements that explain statements, it could only be so in virtue of certain natural relations holding between the worldly things such statements are about.) Since I will argue that events *tout court never* explain or are explained, I do not need to deal separately with the mixed possibilities, on which facts might sometimes explain events or events sometimes explain facts.[7]

If events are even sometimes the relata of the explanation relation, then, at least sometimes, explanation is by a particular event *tout court*, of a particular event *tout court*. Or, alternatively, explanation is at least sometimes of the occurrence of one particular event by the occurrence of another. These come to the same, there being no difference, as far as I can see, between explaining the fire at 10 Downing Street and explaining the occurrence of the fire at 10 Downing Street. This proposal for the relata of the explanation relation can be somewhat broadened to include states, in addition to events, to cover the sort of case in which we might want to say that some unchange, to borrow Ducasse's apt expression, explains or is explained. For simplicity, I shall continue speaking only of events explaining events, leaving it to the reader to understand that other worldly particulars or individual chunks of reality like states or unchanges, as well as events, might be included.

Two writers who accept that there are some explanations of events by events are David Lewis[8] and James Woodward.[9] David Lewis's theory that all explanation is causal explanation is restricted to the explanation of particular events: in reply to an alleged counterexample, he asserts that 'I don't agree that any particular event has been non-causally explained' (Lewis 1986: 223). So there must be at least *some* explanations of particular events, if Lewis is right, whether or not he is right in thinking that all explanations of particular events are causal.

James Woodward, in two very interesting articles, argues that there is a sense of explanation, '. . . causally explains. . . ', which is transparent. In this transparent sense, the explanation relation does hold between events apart from how they are described. 'If what is explained is genuinely an individual occurrence, then the singular term occurring in the effect position will function purely referentially. . . '(Woodward 1986: 279). Woodward's view is supported by the distinction he draws between what an explanation explains and what it presupposes but does not explain. '. . . there is a clear difference between explaining why some particular event, which has a certain feature, occurred, and explaining why that event has that feature.' To take Woodward's example, if the short circuit causally explains the fire, and if the fire was purple and odd-shaped, then it follows that the short circuit explains the purple, odd-shaped fire, which is the same event differently described. (Notice that Woodward uses a rough-grained criterion of event identity: the event of the house being on fire and the event of the house being on purple and odd-shaped fire can be identical, in spite of the fact that two different properties are involved in the two descriptions.)

According to Woodward, the expression 'the purple, odd-shaped fire' functions in the above example purely referentially, to refer to the fire. The explanation does not explain why the fire was purple and odd-shaped; it merely presupposes that the fire has these characteristics, and reference to the fire happens to be fixed via this description. Nor, argues Woodward, should we try to escape the transparency point by thinking of the explanation of the fire as really an explanation of the *fact* that there was one and only one event in the vicinity which was a fire, rather than an explanation of the event *tout court*. To explain the former, I would have to explain why no other fires occurred at the same time in the vicinity. In explaining the fire by the short circuit, it is presupposed that there was only one such fire, but this presupposition is not explained by the short circuit.

On this view, this transparent sense of 'explains' stands for a relation between particular events, occurrences, things in the world, apart from how they are described or referred to or conceptualized. This relation is a natural relation like that of causation, and not a non-natural relation, to revert to Strawson's terminology. It is a natural relation, in the sense that its relata are 'natural', rather than intensional, entities. It is consistent with Woodward's view, that there is, or may be, another explanation relation, to which 'explains', in a second, non-transparent sense, refers, and which is a non-natural relation. But at least for the transparent sense of that term, there is no need to import facts, or statements, or truths, or descriptions, or anything else into the analysis of explanation. In explaining the fire by the short circuit, I explain the occurrence of an event in the world, apart from any linguistic or cognitive considerations about how it is talked about or conceptualized.

The difficulty I have with the Woodward–Lewis view of event explanation is that no explanation sentences are fully transparent, in spite of the sorts of considerations that Woodward adduces. I remind the reader that the topic under discussion is that of explanation, which includes causal explanation, but is not the topic of causation itself. Causation might be a transparent relation, even if causal explanation is not. If 'e *causes* f' is transparent, it does not follow that the corresponding assertion of explanation, 'e causally explains f', must be. Nor, of course, would I deny that we often take the simple assertion of causality as explanatory, but the success of our so doing can only be *insured* when 'e causes f' meets more conditions than would have to be met simply for 'e causes f' to be a literal truth.

Consider the following argument:

(1) The hurricane explains the loss of life.
(2) The hurricane=the event reported in *The Times* on Tuesday.
∴(3) The event reported in *The Times* on Tuesday explains the loss of life.

Or, to pick an example adapted but slightly altered from Mackie:[10]

(1a) Oedipus' marrying his mother explains the tragedy that ensued.
(2a) Oedipus' marrying his mother=Oedipus' marrying the woman he thought least likely to bring tragedy to Thebes.
∴(3a) Oedipus' marrying the woman he thought least likely to bring tragedy to Thebes explains the tragedy that ensued.

What Mackie says is this: the first description 'helps to explain the tragedy in a way that the. . . [latter] does not. What is referentially transparent may be, for that very reason, explanatorily opaque'.

My view is that both (3) and (3a) are literal fasehoods. If the conclusions of these two arguments are false, the best diagnosis of what has gone wrong in the argument is that, despite appearances, the first premiss of each argument is not transparent, not to be construed as stating that a relation obtains between two events, as the Lewis–Woodward proposal for the ontology of explanation proposes. One should take the falsity of the conclusion to throw doubt on the conception that particular events (or states, or whatever) can transparently explain events. Explanation is *never* a natural relation. It *never* touches things that directly and immediately, but is always mediated through the features or characteristics which are appropriate for explanation. Oedipus' marrying his mother is the same event as Oedipus' marrying the woman he thought least likely to bring tragedy to Thebes, but the event is explanatory as conceptualized in the first way, but not as conceptualized in the second way.

Are the conclusions of the two arguments really false, because the one event doesn't explain the second at all, or are the conclusions literally true but just poor(er) explanations? This raises a very complicated question about the nature of such a distinction, which I have already touched on in the first chapter, but let me say here, partly by way of repetition, just enough to produce what I hope will be an adequate underpinning for the thought that the conclusions of the argument are literally false.

There are pragmatic considerations in giving explanations. First, it is legitimate to give less than the whole explanatory truth to an audience, given one's knowledge of its interests and existing knowledge. The audience may only want to know about some part of the full cause. Or it may not want a very specific description of that cause, but only a more general description – an audience of historians might want to know only that a plague in tenth-century China reduced the population level, but not need to know what the plague was. Or, there may be two levels of relevant description of the cause, a macro-description and a micro-description for example, and one rather than the other of the descriptions might be appropriate for the audience one was addressing.[11]

Poor explanations are ones that make these choices between relevant descriptions, or between parts of the relevant description, in the wrong way ('relevance', let us suppose, being cashed out for us by the theory of explanation at hand; I shall discuss the issue of relevance more fully in chapters VI and VII).

But none of these pragmatic considerations covers the case of the introduction of an outright *irrelevant* description, even though the irrelevant description is a true description of the cause. The connection between the event irrelevantly described and the topic at hand can only be seen in a derivative and parasitic sort of way by someone who happens to know the irrelevant description and knows that it fits this event. To select inappropriately from the relevant information is a poor explanation for the purposes at hand; to offer explanatorily irrelevant information is to fail to explain at all. In the conclusions of the above two arguments, just such wholly irrelevant descriptions are being introduced. Although true descriptions of the cause, they are entirely irrelevant descriptions from the point of view of explanation.

The conclusions of these arguments *are*, then, false. I grant that the person who knows the identities might feel reluctant to count the conclusions as wholly literal falsehoods, since there is a sense in which he can see what the conclusions are trying to get at. The conclusions mention events which, *when differently described*, do explain.

One might draw the distinction in this way: there is a difference between *giving* an explanation of something on the one hand, and asserting or implying that there is *some* explanation of that thing, without actually giving it, on the other. So there are two different and incompatible ways in which one might understand (3) and (3a). If they are taken as giving an explanation, as the Lewis–Woodward thesis must suppose, then they are simply false. If, on the other hand, they are taken as asserting or implying that there is some explanation of the explanandum event, which involves the first event when differently described, they are truths.

Someone who does not know that the hurricane was the event reported in *The Times* on Tuesday may take (3) to be implying that *there is some explanation* of the loss of life which involves a different description for that very same event described as 'the event reported in *The Times* on Tuesday'. But he will not take (3) as giving that explanation. The theory of singular event explanation is, as it stands, false. Explanation, even causal explanation, can never just be of events by events *sans* qualification.

When discussing explanation, writers often slip naturally, and sometimes unconsciously, into the terminology of facts. Strawson spoke, in the quotation at the beginning of the chapter, of facts standing in the non-natural explanation relation to other facts. We have already noted the vagaries of Hempel's remarks on this point, and we decided to take as his considered view the one he expresses in the extended discussion in his later article,[12] in which he distinguishes between

164

concrete events and sentential facts and events, and argues that it is 'sentential facts and events' which are explained in an explanation.

Facts are the second candidate for the relata of the explanation relation: 'the fact that p explains the fact that q', where typical expressions referring to facts contain whole sentences, here represented by 'p' and 'q'. Adopting facts as the relata might still yield a theory of singular explanation of a sort, if facts, like events, are a kind of individual entity, in the widest sense. But the relation that relates facts, if such there be, will be, unlike causation, and in some sense yet to be explored, a non-natural relation.

If facts are to come on the stage as a serious ontological candidate, it would be nice if we had a catalogue of the various kinds of facts that there might be. I introduced various species of facts in chapter IV: singular facts, existentially general facts, universally general facts, stochastic facts, and facts of identity. I do not have a complete catalogue (for instance, I do not discuss the 'Russellian' questions of whether there are conjunctive facts, disjunctive facts, and negative facts). I shall be mostly concerned, in this chapter, with singular facts. A singular fact is a fact about a particular, namely the fact that that particular, o, has some property P (the fact that the fire was purple and odd-shaped). 'P' might be a relational property, and so the fact might be about two or more particulars.[13] Facts of identity are singular facts; even so, they deserve special mention. Some of the issues about extensionality and transparency will be irrelevant to some kinds of facts (e.g. there are no questions of transparency for universally and existentially general facts), but this should be fairly obvious.

Other accounts of explanation make statements, or propositions, the relata of the explanation relation. Peter Achinstein, for example, holds that an explanation always includes as a constituent, in addition to an act type, a certain kind of proposition.[14]

Donald Davidson has an account of the logical form of explanation sentences, and a proposal for their analysis.[15] (Proposals concerning logical form and analysis constrain one another, but I ignore these issues here.) First, consider his remarks about their logical form. Suppose Jack's falling down explains his breaking his crown. For him, this, in correct logical form, is (with Davidson's numbering):

(8) *The fact that* Jack fell down *explains the fact that* Jack broke his crown.

'In. . . . (8), intensionality reigns, in that similar substitution [i.e. of equivalent sentences or co-extensive singular terms or predicates] in or for the contained sentences is not guaranteed to save truth' (Davidson 1975: 86). Note that Davidson's remarks about (8) should not be confused with his better-known remarks about (again, with Davidson's numbering) (2): '*The fact that* there was a short circuit *caused it to be the case that* there was a fire' (Davidson 1975: 84–5). Davidson does not think that (2) does finally reveal the logical form of causal sentences (his argument that this is so uses the slingshot). But there is never any hint that (8) does not adequately reveal the logical form of (causal) explanation sentences.

As for the analysis of such explanation assertions, Davidson makes only a single remark. What, for Davidson, does the explanation relation relate? Davidson says, at least in one passage, that explanation is a *relation* that relates *statements*: 'Explanations typically relate statements, not events' (Davidson 1975: 93). Perhaps Davidson's well-known dislike of facts is what inclines him, and should incline us, to statements rather than facts.

Davidson's arguments against facts are only against the use of facts for certain purposes. In 'Causal Relations', the argument, relying on the slingshot, runs as follows.[16] Suppose the logical form of a causal sentence was: (2) the fact that p caused the fact that q. Clearly, the connective, 'the fact that . . . caused the fact that. . . ' is not truth-functional, since substitution of contained sentences by sentences with the same truth-value does not preserve the truth-value of the whole. However, substitution of singular terms for others with the same denotation should not touch their truth-value; if, for example, Smith's death was caused by a fall from the ladder and Smith was the first man to land on the moon, then the fall from the ladder was the cause of the death of the first man on the moon. But, by the slingshot, substitutability of singular terms with the same denotation entails truth-functionality, contrary to the original supposition. So (2) cannot give the logical form for causal sentences.

In another well-known paper on the correspondence theory of truth, Davidson slingshoots in this way.[17] Suppose 's' is some true sentence. On any correspondence theory, the statement that s corresponds to the fact that s. These correspondence contexts must be transparent: if 'Smith fell from a ladder' corresponds to the fact that Smith fell from a ladder, and if Smith was the first man on the moon, then 'Smith fell from a ladder' corresponds to the fact that the first man on the moon fell from

166

a ladder. So, by the slingshot, since 'the statement that s corresponds to the fact that s' is transparent, then for any true sentence 't', the statement that s corresponds to the fact that t. In general, 'the statement that . . . corresponds to the fact that. . . ', if transparent, is truth-functional. If a statement corresponds to any fact, it corresponds to them all. There is, on this account, just One Great Fact, if there is any.

Both applications of the slingshot suppose that the context under discussion is transparent (and that logical equivalents are substitutable *salva veritate*), and argue that if it were transparent, it would be truth-functional. And if facts were to do what causation and correspondence would require of them, then expressions referring to facts must be transparent; causation and correspondence contexts should permit replacement of singular terms by coextensive singular terms, *salva veritate*. It isn't facts *per se* that Davidson doesn't like, but rather his point is that, if there are facts, they aren't any good for causation or correspondence.

Pari passu, if one fact explains another, won't it explain all facts? It depends on what facts are like. Our intuitions *may* tell us that 'the fact that p explains the fact that q' is not even transparent (we shall have to see); if explanation contexts are not even transparent, the slingshot cannot get started towards the conclusion that if one fact explains another, it explains them all.

This may help disarm an argument against facts. Is there any reason to choose facts over (true) statements as the relata of the explanation relation? As the discerning reader will note by the end of this chapter, this is a pressing problem for me, because the facts required for explanation are more like true statements or propositions than facts might even ordinarily be thought to be.

But there is still an important metaphysical difference between statements and even these unordinary facts required for explanation. Facts (empirical ones, at any rate) *include* worldly particulars (like persons and physical objects, for example) as constituents.[18] Facts may include more than just these worldly particulars, but they do include at least them. Statements, even true ones, are not so composed. Having rejected the Woodward–Lewis idea that worldly events can explain worldly events *tout court*, my strategy is to keep explanation as worldly as possible, for as long as possible. I start with particulars and their properties, and *add* conceptualization or description to them. In the end, I have to admit a great deal of this additional conceptualization and description.

There are, then, two competing theories that survive the elimination of event explanation: (a) the theory that makes facts the relata of the explanation relation, and (b) the theory that casts true statements in this role, but adds that statements can explain statements only in virtue of the natural relations obtaining between worldly things. If the reader were to insist that (a) and (b) are equivalent, the difference between them being merely stylistic, I have no strong reason to resist the claim, other than the metaphysical thoughts above. N. L. Wilson,[19] for example, says that 'fact' and 'true proposition' are 'synonyms' (Wilson 1974: 305). Even if Wilson and others are right, though, my discussion still has a point. Many of those who write on explanation use the idea of facts explaining facts quite uncritically. What follows is an attempt to spell out what is involved in the idea. If it turns out that it is equivalent to the idea of statements explaining statements, so be it. But, to repeat, I do not think that the concept of a fact and the concept of a true statement or proposition are the same; there are, I believe, metaphysical differences between them.

Explaining facts

Let's return to Woodward's distinction. Suppose I want to explain the house's burning with a purple, odd-shaped flame, and not just to explain the house's burning, which burning happened to be a burning with a purple, odd-shaped flame. That is, I want to direct the explaining *onto* the purpleness and odd-shapeness of the flame. The explanation of the house's burning with a purple, odd-shaped flame demands something that is not equally demanded by the explanation of just the house's burning.

If (counterfactually) we had agreed to the idea of event explanation, and if we were also prepared to adopt a very fine-grained criterion of event (and state) identity, according to which if two event descriptions use different properties, it follows that the descriptions describe different events, then we could see this second explanation as an event explanation too. On this fine-grained criterion, the house's burning and the house's burning with a purple and odd-shaped flame would count as two different token events, and it would be no surprise that their explanations were different. We could then refuse to accept that an explanation of the burning is an explanation of the burning with a purple and odd-shaped flame. We could say that the short circuit is the explanation of the house's burning; the presence of a certain impurity in the combustible material (say, titanium) is the explanation of the house's burning with a purple and odd-shaped flame, and that both explanations are event explanations, being explanations of (two different) particular or token events.

But I have already rejected this fine-grained criterion of event and state identity, and the view that explanation can be of events. (Even if we adopted the fine-grained analysis at this point in my argument, it would not survive, because of additional problems I raise later.) We need some other way to get at the difference between the two explananda, the house's burning and the house's burning with a purple and odd-shaped flame. The explanation of the house's burning with a purple, odd-shaped flame is best understood, according to me, as an explanation of the *fact* that an event, the house's burning, has a specific feature, viz. being a burning with a purple and odd-shaped flame. Any concrete particular has an indefinitely large number of characteristics or features; what we want to explain may be not just the particular's occurrence, and certainly not its having *all* the features that it does have, which would be an impossible task.

What is needed is what I would call 'a feature-introducing operator', which introduces a (usually short) list of features of the particular for which an explanation may be required. In 'the fact that the fire is purple and odd-shaped', at least two features of the fire seem to be introduced: that the fire is purple, and that it is odd-shaped. Not every explanation explains all the features introduced by the fact locution, for context might make it appropriate to explain some features and to ignore others. *Selection* of introduced features for explanation is a different and pragmatic, context-dependent matter; we often indicate such selection by stress, emphasis, and so on.

But features cannot even be selected for explanation which are not introduced by the fact locution at all. The fire was, no doubt, a fire that occurred at some time, t, but the fact that the fire occurred at t is a different fact from the fact that it was purple and odd-shaped, and its occurring at t is not a feature introduced by the latter fact. Even Woodward's alleged example of explaining the occurrence of the fire *sans* phrase can be construed as explaining the fact that the fire occurred, where *this* fact locution, unlike the fact that the fire had certain features, introduces the occurrence, but nothing else, as the feature of the fire which matters for the explanation.

Aristotle's terminology was, as we saw, designed for a similar purpose: it isn't Polyclitus *qua* the pale or the musical man who explains the statue, but Polyclitus *qua* sculptor or *qua* sculpting. Aristotle was alive to the non-extensionality of '... explains...', and my discussion here is intended to build on his insight. *'qua'* is Aristotle's feature-introducing operator; 'the fact that...' is mine.

Since the point of a feature-introducing operator is to introduce features for explanation, all of the features introduced by 'the fact that ...' are assumed to be explanatorily relevant. When this assumption is not met, the whole explanation claim is false. For example, to return to an example mentioned briefly in chapter I, it is a truth that the fact that Jones is a man explains the fact that Jones did not become pregnant. But it is false that the fact that Jones is a man who regularly takes birth control pills explains the fact that Jones did not become pregnant. In that falsehood, Jones's regularly taking birth control pills is an introduced feature. A presupposition of that explanation claim is that the feature, regularly taking birth control pills, is explanatorily relevant to Jones's failure to become pregnant. Since the presupposition is false, the explanation claim which presupposes it is false too.

If I were asked to explain the fact that the fire was purple and odd-shaped, there are not just two, but *three* features which fall within the scope of the explanation. I mentioned above the two obvious features: the purpleness and the odd-shapeness of the fire. I agree with Woodward, that an explanation of why the fire was purple and odd-shaped presupposes that, but does not explain why, there was a fire. But – and this can be brought out by appropriate stress or emphasis – I may want to know why it was a fire to which the purpleness and odd-shapeness attached themselves, as it were. Here, the 'rather-than' locutions are helpful: knowing that something or other was so oddly coloured and shaped, why was it a fire and not something else (perhaps a cloud)?

So, being a fire, in spite of the fact that it finds its place in the explanandum not by means of a predicate but rather by means of a definite description, is also a feature introduced for the purposes of explanation. In 'the fact that the D is P', the feature, being a D, is also introduced, even though the logical function of 'the D' is to fix reference. The same applies, *mutatis mutandis*, when 'the fact that the D is P' is the explanans. Explanatory weight can be carried by the referring expression when it is a definite description, as well as by the predicates.

If the fact that the hurricane measured force 10 explains the fact that there was a subsequent tidal wave, and even though the hurricane was the event reported in *The Times* on Tuesday, the fact that the event reported in *The Times* on Tuesday measured force 10 does not explain the fact that there was a subsequent tidal wave. (Intuitions to the contrary may arise only because, given that the property in the explanans is the property of measuring force 10, it is easy to work out what the relevant definite description of the event referred to as 'the event reported in *The Times* on Tuesday' must in fact be; viz. the hurricane.) The event which figures in the explaining fact must be relevantly referred to, as well as relevant properties or features attributed to it, to make explanation work.

This confirms the idea that the slingshot argument has no toe-hold in explanation, in contrast to correspondence and causation. The expression, 'the fact that . . . explains the fact that. . . ' is *not* transparent, at least not for definite descriptions; unlike causation and correspondence contexts, there is no substitutability of co-referring definite descriptions in explanation contexts *salva veritate*. Two different definite descriptions of a particular may utilize two different properties, and when this is so, since fact locutions make properties matter, definite descriptions are not replaceable *salva veritate* in 'the fact that . . . explains the fact that. . . '.

The non-extensionality of facts

I now propose to speak freely of facts, as well as fact locutions. I assume that if I specify truth conditions for the fact locution, 'the fact that p=the fact that q', I am entitled to speak, with serious ontic intent, of identity conditions for *facts*. I shall always mean by 'a fact locution', a locution with the form, 'the fact that p=the fact that q'. If, in what follows, I say that facts, or their identity conditions, are, or are not, transparent, predicate extensional, etc., the reader will understand how to translate such remarks from the material to the formal mode, if necessary. My strategy is first to establish the truth conditions for fact locutions, and then to look at 'the fact that p explains the fact that q', in the light of that discussion.

Are the identity conditions for facts predicate extensional? They are not, as the invalidity of the following argument makes clear:

(1) The fact that x is P= the fact that x is P.

(2) $(x) (Px \equiv Qx)$

(3) The fact that x is P=the fact that x is Q.

Since, if $P \neq Q$, (3) will be false, (1) does not permit substitution of coextensive predicates *salva veritate*. An argument similar to the one above shows that the identity conditions for facts are not sentence extensional (truth-functional) either.

That the identity conditions for facts are not predicate extensional suits them for their feature-introducing role in explanation. The fact that x is cordate is a different fact from the fact that x is renate, even though the properties of being cordate and renate are coextensive. Happily so, because an explanation of the fact that x is renate will not do as an explanation of why x is cordate. A feature introducer introduces a feature, without thereby introducing all other features coextensive with the first feature. Fact locutions offer a means for introducing the property and making the property matter, in a way that events and state of affairs do not (or, do so only at best controversially).

So far, my facts are similar to those of N.L.Wilson:

> For consider a domain consisting solely of sugar cubes, one of which is a. For such a domain the class of white things is identical with the class of cubical things. Nevertheless, the fact that a is white is not identical with the fact that a is cubical. And that is because the properties, whiteness and cubicalness, though coextensive, are not identical.

> (Wilson 1974: 306)

I discussed the non-transparency of 'the fact that . . . explains the fact that. . . ' for definite descriptions in the preceding section. It is also true (this is a different but related claim) that 'the fact that. . . is identical to the fact that. . . ' is non-transparent for definite descriptions. The fact that Cicero was the greatest Roman orator is identical to the fact that Cicero was the greatest Roman orator. Cicero=the man who denounced Cataline. But the fact that Cicero was the greatest Roman orator is not the same fact as the fact that the man who denounced Cataline was the greatest Roman orator. Failure of fact locutions to be transparent (with reference to definite descriptions), like failure of predicate and sentence extensionality, makes them suitable (thus far, at any rate) to be the relata of the explanation relation.

Facts: worldly or wordy?

Some have argued that facts are a special kind of combined linguistic and non-linguistic item. J.L. Austin, in his debate with Strawson on truth, claimed that: 'and so speaking about "the fact that" is a compendious way of speaking about a situation involving both words and world'.[20] My denial of sentence and predicate extensionality and definite description transparency for fact locutions does not suggest the involvement of words or conceptualization in the constitution of facts. My remarks on the feature-introducing character of facts bring properties or features or characteristics onto the scene but do not bring words or concepts to the fore. In what way are facts on the side of the words (or concepts) at all, as Austin says?

The fact that the fire is purple introduces the purpleness of the fire, whether for explanation or whatever. It isn't the word, 'purple', that is relevant, or even the concept of purpleness, but the real colour of the real fire, however described or conceptualized. In order to see the 'words' character of facts, I think one needs to look at the questions of the co-typical predicate extensionality and the name transparency of facts. Unlike Austin, I prefer to speak where possible of the conceptual component rather than the words component of facts. It will turn out that what often (although not always) matters in explanation is how we conceptualize or think about something, not what words we use in the thought or conceptualization.

The co-typical predicate extensionality of facts

For each of name transparency and co-typical predicate extensionality, there are the following two separate questions: (1) Are fact locutions name transparent (co-typical predicate extensional)? (2) Given the answer to (1), can facts so conceived be the relata of the explanation relation?

So far, given the failure of fact locutions to be definite description transparent, sentence extensional (truth-functional) and predicate extensional, facts were suited to be the relata of the explanation relation. Suppose the answers to the questions about the name transparency and co-typical predicate extensionality of fact locutions make facts unsuitable for explanation? Rather than impose a theory of explanation onto facts to begin with, to ensure their suitability for explanation, I try to answer (1) on the basis of my (and hopefully your) intuitions. My claim will be that facts, if the deliverances of intuition are as I think they are, won't do the whole job required by explanation. I refer to such ultimately inadequate (for the purposes of explanation) facts as 'ordinary facts'. They pass the test for explanation by failing the test for definite description transparency, predicate and sentence extensionality, because facts can make properties matter. But in the case of co-typical predicate extensionality and name transparency, we move beyond the mattering of just properties; here, facts fail the test for explanation by passing it for name transparency and co-typical predicate extensionality. To this extent, they won't fully do what explanation requires of its relata.

Let me take the co-typical predicate extensionality question first. Suppose property P=property Q. Are the identity conditions for facts co-typical predicate extensional? N.L. Wilson thinks that they are, for the following reason: '. . . red is the color of ripe strawberries. From which it follows that the . . . [fact] that Socrates is red is identical with the . . . [fact] that Socrates is the color of ripe strawberries' (Wilson 1974: 305). Wilson argues in this way: 'two facts will be identical if they have the same constituents in the same order' (p.306). On Wilson's view, since the fact that Socrates is red and the fact that Socrates is the colour of ripe strawberries 'contain' the same individuals and the same properties, they must be the same fact. Neither fact introduces anything not introduced by the other. How could the facts be different? There is no property or object or any other item which is a 'constituent' in one that is not in the other.

I agree with Wilson's general view (although I have doubts about Wilson's specific example). Facts are co-typical predicate extensional. Suppose the property P=the property Q. (Let 'P' and 'Q' both be names of properties rather than descriptions of them. Recall that it makes no difference to my argument whether the identity statement is necessary or contingent; let readers suppose whatever they wish about the epistemic status of statements of property identity which use names of properties.) The fact that x is P and the fact that x is Q, in such a case, differ neither in the individuals they are about nor in the features of the individuals that are introduced. The first fact introduces the feature P; the second, the feature Q. And, *ex hypothesi*, these are the same feature.

There are examples other than Wilson's which lead me to think that the identity criteria for facts, on any theory of facts which is true to how facts are ordinarily thought about, *are* co-typical predicate extensional. These are examples such as: the fact that a gas has temperature t=the fact that its constituent molecules have mean kinetic energy m; the fact that ice is water=the fact that ice is composed of H_2O molecules. I do take the relevant property identities on which these fact identities rest to be a posteriori, for otherwise the examples would be of little interest for scientific explanation. As I said above, it is controversial whether these identities are contingent or necessary, but a decision on this is irrelevant

174

for what I have to say here. (There is also a question about the identity conditions for facts in those cases in which the property identities are a priori; e.g. there is the question whether to count the fact that Harry is an eye doctor as the same fact as the fact that Harry is an oculist. If facts are the same when the relevant property identity is a posteriori, they surely would be the same when the relevant property identity is a priori.)

But now we must turn to the second question that I mentioned about the co-typical predicate extensionality of facts. If facts as ordinarily understood are co-typical predicate extensional, can such facts do what explanation requires? I assume that the following is an explanation (of a macro-state by a micro-state): an explanation for the fact that a sample of ideal gas b has temperature t is the fact that b's constituent molecules have mean kinetic energy m. Such an explanation relies on the property identity, temperature=mean kinetic energy.

There are *other* explanations, at other levels, for this fact. For example, another explanation of the fact that b has temperature t is that I stuck b in the oven at gas mark 4. But *an* explanation for its having temperature t, and the one most appropriate in certain scientific situations, is in terms of the mean kinetic energy of its molecules. In any case, if the reader is inclined to dispute that this is a bona fide example of an explanation, let him take as an example whatever example he wishes, of an explanation of a macro-state by an underlying micro-state, such that the property of being in that macro-state is reductively identified with the property of being in that micro-state. Reduction of one science to another has often been taken as paradigmatic of explanation; whether paradigmatic or not, such reductions must yield *some* examples of property identities which are explanatory.

Consider the following four claims:

(1) No (empirical) fact explains or even partly explains itself (the explanation relation is irreflexive).
(2) Having temperature t=being composed of molecules with mean kinetic energy m (a statement of property identity, whether it be metaphysically necessary or contingent).
(3) The fact that b has temperature t is explained (or partly explained) by the fact that b's molecules have mean kinetic energy m.
(4) Facts are co-typical predicate extensional.

But (1)–(4) are inconsistent, because (2)–(4) jointly imply that the (empirical) fact that b has temperature t explains or partly explains itself, which (1) says is never so.

I take this argument as demonstrating that explanation is not just a relation between facts as constituted by worldly particulars and their properties, apart from how they are conceptualized. If P=Q, the fact that x is P and the fact that x is Q introduce the *same* feature. What matters in explanation isn't only property introduction, but the way in which we conceptualize the property, viz. whether the property P is introduced *as* property P or *as* property Q.

If facts are thought of in the ordinary way, Austin was wrong. Ordinary facts as co-typical property extensional entities are *not* combinations of words (or concepts) and the world. Even ordinary facts are not wholly extensional, it is true, since properties matter to them in a way for which predicate and sentence extensionality cannot account. But their co-typical predicate extensionality makes ordinary facts unsuitable as the relata of the explanation relation. We need relata for that relation, for which not only properties or features matter, but the way in which we conceptualize or cognize them matters too.

I therefore introduce 'special' facts, which are constructed to do just what explanation requires of its relata.[21] If readers think that the deliverances of my intuition about facts are in error, and that what below I call 'special facts' are what they think ordinary facts are like, I have no great objection. The philosophical point about what we need, to do the work that explanation requires, remains unaltered.

I continue to call such things 'facts', but 'in the special or epistemicized sense'. Such a special fact might also be thought of as an ordered pair of an ordinary fact, and a complete conceptualization of that fact. (Alternatively, instead of thinking of explanation as a relation between such ordered pairs, it might be thought of as a four-place relation, whose terms are: an ordinary fact, a complete conceptualization of that fact, a second ordinary fact, and a complete conceptualization of the second fact.)

What I call 'conceptualizations' are, I think, very much like what Nathan Salmon, if I understand him rightly, calls that 'by means of which a proposition is grasped'.[22] Just as he thinks that a proposition can be grasped in different ways, so that belief has to be thought of as a triadic relation between a believer, a proposition, and a way of grasping that proposition ('a mode of presentation'), so similarly I say that explanation is a relation between ordinary facts plus the ways in which those facts are grasped or their modes of presentation (see Salmon 1986:

117–20). Both in the case of his modes of presentation and for my conceptualizations, there is a connection not just with the semantic (in his case) and not just with properties (in mine), but also with the epistemological (see p.120).

I also continue to speak of facts as the relata of the explanation relation, but one must remember that I intend 'fact' in this special, 'epistemicized' sense, which may not accord with the way in which 'fact' is normally understood. Whether a fact as normally understood explains or is explained depends at least in part on the way in which the properties involved are conceptualized; relative to the conceptualization of a property in one way, the fact may be explanatory, relative to a different conceptualization of the same property, the fact is not explanatory. To this extent, it must be admitted that explanations are not fully independent of how we think about things.[23]

In the argument sketched above, (4) is true of facts in the ordinary, non-epistemicized sense; (3) is true only for the special facts which include a conceptual component. So the argument is invalid, since it turns on an ambiguity in the meaning of 'fact'. (1) is true, on my view. The relata of the explanation relation are two different 'epistemicized' facts: the fact that it has temperature t and the fact that its constituent molecules have mke m. These are two different epistemicized empirical facts, and so no epistemicized empirical fact explains itself.

The name transparency of facts

We still have to deal with the question of the name (as opposed to the definite description) transparency of fact locutions. Zeno Vendler argues that 'facts are referentially transparent; propositions, even true ones, are opaque'.[24] And Wilson again: 'it follows . . . that the [fact] that Socrates is red is identical with the [fact] that the teacher of Plato is red'. On their view, if o=i, the fact that i is P=the fact that o is P.

We can see a certain ambiguity in Vendler's and Wilson's assertions. In my view, they are both wrong for the cases they mention; I have already covered these sorts of cases before, in my discussion of definite description transparency. My intuitions tell me that the fact that Socrates is red is not the same fact as the fact that the teacher of Plato is red. I can account for the difference in terms of property introduction. Even though 'the teacher of Plato' is functioning as a referring term, as such it has descriptive content. Thus, it brings additional or different properties into the fact. Although the first fact is constituted by (they 'are the joint full inventory constituents of' the fact, in Wilson's parlance) Socrates and the property red, the second fact has more constituents, to wit: Socrates, Plato, the property, red, and the relational property, being the teacher of.

(An exception to the above will have to be made for the following sort of case: the fact that the water in the glass is warm, and the fact that the stuff in the glass composed of H_2O molecules is warm. If being water=being composed of H_2O molecules, the two definite descriptions employ the same property. So this sort of example will have to be handled like the case of proper names, below.)

However, Wilson and Vendler are right for names; ordinary facts *are* name transparent. Consider the fact that Cicero died in 43 BCE.[25] Since Cicero and Tully are the same person, the fact that Cicero died in 43 BCE and the fact that Tully died in 43 BCE are one and the same fact. To repeat the argument used above in the case of property identity: how could the facts be different? They involve the same individual or particular, and all the same properties or features of that individual. Nothing is a constituent of one that is not a constituent of the other. Fact locutions *are transparent*, for proper names of individuals or particulars.

The identity conditions for ordinary facts are sensitive to the rigidity or otherwise of contained singular terms. The fact that the greatest Roman orator died in 43 BCE, the fact that the greatest Roman Stoic philosopher died in 43 BCE, and the fact that Cicero died in 43 BCE, are three different facts, and only the last mentioned fact is the *same* fact as the fact that Tully died in 43 BCE.

Given these identity conditions, how do facts so identified fare for the purposes of explanation? I have already argued that the definite description non-transparency of facts suits them for explanation. Someone who does not know the identity, the event reported in *The Times* on Tuesday=the hurricane, can do nothing with 'because of the fact that the event reported in *The Times* on Tuesday occurred at midnight' as an explanation for the fact the tidal wave occurred in the early hours of the next morning. If the person does not know that the referent of 'the event reported in *The Times* on Tuesday' and 'the hurricane' are the same, the reply, far from being an explanation, is simply mysterious. We didn't need to tamper with the identity conditions for ordinary facts, in order to take on board this point about their role in explanation.

On the other hand, let's consider the case of proper names. We have agreed that the fact that Tully died in 43 BCE and the fact that Cicero died in 43 BCE are the same (ordinary) fact. They differ with regard to no constituent, neither a particular nor a property nor feature. So, unlike the case of definite descriptions, the criteria for ordinary fact identity are not already 'epistemicized' in the case of proper names of individuals, any more than they were in the case of co-typical predicates.

We have no slingshot problems with the concession that facts *are* name-transparent, for the slingshot argument only goes through for definite descriptions, not names. But if differences in how one *names* an individual make no difference to the identity criteria for facts, such facts will not be adequate for the requirements of explanation. Suppose the question is raised why Cicero's speeches stop in 43 BCE. We can make the same general point that we did before about the hurricane and the event reported in *The Times* on Tuesday. Someone who does not know that Cicero is Tully can do nothing with 'because Tully died in 43 BCE' as an explanation for the fact that Cicero's speeches stop at that date. Without knowledge of the identity, this retort is also simply mysterious.

So if we want entities suitable to be the relata of the explanation relation, our special facts should be ordered sets of ordinary facts and conceptualizations and/or names *both* of the properties and of the individuals who are the constituents of the facts. Cicero named as 'Cicero' might explain, whereas Cicero named as 'Tully' may fail to explain. Here it seems more appropriate to speak in terms of names rather than conceptualizations. It makes perfectly good sense, I think, to speak of mean kinetic energy conceptualized as mean kinetic energy and mean kinetic energy conceptualized as temperature; these are two different ways in which to conceptualize one and the same property. But there are no *concepts* of Cicero and of Tully, which might be variously applied to one and the same person. 'Cicero' and 'Tully' are, rather, different names which might be variously applied to him.

Are the doubly epistemicized facts required for explanation, to borrow an apt term from Stephen Schiffer, 'pleonastic' or 'non-pleonastic'?[26] So far, it might seem that they are to be taken as non-pleonastic. They are non-pleonastic, because I take the expression, 'the fact that p explains the fact that q', even when 'fact' is employed in the epistemicized sense, to have a relational analysis, and I take 'the fact that p' and 'the fact that q' as singular terms which refer to facts (or ordered pairs of facts and 'modes of presentation' of such). (If one thinks of the fact that p and the fact that q as two intensional objects, and calls them 'a' and 'b', then the sentence 'a explains b' is transparent, since any singular term that designates the same fact (understood in my special way) is substitutable *salva veritate*.) On the other hand, Schiffer connects up the idea of ontological commitment with that of existence which is 'language-independent' (Schiffer 1987: 145). That seems to me a conflation. The special facts required as the relata of the explanation relation may not be language-independent (and not conceptualization-independent), any more than the existence of words is language-independent or the existence of concepts is concept-independent. So, this commitment to facts does not entail full-blooded realism about them, in one sense of that word. To this extent, since the facts I require for explanation turn out to be entities dependent on human conceptualization and thought, any realist ontological commitment to them would have to be so qualified.

My argument shows that there is an epistemic requirement in explanation; facts explain facts only when the features and the individuals the facts are about, are appropriately conceptualized or named. The concept of explanation is partly 'epistemological.' But this is by itself no concession to a pragmatic theory of explanation, for the explanatory relevance of the way in which things are conceptualized may not be audience-relative. In one important sense of the term, an epistemological conception of explanation can be objective. Knowledge is, uncontroversially, an epistemic concept, and no one argues from that fact alone that objective knowledge is impossible.

In the remainder of the book, I assume that such special or epistemicized facts are the relata of the explanation relation, even when looseness or ease of expression may have me speaking of events explaining events. This can always be translated as the fact that such an event occurred. What counts as an appropriate conceptualization? This introduces a new topic, to which I also return in the next and the final chapter.

CHAPTER VI

Arguments, Laws, and Explanation

Although I use this chapter and the next to pronounce on a number of the claims about explanation that I have described in the historical section of the book, there are two issues to which I want especially to attend. The first, which I tackle in this chapter, is the thesis common to Aristotle, Mill, and Hempel, that full explanations are valid arguments; the second, which I treat in chapter VII, is Hempel's view that some singular explanations are non-causal explanations. On the way to making these two points, something like a general view of explanation will emerge. That general view is put tentatively, and with some hesitation. I regard it more as a research project, than as a finished theory that is able, as it stands, to meet all difficulties.

The first issue for discussion, then, concerns the claim that explanations are arguments. On Aristotle's, Mill's, and Hempel's accounts of explanation, explanations are arguments, although sometimes elliptically or enthymetically presented. Probabilists and deductivists, although they disagree about whether there are any explanatory arguments with a non-deductive form, both hold an argument theory of explanation. If an explanation is an argument, then (on any plausible account of what sort of argument this will be) it will have to include at least one lawlike premiss.

Since argument theorists include laws as premisses in their account of explanation, the first issue also involves the question of the relationship between explanation and laws. What is a law of nature? There are widely different responses to this question in the literature. In what follows, and indeed throughout the book, I assume(d) that the 'orthodox' answer is correct: a necessary condition for a sentence's stating a deterministic law of nature is that it be a true, universally quantified generalization. On the orthodox view, sentences which state deterministic

181

laws of nature typically have, or entail something with, this form: (x) (Fx⊃Gx). Although the universally quantified conditional might also be more complicated than this (e.g. the consequent might also be existentially quantified), it will make no difference to the argument if we only consider sentences with this simple conditional form. I consider in these remarks only the case of deterministic laws and neglect stochastic laws.

No orthodox theorist would consider this condition by itself sufficient. Accidental generalizations have this form, too. Further, universally quantified material conditionals are true when their antecedent terms are true of nothing. So, if this condition were by itself sufficient for lawlikeness, and if nothing in the universe was an F, then both of the following would state laws of nature: (x) (Fx⊃Gx) and (x) (Fx⊃ ~Gx).

There are various proposals for adding further conditions to the one above. Some are proposals for strengthening the generalization by adding a necessity-operator: laws of nature are stated by nomically necessary universally quantified generalizations.[1] Others ascribe to the universally quantified generalization an additional special epistemic status, or a special place in science, or impose further syntactic requirements.[2] My argument is neutral between all of these variants of the orthodox proposal.

On the other hand, suppose that the orthodox view does not provide even a necessary condition, let alone a sufficient one, for something's being a law of nature. If so, my argument would have to proceed somewhat differently. I am sympathetic to some of these non-orthodox views, but I do not deal with any of them here, nor with how their acceptance would alter my argument.[3]

I start by way of outlining some of the standard counterexamples to Hempel's account of full explanation, which will be useful for the discussion in this and in the next chapter. Whether or not they are counterexamples to Mill's or Aristotle's accounts as well will depend on the efficacy of the proposed cure in Hempel's case. My view will be that some are counterexamples to the accounts of all three thinkers, but I propose to begin the discussion by taking them to be alleged counterexamples only to Hempel.

These counterexamples cluster around two difficulties: (a) irrelevance and (b) symmetry. I do not say that Hempel's account has no resources for replying adequately to *any* of these standard counterexamples, although I do think that this is true in some cases. I indicate where I believe that this is so. The counterexamples purport to show that

Hempel's account of explanation, even if necessary, could not be sufficient. However, I argue that in thinking through an adequate response to the counterexamples, we will see that Hempel's requirements are not even necessary for (full) explanation. Those requirements were described in chapter IV, pp. 138–9.

The standard counterexamples: irrelevance

The first reason, (A), for holding that Hempel's conditions for explanation could not be sufficient turns on the fact that there can be derivations that meet all of Hempel's requirements for D-N (or I-S) explanation, but whose premises are obviously irrelevant to the explanation of the conclusions of those derivations. In the main, I shall only be concerned in this chapter with the explanation of singular facts (as I have so restricted myself throughout the book), but we might note some counterexamples which concern the explanation of laws as well. Here is one, taken from Ardon Lyon, which concerns the explanation of empirical laws by deductive subsumption:[4]

    (1) All metals conduct electricity.
    (2) Whatever conducts electricity is subject to gravitational
        attraction.
  ∴(3) All metals are subject to gravitational attraction.

As Lyon points out, no one would regard the conjunction of (1) and (2) as explaining (3), in spite of the fact that the latter does follow from the former, because (1) and (2) are irrelevant to the truth of (3). 'Metals are not subject to gravitational attraction because they conduct electricity: non-conductors are subject to gravitational attraction to just the same degree' (Lyon 1974: 247). Lyon's counterexample is directed against Hempel's account of the explanation of laws, but it is easy to construct a parallel counterexample to Hempel's account of the explanation of singular facts. The explanandum in question would be that this bit of metal is subject to gravitational attraction, and the explanans will include the fact that this bit of metal conducts electricity.

    Another alleged counterexample to Hempel's analysis of the explanation of laws is offered by Baruch Brody:[5]

    (1) Sodium normally combines with bromine in a ratio of one-
       to-one.

(2) Everything that normally combines with bromine in a ratio
of one-to-one normally combines with chlorine in a ratio of
one-to-one.

∴(3) Sodium normally combines with chlorine in a ratio of
one-to-one.

Brody claims that this derivation has no explanatory power whatever,
and I agree with him. But even if the reader were to insist that it has
some such power, it doesn't have much, and Hempel's analysis does not
offer us the materials for saying why that should be so. Although Brody
does not say so, one could say that the problem here too is one of
explanatory irrelevance. The ratio in which bromine and chlorine
combine is surely irrelevant for explaining (but not necessarily
irrelevant in other ways) the ratio in which sodium and chlorine
combine, even though the two ratios *are* related in a lawlike manner. As
with Lyon's counterexample, it is simple to convert Brody's counterexample to one concerning the explanation of a singular fact: the fact
that this bit of sodium combined with this bit of chlorine in a one–one
ratio.

Two further counterexamples which I wish to mention are
specifically directed to irrelevance in the case of the explanation of
singular facts. The first example is adapted from Peter Achinstein.[6]
Suppose that poor Jones (he is so often ill) eats at least a pound of
arsenic and dies within twenty-four hours, and that eating at least a
pound of arsenic inevitably leads to death within twenty-four hours.
Does it follow that the argument below is an explanation of Jones's
death?

(1) Jones ate at least a pound of arsenic at time t.
(2) (x) (x eats at least 1 lb arsenic at t ⊃ x dies within 24 hours
after t).

∴(3) Jones dies within 24 hours of t.

Suppose, consistently with the above suppositions, that Jones was run
over by a bus and died soon after ingesting the arsenic. In this case, the
deduction will not be explanatory, since Jones, although he would have
died from the arsenic had he not been run over by a bus soon after eating
the poison, was actually killed by the bus. It is the bus, and not the
arsenic, which explains his death, in spite of the argument given above
meeting all of Hempel's conditions.

One can generalize Achinstein's example, to any case in which there is causal pre-emption. Suppose some event, e, has two potential causes c and d, in the sense that c occurs and causes e, and that d also occurs and does not cause e, but would have caused e if c had not occurred. d is a potential alternative cause of e, but is pre-empted by the actual cause c.[7] In any such case, there will be an Achinstein-style counterexample to the D-N account of the explanation of singular facts, since there will be a derivation (with all true premisses, etc.) to the explanandum via a premiss set which includes a premiss about the pre-empted cause but not one about the actual cause, and hence no explanation of the explanandum so derived. The pre-empted cause is explanatorily irrelevant to the explanandum thus derived.

I do take the lesson of this counterexample to be important, so it will be worth dwelling on it. Is there a way of meeting this alleged counterexample from the existing resources of Hempel's theory? One might think that it can be met by the introduction of a *ceteris paribus* clause in the statement of the law, (2), and the addition of a further premiss (which will in this case be false) that says that other conditions are in fact equal.[8] So the 'irrelevant explanation', since it includes a false premiss, will fail to be an explanation on Hempel's own account. After all, the rejoinder goes, no one can die who is already dead; the arsenic will be what kills Jones only if he hasn't already died from some other cause. The arsenic ingestion is relevant, only if the *ceteris paribus* clause in the law is met, and the clause will exclude the case in which an alternative cause operates.

I fail to see how the *ceteris paribus* clause response will meet the difficulty at hand. A *ceteris paribus* clause is inserted in a law, as a means of saving an *apparently* falsified law from real falsification: other things are not equal, so the law is true after all. However, in the counter-example, Jones's being run over by a bus does not *even apparently* falsify the law that whoever eats at least a pound of arsenic dies within twenty-four hours. After all, after eating the arsenic, Jones *did die* within the required time period. So how could Jones's bus-related death present any kind of even apparent difficulty for the law about what happens to people after they ingest at least a pound of arsenic? Any difficulty for that law must involve someone's failure to die in some circumstances or other, and poor, dead Jones is no example of that.

In general, when c (the bus hitting Jones) causes e (the death of Jones), there is no argument from this fact to the falsity of the law that whenever a D (an ingestion of at least a pound of arsenic), then an E (a death). In particular, one does not need to rephrase the law as: Whenever a D, then an E, unless there is some alternative cause that operates to bring about an E. It is *true* that whoever eats a pound of arsenic at t dies within twenty-four hours, even when sometimes death of arsenic ingestors is actually brought about by buses or something else.

One further reply to this counterexample might dispute that (2) correctly expresses the intended law. Suppose we interpret the law as itself *including* a causal claim: eating a pound of arsenic *causes* death within twenty-four hours. If laws are universally quantified generalizations (remember that we are assuming throughout that this is so), how should we represent 'eating 1 lb arsenic at t *causes* death within 24 hours', in such a way that it would retain an explicit causal claim? Perhaps in this way: (x) (x eats at least 1 lb arsenic at t ⊃ x's eating at least 1 lb arsenic at t causes x's death within 24 hours). There may be some other way in which to capture the causal claim in an explicit way within the universally quantified generalization, but I cannot see what it might be.

This generalization *is* falsified by the case in which Jones eats the arsenic but the bus causes his death, so a *ceteris paribus* clause would have to be inserted into it after all. If this is the law, it surely intends to assert that one's eating that much arsenic will cause death, *unless* something else causes it instead. The qualification, 'unless something else causes it instead', would be included in the *ceteris paribus* clause. The law should therefore be expressed as: (2′) (x) (x eats at least 1 lb arsenic at t & *ceteris paribus* ⊃ x's eating at least 1 lb arsenic at t causes x's death within 24 hours). The explanatory argument which uses (2′) would have to include an additional premiss: (2″) Other things are equal. If the bus and not the arsenic kills Jones, (2″) would be false, and so the argument would fail to be explanatory, on Hempel's own account. Can we conclude then that, on this view of what the law is, the *ceteris paribus* strategy could handle the arsenic-and-bus counterexample to Hempel's account after all?

I think not, for two reasons. First, this strategy is simply not available to Hempel. No supporter (like Hempel) of the orthodox view of laws would accept (2′) as giving the correct form for a causal law. Second, there are additional problems about what the explanandum would be which (2′) would help to explain; the explanandum certainly would not be as given by (3), 'Jones dies within 24 hours of t'. The explanandum explained by (2′) could only be: (3′) 'eating at least 1 lb arsenic caused Jones's death within 24 hours of t'. One might wrongly suppose that this will present no difficulty for Hempel, since (3) follows from (3′). If one explains (3′), and (3) follows from (3′), hasn't one explained (3) as well?

As Peter Lipton has pointed out,[9] this assumption is not available to Hempel. Hempel's D-N model of explanation is itself not closed under logical entailment. Suppose conclusion c is derived from, and explained by, law L and initial conditions i. The disjunction, i or c, logically follows from c. But the explanation of c by the conjunction of L and i cannot, on Hempel's account, be an explanation of i or c, because L is not essential to the derivation of i or c from the conjunction of L and i.

I have no doubt there is *some* way to handle the arsenic-and-bus case, but the introduction of a *ceteris paribus* clause into the law is simply not it. Nor do I think that there are any resources available in Hempel's account as it stands for satisfactorily dealing with it.

The arsenic-and-bus counterexample is interesting for another reason. It provides an additional example of the asymmetry between explanation and prediction. Someone who produces the above argument, (1)–(3), cannot be said to have explained Jones's death, but he certainly will have been able to predict it successfully. He predicts that Jones will die, and his prediction is correct. Moreover, he has offered excellent grounds for his prediction. Given that Jones drank the arsenic, the predictor could be certain that Jones would die. One can predict via a pre-empted cause, even though one cannot explain via one. Any rejoinder which wishes to claim that the above argument yields neither a successful prediction nor a successful explanation will owe us a fuller account of successful prediction than has been, thus far at any rate, provided.

A second example of explanatory irrelevance which constitutes a counterexample to Hempel's analysis of explanation of singular facts is one taken from Wesley Salmon:[10]

> (1) Every man who regularly takes birth control pills avoids pregnancy.
> (2) John Jones has taken his wife's birth control pills regularly.
> ∴ (3) John Jones avoided becoming pregnant in the past year.

The same sort of case can be made out for someone 'who explains the dissolving of a piece of sugar by citing the fact that the liquid in which it dissolved is holy water'. A sentence which states the fact that the sugar dissolved in that liquid can be derived from, but hardly explained by, sentences stating the fact that the liquid is holy water and the relevant law connecting water and the dissolution of sugar. The fact that the water is holy water is not relevant to the explanation of the dissolution. If (1) above is rephrased as a stochastic rather than as a deterministic law, it will serve as an irrelevance counterexample to the Hempelian account of I-S explanation.

A determined advocate of Hempel's models of explanation might try to insist that the inclusion of explanatorily irrelevant material in the explanans in Salmon's counterexamples might make the explanations poor(er), but that they are still explanations none the less. In chapter I, I distinguished between cases in which an explanation is bad and cases in which there is no explanation at all, and in chapter V, I applied that distinction specifically to the example of the inclusion of explanatorily irrelevant information in the explanans. I argued the following case in chapter V: that someone is a man who takes birth control pills entails that the person is a man, and the person's being a man explains why that person does not become pregnant, but the person's being a man who takes birth control pills does not explain in the least why the person does not become pregnant.

I agree with Salmon about this, and my discussion of the inclusion of irrelevant properties within fact locutions in chapter V was intended to support his view. The richer information has the explanatorily relevant information buried in it: its being water is included in its being holy water; the person's being a man is included in the person's being a man who takes birth control pills. But the richer information does not explain some explanandum, just in virtue of the fact that the weaker information which it includes and hence entails does explain it. The additional information which makes it richer but which is explanatorily irrelevant overrides and kills the explanatory power of the weaker information when it is added to it. As Salmon said, irrelevance is *fatal* to explanation.

The examples which I group under (A) all teach the same lesson. There can be derivations which meet all of Hempel's conditions for the explanation of a singular fact, but, whereas they are wonderful derivations, they offer no explanation of what is derived. This is because the premises are explanatorily irrelevant to the conclusion, or contain misleading explanatorily irrelevant additional information, even though they do imply the conclusion.

One might have hoped to explicate this concept of explanatory relevance as statistical relevance (as Salmon once did), but this seems a hopeless task. The thought might be that a man's taking birth control pills is statistically irrelevant to his becoming pregnant, since, if one considers the set of men who do take these pills and the set of men who do not, the incidence of pregnancy is the same, to wit, nil. So the regular ingestion of birth control pills by a man fails the test of statistical relevance, and hence might *thereby* be thought to fail the test for explanatory relevance.

However, the imposition of statistical relevance has a number of unacceptable consequences. Consider this argument, which is due to John Meixner.[11] Assume that the following argument is an explanation at some level, although admittedly not a very powerful or deep one, of the fact that this sample of material dissolved in water. (If the argument is not an explanation of its conclusion, it certainly does not fail to be one as a consequence of the statistical irrelevance of the premises).

    (1) All salt dissolves in water.
    (2) <u>This sample is salt.</u>
∴(3) This sample dissolves in water.

But if statistical relevance were added as an additional necessary condition for explanation, the above argument would not be explanatory. If this sample is salt, then it has a physical probability n of dissolving in water. If this sample had been baking soda or potassium chloride, it would have had the same probability n of dissolving. It is statistically irrelevant to dissolution whether the sample is salt or potassium chloride or baking soda. Moreover, to say that the sample is salt is more informative than to say only that it is either salt, or baking soda, or potassium chloride.

If explanatory relevance were just statistical relevance, it would therefore not be possible to explain why this sample dissolved in water on the grounds that it was salt, since the fact that the sample was salt includes additional statistically irrelevant information, just as we cannot explain why this lump of sugar dissolved on the grounds that it was placed in holy water, since the fact that the water is holy water is statistically irrelevant additional information.

If we take statistical relevance seriously, then the only grounds that will do, in the explanation of why this sample dissolved in water, will be either (a) that it was [salt v potassium chloride v baking soda. . .], or (b) that it was a substance which had a certain molecular structure m, all and only samples of which (including salt, baking soda, potassium chloride, etc.) dissolve in water.

The first horn of the dilemma, (a), seems unacceptable. I can explain the dissolution of the material by its being salt, without having to include all of the other disjuncts which have the same probability of dissolution. The fact that this sample was salt surely does explain its dissolving, in spite of the fact that, when compared to a sample's being one of the other substances, it is statistically irrelevant that it is salt. The second horn, (b), is equally unacceptable. Of course, science strives for depth in explanation; no doubt it is true that a deeper explanation in terms of molecular structure is a better explanation than the shallow explanation in terms of the material's being salt. But we can explain the dissolving of this substance in water on the grounds that it is salt when we do not know what the relevant molecular structure is. Moreover, when we come to know what molecular structure m is, the material's having m may be a *better* explanation than the one in terms of the material's being salt. But a less good explanation is still an explanation. When we possess the better explanation, it does not follow even then that its being salt is no longer *an* explanation at all, on grounds of statistical irrelevance. The lesson of Meixner's discussion is this: we can sometimes explain with information, some part of which is statistically irrelevant to what we are explaining, so explanatory relevance cannot be understood as statistical relevance.[12]

If applied to Achinstein's arsenic-and-bus case, Meixner's argument would have an even more telling point to it. Surely, we can explain Jones's death by the ingestion of arsenic, when that is what kills him, and by a large and fast-moving bus, when it is that which does the dirty work. The probability of Jones dying after ingesting a pound of arsenic is, let us say, only 0.98. Suppose also that, coincidentally, the probability of Jones dying after getting hit by a large, fast-moving bus is 0.98. Whether it is a bus or the arsenic is therefore statistically irrelevant to Jones's dying, so each disjunct would be ruled out as having explanatory power on its own on the statistical relevance theory. Only the disjunction itself, which includes all the disjuncts which give the same probability of death, will be explanatory; or, if not the disjunction, then some very vague formulation as 'something happening which gives a 0.98 probability of dying'. Yet this seems wrong. Each of ingesting arsenic and being run over by a bus can explain death, when appropriately cited on its own, whether or not dying has the same statistical probability on both.

The standard counterexamples: symmetry

The second reason, (B), for holding that Hempel's conditions could not be sufficient for singular explanation has to do with 'explanatory' symmetries. Hempel's account of singular explanation in terms of derivability from true, empirical premisses permits intuitively objectionable cases in which (part of) the explanans can be explained by the explanandum, as well as explain it. How can we amend the account, so that such symmetries of 'explanation' will not arise?

Both James Woodward and Peter Achinstein have argued (or implied) that the explanation relation is not an asymmetric relation, as is usually supposed, and that there are or can be bona fide cases of acceptable symmetrical explanation, explanatory mutual dependence between two singular facts.[13] However, both would of course concede that there are some cases in which symmetrical explanation must be ruled out (i.e. in the case of causal explanation). The explanation relation, even if not asymmetric, is surely not symmetric. If not asymmetric, it must be non-symmetric. This is enough for my argument here. All the examples I shall consider in this part of the chapter are cases in which symmetrical explanations are intuitively unacceptable; I do not need to retain the stronger claim that the explanation relation itself is asymmetric. At the end of chapter VII, I offer (following Achinstein) an example of what I think is a bona fide case of symmetric explanation, and show why and how symmetric explanations may sometimes be acceptable.

There are a number of these 'symmetry' counterexamples which challenge Hempel's account of singular explanation, many of which derive from Sylvain Bromberger and Michael Scriven.[14] We have already touched on some of these examples in the discussion of Hempel. There are really two kinds of cases that generate these unacceptable symmetries. First, there are equations which show that the numerical value assumed by some property of a system at time t is a function of the values assumed by other properties of a system at time t or an earlier time, t-Δ (Ohm's law, Hook's law, the Boyle–Charles laws for ideal gases, the length and period of a pendulum).

Second, there are laws with biconditionals, which can include cases both of laws of coexistence and of laws of succession. A barometer falls iff a storm is approaching; the light received from the galaxies exhibits a shift towards the red end of the spectrum iff the galaxies are receding from us; and (Aristotle's case) a planet twinkles iff it is not near. To this, we can add Salmon's confused rooster who explains the rising of the sun on the grounds of his regular crowing.[15] These equations or biconditionals will allow the *derivation* of the height of the flagpole from the length of the shadow and the length of the shadow from the height of the flagpole; the length of the pendulum from its period and its period from its length; the approaching storm from the fall in the barometer as well as the fall of the barometer from the approaching storm; the receding of the galaxies from the red shift as well as the red shift from the recession of the galaxies, the rising of the sun from the crowing of the cock as well as the crowing of the cock from the rising of the sun.

But, in each of these pairs, the first derivation would be non-explanatory; the second, explanatory. Equations and biconditionals permit symmetric derivations; but since at least these examples do not provide symmetric explanations, there must be more to singular explanation than what Hempel's theory thus far allows.

Hempel, as we saw, 'dealt' with this by suggesting that there may not really be true biconditionals in such cases (he supposed, it will be recalled, that there might be cases of Koplik spots without measles). But what we have to establish is how, given that there may really be true biconditionals or equations of this kind which allow derivations 'in both directions', we are able to distinguish the explanations from the derivations which fail to explain.

A proposed cure and its problems: the causal condition

It is not a novel thought that the cure for the problems of irrelevance and symmetry, (A) and (B), that Hempel's analysis of D-N explanation faces (at least for the explanation of singular facts; explanation of laws would be quite a different matter) is to be found by stipulating that the premisses include something about the cause of the event to be explained. This was Aristotle's suggestion in chapter III for the examples of the twinkling planets and the deciduous vines. Mill's official theory, which requires that the premisses include the statement of a causal law, has similar resources for dealing with the counter-examples. At least some explanations are, on such an account, deductively valid arguments with true premisses which have empirical content, one of which is a lawlike generalization (thus far, Aristotle, Mill, and Hempel can agree), but also one of which mentions or specifies in some way the cause of the explanandum event (the final requirement would have to be added to the Hempelian account, but is already explicit in the accounts of the other two).

How would the causal requirement help with the problem of symmetry? Given the angle of the sun's elevation, it is the height of the flagpole that causes the length of the shadow, and not vice versa; the change in atmospheric pressure that causes the rise or fall of the barometer, and not vice versa; the receding of the galaxies that causes the red shift, and not vice versa. The causal requirement will also help with irrelevance. It was the bus but not the arsenic, his being a man but not his taking birth control pills, the substance's being water but not its being holy water, which is causally relevant to the death of Jones, the pregnancy failure, and the dissolution of the sugar. So causation seems a way both to rule out symmetric 'explanations' (anyway, where these are unwelcome) and irrelevant 'explanations'.

One might doubt whether causation will in fact help with irrelevance. Suppose we have a jar in which there is some sugar. We add to the sugar some water appropriately blessed by the local priest. What caused the dissolution of the sugar? In part, its being immersed in the water. But, the sample of water just *is* a sample of holy water, so if the immersion in the water caused the dissolution, then the immersion in the holy water caused it. If the immersion in the water not only caused but also explains the sugar's dissolution, doesn't the immersion in the holy water explain it too?

No, for we have distinguished in chapter V between causation and causal explanation. It is true that the immersion in the water, and hence in the holy water, causes the dissolution of the sugar. But it is the *fact* that it was immersed in the water in the jar that *causally explains* the fact that it dissolved, and even though the water is holy water, the fact that it was immersed in the holy water in the jar is a different fact from the fact that it was immersed in the water in the jar. The fact that it was immersed in the holy water in the jar introduces a feature that the other fact does not introduce. And that additional feature, the water's being holy, is causally irrelevant to the dissolution and hence irrelevant to the explanation of the dissolution. A similar diagnosis will be available in the other cases of explanatory irrelevance we have looked at. The purported explaining facts introduce features which are causally irrelevant to what is being explained.

Many contemporary writers have converged on the necessity of including such a causal requirement. Thus, Salmon, reversing his earlier attempts to explicate explanation on the basis of statistical relations and without mention of causation, says that 'The explanatory significance of statistical relations is indirect. Their fundamental import lies in the fact . . . that they constitute evidence for causal relations', and 'The time has come . . . to put the "cause" back into "because"'.[16] Or, 'To give scientific explanations is to show how events and statistical regularities fit into the causal network of the world' (Salmon 1977: 162). Others, including Baruch Brody, have hit upon the same idea, of supplementing Hempel's account with some sort of causal information.[17]

The difficulty with this otherwise extremely attractive view has been pointed out by Timothy McCarthy.[18] It is easy to construct examples of derivations which meet all of Hempel's conditions, plus the condition that there be a premiss which mentions the actual cause of the event to be explained, but which still fail to be explanatory. McCarthy has given several such examples.

His first example (slightly amended) is this. Let e be any event; let 'D(e)' represent any sentence describing e, and let 'C(e)' be a sentence which describes c, e's actual (and not its pre-empted potential) cause (c is described under its causally relevant description). Let '$(x)(Ax{\supset}Bx)$' represent any law utterly irrelevant to the occurrence of e. (It won't matter if you want to strengthen the requirement and make the law a causal law). Finally, let o be any object such that Ao. Consider the following derivation:

(1) $(x)(Ax{\supset}Bx)$
(2) $C(e)$ & Ao
(3) $\sim B(o)$ v $\sim C(e)$ v $D(e)$
∴(4) $D(e)$

This derivation of 'D(e)' from premisses (1)–(3) meets all of Hempel's conditions + the suggested causal supplement. e's cause is described by 'C(e)' in premiss (2). Moreover, 'C(e)' is essential to the derivation (as is the law). Yet, no one would say that we have here an explanation of e, because even though c, e's cause, is described in or mentioned by a premiss, it is not made causally and hence explanatorily relevant to e's occurrence. There is still a notion of 'explanatory relevance' that 'derivation + mention of cause of what is to be explained' simply isn't getting at. As McCarthy says,

> One might suppose that the idea is to mirror the causal dependence of e on its cause by the deductive dependence in d [the derivation]

of a description of e upon a description of e's cause. That is an interesting idea; immediately, however, we may begin to suspect a gap in the argument. The basic worry may be put in this way: why should it follow, merely because a D-N derivation of a sentence describing e ineliminably involves, in some way or other, a description of e's cause that this description functions in the derivation to show (causally) why e occurs? No obvious reason exists why a D-N derivation of a sentence describing e could not depend on a description of e's cause in some way quite unrelated to the causal dependence of e on that cause.

(McCarthy 1977: 161)

McCarthy shows that various attempts to outmanoeuvre this objection will fail. In particular, his argument can be sustained even if an additional condition due to Kim is imposed.[19] That condition is this: let all the singular sentences in the premisses be put in complete conjunctive normal form. Then the condition requires that none of those singular sentences is a logical consequence of the explanandum itself. However, the following derivation meets all of Hempel's requirements + the causal requirement + Kim's conjunctive normal form condition. In the derivation below, 'C(o)' describes the cause of o's turning black, which, let us suppose, is o's being immersed in a bucket of black paint.

(1) All crows are black.
(2) (x) (y) (x turns the colour of y & y is black ⊃ x turns black).
(3) C(o) & Henry is a crow.
(4) ~C(o) v o turns the colour of Henry.
∴(5) o turns black.

Even though (1)–(4) meet all of Hempel's requirements + the causal supplement + Kim's condition, no explanation of (5) has been given.

There is surely something right in the demand that 'cause' be put back into 'because'. But what has gone wrong in the above examples? To simplify, in both derivations, call the cause 'c' and the effect to be explained, 'e'. Although it is true that one of the premisses in both of the above derivations says that c occurs, and although it is true that this premiss is essential to the derivation, no premiss asserts, *of c, that it is the cause of e*. The derivation gets us, as it were, to e's occurrence from c's occurrence, *not* via the fact that c causes e, but rather via a law irrelevant to c's causing e. There is no connection between c and e other than that of logical derivability of the latter's description from the former's (plus an irrelevant law), and that type of connection simply isn't enough to ensure explanation of the conclusion by the premisses. As McCarthy puts it:

> The reason is precisely that the logical dependence of 'D(e)' on 'C(e)' has nothing at all to do with the causal dependence [and hence the explanatory dependence] of e on the event described by 'C(e)', because the law mediating the deductive relation between 'C(e)' and 'D(e)' is causally irrelevant to the occurrence of e.[20]

In the note to the preceding sentence, I argue that various further attempts to strengthen the causal requirement, which require that the law *not* be irrelevant to the occurrence of the effect, will still leave us with non-explanatory derivations.

There is a very simple way to bring the cause and the explanandum event together in the right and relevant way, in order to ensure explanation: not by including as a premiss a singular statement which merely describes or mentions the cause of the explanandum event, e, but rather by including as a premiss a singular statement which asserts, of that cause, that it is the cause of e. *The relevant premiss in McCarthy's arguments would say, for example, not only that c occurs, but also that c is the cause of e.*[21] If this were added, it seems that the derivation would become explanatory. And surely it is this that is lacking in McCarthy's examples, which accounts for the fact that they are not explanatory. This simple and expedient method avoids all the difficulties we have found in trying to capture explanatory dependence or relevance by logical dependence of conclusion on premisses. Explanatory dependence, at least in this example, is captured by an explicit statement of the causal dependence of the effect on the cause. Why just mention the cause in one of the premisses? Why shouldn't a premiss actually assert the causal dependence of explanandum event on explanans event?

I do not think that every such additional premiss must use the word 'cause'. The premiss might assert that e occurs *because* c occurs, or that the *reason* for e is c, or some such.[22] In so far as we are here restricting ourselves to singular causal explanation, all of these will be ways of saying roughly the same thing. The point is this: the premiss under consideration will have to itself assert the dependence of effect on cause, and this dependence cannot be captured by logical dependence. The occurrence of the expression, '. . . is the cause of . . .', although frequently the way in which this is done, is hardly essential (remember that throughout I assume that the descriptions in the causal claim are the ones relevant for explanation); other alternative expressions, like ones which use 'because' or 'is the reason for', and which also capture this sense of non-logical dependence, will do equally well.

However, there are at least two important consequences of this last suggestion that we must note. First, *Hempel's (and Mill's) requirement that there be a lawlike generalization in the premisses which is essential for the derivation is rendered unnecessary*. On the suggestion being canvassed, we have in the argument a premiss that explicitly says: the cause of the explanandum event is such-and-such, and that premiss *by itself* will entail the statement that the explanandum event occurred, without the addition of any further premisses at all. In particular, no premiss stating a universal general fact, no law, will be required for the derivation of the explanandum. So the first consequence is the redundancy of laws in (at least some) explanations.

There is a second important consequence of this suggestion. Why think of explanations as arguments at all? True, we could think of the explanation as an argument with a single premiss:

(1) <u>c is the cause of e.</u>
∴(2) e.

But the derivation of 'e' from 'c is the cause of e' is trivial. It is simpler, and nothing is lost, if we think of this explanation as composed of a singular sentence, 'c is the cause of e' (or, 'e because of c', etc.). Since in fact all of the premisses save this one will be redundant, the explanation really just consists in the one remaining sentence that says that the cause of the event to be explained was such-and-such.

Deductivism and probabilism agreed that *all* full explanations are arguments; if McCarthy's argument and my elaboration of it above are sound, then at least sometimes full explanations are *not* arguments, but sentences. McCarthy's argument, in conjunction with my suggestion for remedying the defect to which it points, does not show that full explanations are *never* arguments; that conclusion would be too strong. But I would go further; *typically*, full explanations are not arguments, but singular sentences, or conjunctions thereof.

Is construing a specific bit of discourse as a sentence rather than an argument simply a matter of personal aesthetic preference on my part? McCarthy's argument and my subsequent remarks were intended to motivate the choice of sentence over argument. The explanation must explicitly include some word like 'because', 'reason', 'causes', etc., and

197

it is just this that the idea of an explanatory argument was meant to avoid, by attempting to capture the dependence which such expressions get at by the idea of deductive or inductive logical dependence of a conclusion on premisses. We have seen how this strategy fails, and have seen that only explicit assertions or statements of the relevant dependence will do. Hence, such explanations typically consist, on my view, of sentences rather than arguments.

Let me mention one not very promising line of reply to this. Is there any *real* difference between an argument theory and a non-argument (or, specifically, a sentence) theory? Isn't the difference between an argument and a sentence theory somewhat superficial? There is, indeed, a way to trivialize the distinction between an argument and a sentence. Any argument can be rewritten as a conditional sentence, with the premisses as the antecedent and the conclusion as consequent. Such a conditional sentence, if true, is necessarily true. The explanatory sentences envisaged by a non-argument theory, if true, are contingently true. Explanations are typically contingently true sentences or conjunctions thereof. The sentence, 'o is G *because* o is F and all F are G', is, if true, contingently true, even though the corresponding assertion of entailment, 'if all F are G and o is F, then o is G', is a necessary truth.

Moreover, any attempt to minimize the difference between an argument theory and a non-argument sentence theory works more to my advantage than to Hempel's. It is a doctrine central to Aristotle's, Mill's, and Hempel's accounts that explanations are arguments. In so far as the distinction between an argument and a sentence is minimized, it is a central doctrine of theirs whose importance is being reduced.

We have, at a sweep, a convincing reason for dismissing any argument theory of explanation, whether deductivist or probabilist. (We still have the choice between certainty, high, and low epistemic probability theories of explanation, the first two being the non-argument analogues of deductivism and probabilism.) In particular, this criticism strikes at the very heart of the Mill-Hempel theory, and the Aristotelian theory of scientific explanation, for all three thinkers held that all full explanations were deductive or inductive arguments. These accounts of explanation not only fail to offer sufficient conditions for full explanation, but more importantly they fail even to provide *necessary* ones. The criticism is not that explanations are not just arguments, but rather arguments plus something more; explanations are, typically, not arguments at all.

McCarthy's reason, although the only one I here discuss, is not the only one advanced by non-argument theorists for not taking explanations to be arguments. Achinstein offers two reasons against construing explanations as arguments: the illocutionary force view (which I have already discussed and dismissed in chapter I) and the problem of accounting for emphasis.[23] Salmon's reason, among others, is rather different: an argument theory of explanation cannot deal with explanations which confer low probabilities. There is no such thing as an argument whose conclusion has a low probability on the premises, so if there are low epistemic probability explanations, at least they cannot be arguments.[24] I remain uncommitted concerning Achinstein's second, and Salmon's, reasons for adopting a non-argument theory of explanation.

If explanations are typically not arguments, what place do laws have in explanation? Can we argue that, since explanations typically are not arguments, therefore explanations typically do not include laws? Although I do believe that many full explanations do not include laws, I do not think that the absence of laws from even some explanations at all follows from the fact that some explanations are not arguments.

The requirement that explanations always include at least one lawlike generalization has been closely bound up with argument theories of explanation. That is to say, if all explanations were deductively valid or inductively good arguments, they would (given the addition of some further uncontroversial assumptions) have to include a lawlike generalization as a premiss.[25] But the inverse is not true; it does not follow from the fact that not all explanations are arguments, that a law is not a part of every full explanation. It only follows that, if laws are a part of full explanations which are not arguments, the idea of their parthood in such cases is not to be cashed out as that of a premiss in an argument. For example, suppose (S) is an explanation of why e happened: (S) 'e occurred because of the fact that c occurred and that whenever a C, an E.' (S) is a sentence, not an argument, and yet it includes the statement of a law.

However, McCarthy's example, in conjunction with my additional remarks about the solution for the difficulty he detects, and Scriven's example below, *also* convincingly show that laws are *not* part of *every* full explanation, in any sense of parthood. The idea that full explanations do not always include laws (and therefore are not always arguments) is not a novel one. In different ways and from different points of view, Ryle, Scriven, Salmon, and Achinstein (and others too; the list is not intended to be exhaustive) have said this, or similar things, about the role of laws in explanation.[26] For example, in numerous papers, Michael Scriven said things similar to what I would wish to maintain about the role of laws or generalizations in explanation (although I do not need to agree with any of his specific examples). In 'Truisms as the Grounds for Historical Explanations', he defended the view that the following was a perfectly *complete or full* explanation as it stood: the full explanation of why (a) William the Conqueror never invaded Scotland is (b) that 'he had no desire for the lands of the Scottish nobles, and he secured his northern borders by defeating Malcolm, King of Scotland, in battle and exacting homage' (Scriven 1959: 444). The explanation, (b), is a conjunctive statement formed from two singular statements and contains no laws. Explanations which lack laws are 'not incomplete in any sense in which they should be complete, but certainly not including the grounds which we should give if pressed to support them' (p.446). Notice that Scriven can be taken as making a weaker and a stronger point: (a)'s full explanation, whatever it is, includes or may include no law; (b) – which includes no law – is (a)'s full explanation. I agree with the weaker of Scriven's points; there are some full explanations which do not include laws, and (a)'s full explanation is likely to be such an example. I do not necessarily agree that (b) is (a)'s full explanation. I return to this distinction below.

Scriven's example above is an explanation of a human action. It is sometimes argued in the case of human actions that they are explicable but *anomic*. The thought here is rather different. Human actions might be, perhaps must be, nomic, law-governed. The first of Scriven's claims is that although or even if human actions are always nomic, sometimes the laws or 'truisms' which 'cover' them form no part of their full explanation.[27]

Scriven makes it clear that he intends the point as a point about explanation generally, not just as a point about the explanation of human action.

> . . . abandoning the need for laws . . . such laws are not available even in the physical sciences, and, if they were, would not provide explanations of much interest. . . . When scientists were asked to explain the variations in apparent brightness of the orbiting second-stage rocket that launched the first of our artificial satellites, they replied that it was due to its axial rotation and its asymmetry. This explanation . . . contains no laws.
>
> (Scriven 1959: 445)

I have been arguing that some full explanations do not include laws. But laws are still important, even to those cases of explanation which do not include them, in other ways. Indeed, the argument view, by insisting that laws are a part of every full explanation, has tended to neglect the other ways in which laws are important to explanation. Let me add some remarks about how laws are still important for the explanation of the world about us, all consistent with my above claim; the remarks will also permit me to sharpen my view somewhat on the role of laws and generalizations in explanation.

First, to repeat what I mentioned above, I have argued that there are *some* full explanations of which laws form no part, in any sense. But many full explanations do include laws, and this seems to be especially so in the special sciences. Indeed, this is one way in which actual explanations, whether 'ideal' or not, in science and ordinary affairs typically differ. Explanations in science typically include relevant laws, although even when this is so, their inclusion in the explanation will not necessarily be as a major premiss of an argument: 'o is G because o is F and all F are G' is a (contingently true) *sentence* which includes a law, but is not an *argument*.

Second, laws are important for the resolution of many types of puzzlement. Clearly, citation of an appropriate regularity can show that the phenomenon about which I may be perplexed or puzzled is, in any case, not atypical or extraordinary or irregular in any way. Given Mill's view of the epistemic circularity of deduction, it was not easy to see why he thought explanations had to be deductive arguments with at least one lawlike premiss. One line of response I proposed on his behalf was that what a covering law 'explanation' of, for example, the Duke of Wellington's mortality could do, was to show how the good Duke's mortality fits into a pattern of nature; the deductive 'explanation' places his mortality within the context of a wider generalization, and hence within the context of a uniformity of nature. I believe that Mill was thinking along such lines as these, since explanation for him was always the fitting of facts into ever more general patterns of regularity. But the answer that I gave on his behalf invites the following observation: explaining the Duke's mortality is one thing; fitting his mortality into a more general pattern, however worthy that may be, is something else. To learn that something is not irregular is not the same thing as to explain it. Not all resolutions of puzzlement or perplexity are *ipso facto* explanations.

There is a *third* way in which laws can be important. Does the explanans really fully explain the explanandum? Perhaps it is not adequate to explain it fully; something may be missing. How can I justify my claim that the explanans fully does the job it is meant to do? On Scriven's (1959: 446) view, suppose I claim that the full explanation of e is c. If I am challenged about the adequacy or completeness of my explanation, I can justify my claim to completeness, and thereby rebuff the challenge, by citing a law (or truism), e.g. that all C are E (c being a C; e being an E). This is what Scriven calls the 'role-justifying grounds' that laws provide, in support of a claim that one has given a full explanation. The law or truism can justify my assertion that c is the full and adequate explanation of e, without being part of that explanation. Although Scriven does not say so, there can be no objection to offering the full explanation and the justification for its fullness in a single assertion, but if this is done, we should be clear that what we have is a full explanation *and* something else, and not just a full explanation.

It is for this reason that I distinguished Scriven's weaker and stronger claims above. I agreed that a full explanation for (a) included no laws, but I did not necessarily agree that (b) – which included no laws–was (a)'s full explanation. The full explanation of o's being G is the fact that o is F, only if it is a law that all F are G, *sans* exception. Suppose the law in question is a more complex law which says: (x) (Fx & Kx & Hx & Jx ⊃ Gx). A full explanation of why o is G would be the fact that o is F&K&H&J. In this way, my view of full explanation is, in at least one way, close to Hempel's, in spite of my rejection of his, or any, argument theory of explanation. Full explanations, on my view as on his, may well be close to ideal things; if almost no one ever gives one, that tells us a lot about the practical circumstances of explanation-giving, but provides no argument whatsoever against such an account of full explanation.

There may be perfectly good pragmatic reasons why we are entitled to give a partial explanation of o's G-ness; it may be that o's being K&H&J is so obvious, that one never needs to say anything more than that o is F. But the law (or 'truism') provides the criterion for what a complete or full explanation is. I do not want to commit myself about the 'fullness' of Scriven's explanation for William's non-invasion of Scotland, since this raises issues about whether there are any laws which 'cover' human actions and which are also expressible in the vocabulary of human action itself, as Aristotle seemed to believe. This would also involve a discussion of how 'truisms', in Scriven's parlance, differ from laws, and I avoid this issue here.[28]

But, to turn to his second example, I am sure that the explanation of the variations in apparent brightness of the orbiting second-stage rocket that launched America's first artificial satellite, in terms only of its axial rotation and asymmetry, cannot be its full explanation. I agree that its full explanation, whatever it is, need not include a law, but since the explanation Scriven offers fails to contain any particular information about, for instance, the source of light that was present, it could not be a full explanation. Scriven's own remarks about the role-justifying grounds that laws provide helps make this very point. The particular explanation Scriven offers as full can be seen to be only incomplete, not because it does not include a law, but because the law provides the test for fullness which Scriven's explanation fails.

Fourth, on my view, there is still a connection between singular explanation and generality, but not through the presence of a law. Suppose it is argued that the following is a full explanation:[29] (F) object o is G because o is F. It seems to me that someone who insists that this cannot be a full explanation because of the absence of a law has to motivate the thought that (F) could not really be a full explanation, by showing what it is that (F) omits, which is not omitted once a law is added to the explanation. (Recall that we are already assuming that argument theories of explanation have been rejected, so he can't fault the absence of the law on the grounds of non-derivability of explanandum from explanans without it.) He must, I think, say this: the real full explanation is only (FL): object o is G because o is F and (x) (Fx⊃Gx).

But can we pinpoint what it is that the law is meant to add to (F)? What has (FL) got that (F) lacks? Return to the thought, developed at length in chapter V, that what matters to explanation are properties.[30] When o's being F fully explains o's being G, it isn't (to put it crudely) that *o*'s being F explains *o*'s being G; there is nothing special about o in any of this. Rather, it is o's *being F* that explains o's *being G*. Explanatory impact is carried by properties and there is generality built into the singular explanation by the properties themselves, without the inclusion of a law. This implicit generality surely implies that other relevantly similar Gs which are F will get the same full explanation that o got.

Of course, there is one obvious sense in which an explanation of o's being G, in terms of o's being F, could be incomplete. The explanation might fail to specify or cite all of the explanatorily relevant properties or characteristics of o. But all of the relevant properties of o can be cited without inclusion of any law generalization.

Suppose, for the sake of argument, that it is an exceptionless law of nature that (x) (Fx⊃Gx). In this case, the only property of o, relevant for explaining why o is G, is o's F-ness. In such a case, it seems that o's being G can be fully explained by o's being F. What could the inclusion of the law or generalization add to the explanation that o is G because o is F?

In '(x) (Fx⊃Gx)', the only information that could be relevant to the explanation of o's being G is already given by the property linkage between being F and being G which is already expressed by (F). That part of the information in the generalization which is about (actual or possible) Fs other than o which are also G, is simply irrelevant to the explanation of o's being G. In short, everything relevant to the explanation of o's being G is already contained in (F), since that claim already makes the requisite property connection between being F and being G. Assuming that the generalization can connect properties at all (it is unclear that a generalization can do this, even when strengthened by a necessity operator), what (FL) does that is not done by (F) is to extend the connection to cases other than o. And this can't have any additional explanatory relevance to o's case. The case of temporally and spatially distant F-objects which are G is surely not relevant to o. One might ask about explanation the question Hume asked himself (but believed he could answer) about his constant conjunction theory of causation: 'It may be thought, that what we learn not from one object, we can never learn from a hundred, which are all of the same kind, and are perfectly resembling in every circumstance.'[31]

My view is even more radical than the suggestion that emerged in chapter IV, that Mill could have considered a type of real explanation, parallel to his account of the fundamental kind of real, non-deductive inference. Such Millian considerations would certainly dispense with the generalization that all F are G, in the explanation of o, which is F, being G. If the manhood of individual persons does not explain their mortality, how could putting all the cases together, as it were, into a generalization, help get explanation off the ground? How could a generalization have some supervenient explanatory power that each instance of the generalization lacks?

Although such a view dispenses with generalizations, it does not dispense with the relevance to o's case of other Fs which are also Gs. This Millian inspired view of explanation would retain, as relevant to the explanation of o's being G, the F-ness and G-ness of other particulars, a, e, i, u, etc. Mill thought that we could (really) infer (and, let us suppose, explain) the Duke's mortality, not from a generalization, but from his resemblance to other individual men who were mortal. Yet, it is hard to see how, if the Duke's manhood cannot explain his mortality, introducing the manhood and mortality of people other than the Duke (whether by a generalization or by the enumeration of other particular instances) could explain it. What is the relevance to the good Duke's mortality of the mortality of men spatially and temporally far distant from him?

On my more radical view, neither the generalization that all Fs are Gs, nor the F-ness and G-ness of other particulars, is required to be any part of the full explanation of o's being G. In the case being supposed, the only fact required for the full explanation of o's being G, is o's being F, even though the generalization, and the explanation of other particulars' G-ness by their F-ness, and so on, are implied or presupposed by the full explanation of o's being G by o's being F. The question Hume asked, quoted above, if it has any bite at all, bites not only against a constant conjunction theory of causation (which brings a generalization into prominence), but even against a weaker theory of causation which makes part of the analysis of an instance of a causal relation information about *any other* individual instances of that causal relation.

Generalizations get their revenge

The above remarks attempt to spell out a number of ways in which laws and generalizations are important for explanation, without necessarily being part of them. There is yet another way, closely connected with the third and fourth ways mentioned above. It is sufficiently important to separate it from the others. The point assumes that things are explanatory only as described, and hence builds on the discussion of facts in the last chapter.

Aristotle, it will be recalled, thought that laws provided the criteria for the selection of the descriptions under which the explanans explains the explanandum. Why did the match light? I struck it, and my striking of the match was, let us suppose, the penultimate thing that ever happened to the match. Or, my striking of the match was the event that caused the match to light. Why, then, can I *explain* the fact that the match lit by the fact that the match was struck, and not by the different facts that the penultimate thing that ever happened to the match occurred, or that the cause of its lighting occurred, even though these three singular facts (the fact that the match was struck, the fact that the cause of the match's lighting occurred, the fact that the penultimate thing that ever happened to the match occurred) are all facts about the same causal event, but differently described? In virtue of which of the features of a cause is the cause fully explanatory of the effect?

Aristotle's reply would be that the explanatory features are the ones linked in a law (whether deterministic or stochastic). To be sure, that strikings of matches are followed by lightings of matches is itself no law, nor any part of a law, of nature. We must therefore extend Aristotle's point, to include not only features linked in a law, but also features nomically connected in the appropriate way in virtue of underlying laws (more on appropriateness in chapter VII). In virtue of the underlying laws of physics and chemistry, striking and lighting, but not for example being a penultimate occurrence and a lighting, are nomically related. It is not that the laws need be any part of the explanation; rather, the laws provide the criteria for determining under which descriptions one particular explains another (which singular fact explains another). Laws permit selection of the vocabulary appropriate for singular explanation.

The above allows me to make a closely related point about the role of theories in explanation. Scientists often cite theories in explaining a phenomenon. For example: the theory of gravity explains why the moon causes the earth's tides; the law of inertia explains why a projectile continues in motion for some time after being thrown; subatomic particle theory explains why specific paths appear in a Wilson cloud chamber. And theories consist (perhaps *inter alia*) of generalizations. *But (a) it does not follow that theories are explanatory in virtue of their generality, (b) nor does it follow that the way in which they are explanatory is in all cases by being part of the explanation.* I have already argued for (b). But I now wish to argue for (a). Theories help to explain singular facts, in virtue of supplying a vocabulary for identifying or redescribing the *particular* phenomena or mechanisms at work, which are what explain the explanandum facts.

The examples of 'syllogistic explanation' that I used in my discussion of Mill might have struck the reader as exceedingly artificial: whoever would have thought, the reply might go, that the Duke of Wellington's mortality could be explained by his manhood and the generalization that all men are mortal? And, in admitting that some explanations do include laws (especially in the sciences), I gave this example: 'o is G because o is F and all F are G'. These generalizations are 'flat', in the sense that they are simple generalizations that use the same vocabulary as do the singular explanans and explanandum descriptions. Flat generalizations do not contribute at all to singular explanation.

However, from the fact that flat generalizations are explanatorily useless, it hardly follows that all are. What is needed, so the reply might continue, are generalizations which employ a theoretical vocabulary with greater depth than 'man' and 'mortal'. Perhaps the vocabulary should be in *deeper* terms that refer to the fragility of hydrocarbon-based life forms. To explain why o is G, in terms of o's being F, if a law is to be included, typically a scientific explanation will cite a law with a vocabulary which is different from and deeper than the vocabulary of which 'F' and 'G' are part. Only as such could the generalizations be explanatory.

And such a reply is correct. But it confirms rather than disconfirms my view. If generalizations or laws were always *per se* explanatory, then flat ones ought to help explain (perhaps not as well as deep ones, but they should explain to some extent none the less). The fact that *only* ones that are deep, relative to the vocabulary of the explanans and explanandum singular sentences (in general, theories), will help explain *at all* is an indication that they are explanatory in virtue of offering a deeper vocabulary in which to identify or redescribe mechanisms, but not just in virtue of being generalizations. And even so, to return for a moment to (b), the generalizations that make up the wider or deeper theory may help to explain by offering that alternative vocabulary, and without being part of the explanation itself.

I argued before that often full explanations do not include laws, but that they sometimes do, especially in the special sciences. When laws are included within an explanation, as they sometimes are, the purpose of the inclusion is to introduce a vocabulary different from the one used in the explicit descriptions of the particular explanans and explanandum events. On the one hand, if the less deep vocabulary used to describe the particular phenomena were wholly expendable, the theoretic vocabulary could be explicitly used to describe them, and any mention of the law would be redundant. If on the other hand no deeper vocabulary were available, there would be no purpose for a law to serve. Laws find their honest employment in singular explanation in situations between the two extremes: when the less deep vocabulary used to describe singular explanans and explanandum is to be retained at that level, but a deeper vocabulary is available, and needs introduction.

One important role that theories play in science is to unify superficially diverse phenomena.[32] In virtue of a unifying theory, what seemed like different phenomena can be brought under one set of deep structural laws:

> By assuming that gases are composed of tiny molecules subject to the laws of Newtonian mechanics we can explain the Boyle–Charles law for a perfect gas. But this is only a small fraction of our total gain. First, we can explain numerous other laws governing the behavior of gases.... Second, and even more important, we can integrate the behavior of gases with the behavior of numerous other kinds of objects.... In the absence of the theoretical structure supplied by our molecular model, the behavior of gases simply has no connection at all with these other phenomena. Our picture of the world is much less unified.
>
> (Friedman 1981: 7)

On my view, there is a difference between unification and explanation. Unification of a phenomenon with other superficially different phenomena, however worthwhile a goal that may be, is no part of the explanation of that phenomenon. If other men's mortality couldn't explain why the good Duke is mortal when his own manhood doesn't, then the fragility of other hydrocarbon-based life forms couldn't explain the Duke's fragility or mortality when his own hydrocarbon constitution doesn't. It doesn't matter, from the point of view of explanation, whether there are any other phenomena which get explained by the deeper vocabulary; the point is that the vocabulary gives a new and more profound insight into the phenomenon at hand, whether or not the vocabulary unifies it with other phenomena.

CHAPTER VII

A Realist Theory of Explanation

On Mill's official account of explanation, all explanations of singular facts seemed to require laws of efficient causality (although we noted that there was some evidence that Mill himself was prepared to consider the matter differently). Hempel, on the other hand, specifically allows for non-causal explanations of singular facts. Plato and Aristotle used 'cause' so widely that, even though all explanations invoke a 'causal' factor, much more is included than Mill would certainly have allowed. Whose claim is (more nearly) correct?

The question I wish to deal with in this chapter is the question of non-causal explanation. We discussed in chapter VI symmetry and irrelevance difficulties faced by Hempel's account of explanation. Causal asymmetry will ensure explanatory asymmetry in those cases in which the asymmetry of explanation is thought to be desirable. Causal relevance will also provide us with a way to ensure explanatory relevance. So causation seems a good bet for explaining explanation.

But are all singular explanations causal explanations? In my remarks throughout the book I have moved rather freely between 'explanation' and 'causal explanation'. Indeed, when I introduced various distinctions between kinds of theories of explanation in chapter I, I did so by adopting an interim assumption: all explanation of particular or singular facts is causal explanation (this excludes, of course, the case of explanation of laws by more general laws). It is now time to look at this question in a more sustained way.

What hangs on this question? I think that a great deal does. I agree with much of what Kim writes in 'Noncausal Connections', and I apply the lesson it teaches to theories of explanation.[1] He there argues that:

> Events in this world are interrelated in a variety of ways. Among
> them, the ones we have called dependency or determination

relations are of great importance. Broadly speaking, it is these relations, along with temporal and spatial ones, that give a significant structure to the world of events. The chief aim of the present paper has been to show that causation, though important and in many ways fundamental, is not the only such relation, and that there are other such determinative relations that deserve recognition and careful scrutiny.

(Kim 1974: 52)

There appear to be dependency relations between events that are not causal, and, as I shall argue, universal determinism may be true even if not every event has a cause. These non-causal dependency relations are pervasively present in the web of events, and it is important to understand their nature, their interrelations, and their relation to the causal relation if we are to have a clear and complete picture of the ways in which events hang together in this world.

(Kim 1974: 41)

Metaphysically, Kim's point is that the world is structured by various determinative or dependency relations, of which causal relations are only a proper subset. Not all metaphysical relations structure the world, in the relevant sense; accidental correlation relations between types of objects or properties are 'real' metaphysical relations, but they result from the world's structure, rather than help to structure it. Notice that Kim, unlike me, does not distinguish between the concepts of determination and dependency.

On my view, it is the presence of these 'structural' determinative (and dependency) relations that makes explanation possible. They are not all that is required, for as I have stressed, these are metaphysical relations, and explanation is an epistemological idea. Conceptualization must be considered in any complete account of explanation, as I have tried to do in chapter V. Whether the explanation relation relates those real objects or events directly, or only relates statements or facts about them, the basis for explanation is in metaphysics. *Objects or events in the world must really stand in some appropriate 'structural' relation before explanation is possible.* Explanations work, when they do, only in virtue of underlying determinative or dependency structural relations in the world.

If the causal relation were the only type of determinative relation there is, then one might expect all singular explanations to be causal. But if Kim is right, if there are other types of determinative relations, they might provide the basis for non-causal singular explanations. I would have called the theory of explanation I advance 'a determinative theory', to capture this idea that explanation rests on appropriate metaphysical relations, but I do not wish to beg the question of whether causation is a deterministic or nondeterministic idea. To allow for the possibility of nondeterministic causal explanation, i.e. high or low dependency explanations (and indeed for the possibility that there may be nondeterministic relations other than causation that underpin explanations), I prefer to call the theory of explanation 'realist'. The idea behind this realist theory of explanation is that explanation rests on real metaphysical relations, whether they be deterministic or nondeterministic ones. I remain neutral in the dispute between determinative, high, and low dependency theories of explanation.

Are all singular explanations causal explanations?

The literature seems divided in its answer to the above question. Van Fraassen, for example, argues that all explanation is by way of fitting things into the causal net, but 'the causal net' is defined by him as 'whatever structure of relations science describes'.[2] Van Fraassen seems quite uninterested in the details of causation; trivially, whatever science reveals is causal in the only sense in which he appears interested. Similarly, John Forge attempts to salvage Salmon's causal theory of explanation by saying that 'a causal process is one governed by scientific laws (theories)'.[3] If one adopted a concept of causation that was this wide, it would indeed be an easy task to show that all explanation of singular facts was causal. But the victory would be pyrrhic, relying as it would on an unmotivated and *ad hoc* understanding of causation.

Salmon, on the other hand, defends the thesis that all scientific explanation (that is, *singular* scientific explanation; I shall not always repeat this qualification in what follows) is causal explanation, using for the purpose a narrower and more plausible account of causation: 'Causal processes, causal interactions, and causal laws provide the mechanisms by which the world works; to understand why certain things happen, we need to see how they are produced by these mechanisms.'[4] In a similar vein, Richard Miller claims: 'An explanation is an adequate description of underlying causes helping to bring about the phenomenon to be explained'.[5] Although Miller's account of the concept of causation is

211

unusually free of aprioristic restrictions, the concept is based on a core of cases and is extendible to further cases by rational procedures for such extension. So Miller's conception of causation, although malleable and adaptable, is definite enough not to be amorphous and able to cover anything one could wish. For Salmon and Miller, unlike for van Fraassen, all explanations are causal in a specific enough sense of 'cause', so that 'all (scientific) singular explanations are causal explanations' is something more than just a definition or a tautology.

Many, perhaps even most, other writers have disagreed with the claim that ties explanation so intimately with causal explanation, and have produced lists of apparent counterexamples to the thesis. We shall be looking in some detail at a few of those counterexamples below. Let me give a fuller flavour of this widespread disagreement by repeating a random selection of the lists of these allegedly non-causal explanations.

Philip Kitcher's non-causal cases are the explanation of why neon is chemically inert by quantum chemistry and various explanations in formal linguistics.[6] Nancy Cartwright mentions generally explanations invoking laws of association as non-causal: 'the equations of physics . . . [for instance] whenever the force on a classical particle of mass m is f the acceleration is f/m', and the laws of Mendelian genetics.[7] Clark Glymour argues that there

remains, however, a considerable bit of science that sounds very much like explaining, and which perhaps has causal implications, but which does not seem to derive its point, its force, or its interest from the fact that it has something to do with causal relations (or their absence).[8]

Glymour's examples are all concerned with explaining gravitation and electro-dynamics on the basis of some variational principle, and he gives three examples of this. Peter Railton says that 'some particular facts may be explained non-causally, e.g., by subsumption under structural laws such as the Pauli exclusion principle'.[9] John Forge reminds us that

. . .laws of co-existence are not causal laws . . . laws of co-existence do in fact appear in scientific explanations. Some of these explanations are of considerable significance, such as those involving applications of classical thermodynamics in chemistry.[10]

What sort of argument should we accept as decisively defeating a causal theory of explanation? How do we decide which of the above cited examples are bona fide examples of non-causal explanation? Let me mention four such lines of attack which I do *not* think will do the job. *First*, Peter Achinstein provides a number of alleged counterexamples to a causal theory of explanation, some of which are examples of the explanation of an instance of a law, e.g. the fact that since c occurred, e occurred, by means of the law of which it is an instance (the law that Es when Cs). Let's call these 'instance explanations'. Instance explanations, in this sense, are not arguments but *sentences* which assert that some singular relational or conditional fact[11] is an instance of a lawlike regularity. Suppose there are these instance explanations, as Achinstein asserts.[12] There is also the case of the explanation of laws by more general laws (discussion of which I have forsworn). Mill himself pointed out, in a passage I earlier quoted, that the relation of a generalization to one of its instances is not the relation of a cause to its effect.

But I do not think that we should accept any of these cases as a serious counterexample to a causal theory of explanation. An upholder of a causal theory of explanation like Salmon would rightly not be very impressed with this; the causal theory of singular explanation should be expressed in such a way that will allow for these types of explanation.

Suppose the explanandum which figures in one of Achinstein's instance explanations is: fRg ('R' stands for some relation, we know not what as yet, which I have thus far indicated by the rather anodyne 'since' and 'when'). Suppose the explanation is: fRg because all Fs stand in relation R to Gs (as I mentioned in chapter VI, the law will typically be expressed in a different vocabulary than is the singular claim, one dependent on some theory). Is that a non-causal explanation? Surely, we cannot tell, until we know for what relation 'R' stands. If it is a causal relation, then the explanation is causal in an appropriately widened sense; if not, then not. The point of importance is this: the fact that the explanation is an instance explanation, which cites a law as explanatory, is simply irrelevant to the question of whether it is a causal explanation. It is of course true that a generalization or law never causes its instances, but explaining a particular relational causal fact as an instance of a causal generalization cannot be a serious counterexample to a judiciously stated causal theory of explanation.

The *second* way in which I avoid a too easy victory over a causal theory of explanation is this. Many writers (Hempel, Cartwright, and Forge were examples) dismiss the claim that all explanations are causal explanations on the grounds that some explanations involve laws of coexistence,[13] rather than laws of succession. This dismissal assumes that no cause can be simultaneous with its effect. This seems an unwise assumption to make about causation, since it has often been questioned. It is certainly open to the defender of the causal theory of explanation to insist that an effect can be simultaneous with its cause, and such a rejoinder does not seem especially *ad hoc*, or unmotivated.

Any alleged example is bound to be controversial, but two examples of the simultaneity of cause and effect which are sometimes offered are these. First, consider a rigidly connected locomotive and caboose. The locomotive begins to move, and the caboose begins to move simultaneously. Second, when I force my fist into a pillow, the impact of my fist creates a hollow pocket in the pillow, and the impact of my fist on the pillow and the creation of the hollow in it are simultaneous. Or anyway so it might be argued. There are, of course, alleged 'micro' replies to these examples.[14] Perhaps some of the replies are successful; perhaps none is. I wish to avoid all of this controversy, by eschewing this line of attack on the causal theory of explanation. Of course, if it is possible for a cause and effect to be simultaneous, causal asymmetry cannot itself be explicated as temporal asymmetry. The view that allows simultaneous causes and effects will have to find some other way in which to capture causal asymmetry.

Third, there are some cases of explanation which depend on laws which seem to be *non-causal* laws of succession. Explanations in such cases will be explanations by an earlier singular fact, of a later, succeeding, singular fact, where the relationships involved do not appear to be causal. Examples are ones that utilize laws governing self-maintaining processes, like the law of inertia, conservation laws, and in general laws governing the motions of objects.

In order to handle such cases, John Mackie distinguishes between immanent and transeunt causation. When a process is hindered or interrupted 'from the outside', the external event is a transeunt cause of the later, altered stages of that process. On the other hand, when a process continues uninterrupted, the earlier stages of the process itself are the immanent causes of the later stages.

Mackie argues, plausibly to my mind, that laws like the inertia and conservation laws *are* causal laws, namely laws of immanent causation. Therefore, we can say that explanations which presuppose laws like the law of inertia are immanent causal explanations.[15] I throw a projectile, and it moves during the time interval t–t′ at a certain velocity v. Suppose no force acts on the projectile after its release. It will travel at the same velocity v in the interval t′–t″. What causes it to travel with velocity v during t′–t″? Can we say that its travelling at v in the first interval caused it to travel at v in the second one?

Mackie says that if a force acts on the projectile to slow it down, there is a transeunt cause 'from the outside' which, in the circumstances of the projectile moving at velocity v, causes the slowing down of the projectile to less than v. But, if we take the absence of an external force as part of the circumstances, then it would seem perfectly reasonable to say that the cause of the projectile moving at velocity v in the latter time period was its moving with velocity v in the earlier time period. The earlier stage of the process is the immanent cause of the latter stage.

It is true, says Mackie, that we 'ordinarily look for and recognize a cause of a change in a process, rather than for the mere continuance of the process'.

> However, while it seems strange to call this earlier phase a cause, and while our reluctance to do so reveals something about our actual concept of causing, there are analogies which would justify our extending the existing concept to cover this. . . . The earlier phase of a self-maintaining process surely brings about, or helps to bring about, the later phase. If the concept of cause and effect does not yet cover them, it should: we can recognize immanent as well as transeunt causation.
>
> (Mackie 1974: 155–6)

We can speak of causation in the case in which there is a continuation rather than a change, on this view. Of *what* is it a continuance rather than a change? The reply is: motion, or whatever other state of the object is conserved through the relevant time period. One thing that Mackie's view entails is that a cause can be an event like: the moving at velocity v at an earlier time, which is said to be the cause of its continuing to move with velocity v at a later time.

Some have objected to this view, on the grounds that pure motion cannot be a cause. I can see no reason a priori to conclude that moving with velocity v cannot be a cause. Our ordinary conception of cause surely permits causes of this kind. It may be extraordinary to speak of causation where there is continuation rather than change; but there is nothing extraordinary about movings being causes, in the case in which the moving brings about a change. A standard 'scientific' view of causal explanation makes causal explanation 'appropriate when there is transference of energy and momentum in accordance with conservation laws';[16] on such a view, Mackie's immanent causation is certainly a type of causation, and explanations which rely on these laws of succession are causal explanations.

We need not settle the question of whether the idea of immanent causation generally, or its application to these cases, will ultimately withstand scrutiny. The only thing we need to conclude is that the matter is sufficiently unclear for it to be unwise to rest a rejection of the causal theory of explanation on such cases.

Fourth and finally, I will not rest my argument on examples taken from quantum mechanics. These cases arise in discussions of quantum mechanics, and in particular of the so-called Einstein–Podolsky–Rosen paradox, and the contributions to that problem by J.S. Bell.[17] Put very succinctly, assume two half-particles travelling in opposite directions along the x-axis from a singlet spin state. According to quantum mechanics, if the measurement of the component of spin in one direction is +1, the measurement for the second must yield -1, and vice versa. Paradoxically, the two particles can be separated by any distance, and the choice of which of the two particles on which the measurement is first to be made can be taken after the particles leave their singlet spin state, and the result will still be the same. Moreover, Bell showed, in a series of papers, that an assumption of some hidden variable to account for these results is inconsistent with quantum mechanics (and relevant experiments). Does the E–P–R paradox provide us with a case of non-causal explanation?

There are two reasons why I do not pursue the question of whether we have, in quantum mechanics, a type of non-causal explanation. First, it is a matter of some controversy whether the idea of causation is malleable enough to be employed in the description of the E–P–R correlations. Can there be non-local causation? Can there be causation at a distance?[18] Second, and more to the point, it is unclear what lessons there are for explanation in this. Suppose we reject the idea that measuring the component of spin on one half particle can causally influence the measurement of the component of spin we obtain on the other half-particle. But perhaps explanation and causation still go together. Can we, even in the absence of one half-particle *influencing* the other, really explain one measurement by the other? The correlations of values obtained in the measurements of the components of spin of the two half-particles are certainly nomic, but in spite of being nomic, they may fail to be explanatory, in the absence of a causal mechanism.[19] All of this is highly contentious, and justifies my neglect of quantum mechanics in my discussion of non-causal types of explanation. But there is nothing in my final thesis about non-causal explanation, which follows in the next section, that could not be amended to include these cases, if the reader insists that they do provide genuine cases of non-causal singular explanation.

What would make an explanation non-causal?

What sorts of cases, if any, should convince us that there are non-causal singular explanations, if not these? In particular, what is the concept of causation that is being used, in either the assertion or the denial of the causal theory of singular explanation? I indicated earlier that the van Fraassen–Forge concept of causation was too wide. In order to meet the objections to a causal theory presented by laws of coexistence and (apparently) non-causal laws of succession, I have had to widen the idea of cause, or anyway argue that the concept of causation is wider than the opponent of the theory seemed willing to allow. If one is allowed to widen the concept at will, there could never be any definitive refutation of a causal theory of explanation. Where shall the limits of permissible widening be set?

I assume without argument two features of (ordinary, empirical) causation, that are uncontroversial.[20] If we can argue against a causal theory of explanation on the basis of them, I believe that we will have produced a definitive argument against the view that all explanation of singular facts is causal explanation. The two features are these: (1) nothing can cause itself; (2) the causal relation is contingent. I do not claim that (1) and (2) are logically independent. (1) of course has been denied for the case of allegedly necessary beings such as God, or Nature-As-A-Whole, and what we might call 'metaphysical explanation'. It is uncontroversial in its application to contingent beings and empirical explanation, scientific and ordinary, which is what is under discussion here.

In (2), I intend 'the contingency of the causal relation' in the sense that, if c causes e, there is a series of metaphysically possible worlds, viz. one in which c occurs and does not cause e but causes something else, one in which c occurs and causes nothing, one in which e occurs caused by something other than c, and one in which e occurs caused by nothing. The requirement is Humeian in inspiration, and I accept it. There are two grades of contingency that should be distinguished in what I have said: weak contingency says that it is possible that the cause have a different effect, and the effect have a different cause; strong contingency says that it is possible that the cause have no effect, and the effect have no cause.

The contingency is a metaphysical contingency, and has nothing to do with the descriptions one happens to use to refer to the cause and effect. It is sometimes said that the contingency or otherwise of the causal relation depends on which descriptions of cause and effect are selected, so that, for example, even if 'c causes e' is contingent, 'the cause of e causes e' is necessary. This last claim is false, for the relevant scope reading of that assertion. The claim 'Concerning the cause of e, it caused e' is metaphysically contingent, since the event which was the cause of e might not have been. What is necessary is merely this sentence: '(x) (x causes e ⊃ x causes e)'. This necessity is not metaphysical, but analytic necessity.

I now turn to some cases of explanation which I regard as successful refutations of a causal theory of singular explanation.

Identity and explanation

No one, as far as I know, has ever disputed the claim that no (contingent) thing or event causes itself, (1) above.[21] Causation in such cases must be a relation between two distinct existences. Since there are cases of empirical explanation in which there are not two distinct (or even different) existences that figure in the explanans and the explanandum, it follows that there are some cases of non-causal explanation.[22] These cases provide, to my mind, the least controversial examples of non-causal explanation. Identity explanations presuppose that some 'level' of reality in some sense explains itself. How this can avoid the evil of self-explanation, and what it commits us to as far as symmetric explanation is concerned, are issues which we shall have to discuss.

Peter Achinstein has discussed cases of this sort, and I owe much of what follows to him.[23] Achinstein's examples of this type of explanation include: explaining why the pH value of some solution is changing on the grounds that the concentration of hydrogen ions which that solution contains is changing; explaining why ice is water on the grounds that it is H_2O; explaining why some gas sample has temperature t on the grounds that its constituent molecules have a mean kinetic energy m.

In its simplest form, we can sometimes explain why some particular, a, has property P by identifying P with a property, Q, which a also has.

In a somewhat less simple form, we can sometimes explain why a is P, by identifying a with the sum of its parts, [b&c&d], and identifying P with some property of the sum, Q, or, sometimes, with a property Q had individually by each member of the sum. Achinstein argues that identity explanations cannot be a species of causal explanation, since the having or acquiring of property P can't cause the having or acquiring of property Q, if P=Q. It makes no difference to my argument whether these identities are metaphysically necessary or contingent.

Temperature=mean kinetic energy (for some temperature t and some mke m, having temperature t=having constituent molecules with mke m). I can explain a gas's having a certain temperature t by its constituent molecules having mean kinetic energy m, and I can explain a change in a gas's temperature by a change in the mean kinetic energy of its constituent molecules. We explain in these cases, not just by laws of the coexistence of two types of phenomena, but by property or type–type identities. This kind of explanation, relying as it does on identities, cannot be assimilated to causal explanation. Identity is another of the determinative relations that structure the world, and make for the possibility of explanation.

Just as not all statements of causal relation are explanatory (it depends on how the cause and effect are described), so too not all identity statements are explanatory. Temperature t=mean kinetic energy m; temperature t=temperature t. The second identity is not explanatory. The explanatoriness of an identity, like that of a causal relation, also depends on how the things identified are described. The apparatus developed in chapter V permits us to avoid self-explanation. In view of the ontology of explanation for which I there argued, self-explanation would have to mean explanation of a fact f by itself. In terms of the identity conditions for particular changes, since t=mke, the gas's acquiring temperature t and its acquiring mke m is one change (or anyway, let's take this as uncontroversial, to make the case for apparent self-explanation stronger). But in terms of the special or epistemicized facts that we have agreed that we need as the relata for the explanation relation, the fact that it has that temperature and the fact that its molecules have mke m are two distinct facts, because even if there is only one property involved, it is apprehended or conceptualized in two different ways. *So no self-explanation is involved.* A particular's having a property, described or conceptualized in one way, can explain the same particular's having the *same* property, described or conceptualised in another way. Explanation is an irreflexive relation, and *a fortiori*, identity explanation is irreflexive, even though identity is itself a reflexive relation.

There can be explanations of the fact that a is P in terms of the fact that a is Q, where P=Q, even where Q and P are not related as micro-property to macro-property (this example is also due to Achinstein). For example, I can explain the fact that a cow is a ruminant by the fact that the cow chews its cud. Such cases have to do with the place of a thing, or type of thing, within a system of classification. Some may think to dismiss this sort of example, by arguing that what is explained in such a case is nothing but why the cow is *called or classified as* a ruminant, not why it *is* a ruminant. This is not so. If the explanandum were: the cow's being classified as a ruminant, the explanans would have to include information about the classificatory scheme itself, how such a scheme was adopted, and so on. Someone who explains why the cow is a ruminant *uses* that classificatory scheme, but does not, in the explanans, offer any information about it.

Although I agree with Achinstein that this is a genuine sort of explanation, the scientifically more interesting cases rely on micro–macro (or, more generally, whole–part) identities, and it is hardly surprising that this should be so. It has long been the goal of scientific explanation to explain by depth, by identifying things with their 'underlying' counterparts. I have in mind here the sort of strategy sketched in bold and optimistic strokes by Oppenheim and Putnam in 'Unity of Science as a Working Hypothesis'.[24] On their view, the unity of science is advanced by micro-reductions; the ideal is to micro-reduce the science of social groups to the science for multicellular living things; the latter to that for cells; thence to molecular science; and finally to the science of atoms and elementary particles. Such micro-reductions require the identification (or replacement) of the (non-observational) properties that figure in the reduced science by the properties that figure in the reducing science, and the 'decomposition' of the entities of the reduced science into proper parts which are the entities of the reducing science.

So understood, two kinds of relations are required for micro-reduction: property identities (unless replacement is the strategy to be adopted), and the identification of the whole with the sum of its parts. I have elsewhere expressed my reservations about the possibility of the success of this strategy in the case of the social sciences.[25] One might be equally sceptical about the adoption of this strategy for the putative explanation of the mental by the physical. However, one need not sympathize with Oppenheim and Putnam's over-optimistic global enthusiasm for this strategy, in order to see that the strategy of micro-reduction offers a powerful tool for explanation, where it is appropriate.

Let's call explanations which make use of this micro-reductive identification strategy 'mereological explanations' ('mereological' covers not only the whole–part relation between the entities, but, by a natural extension of the idea of mereology, also the micro-reductive identity relation between the properties themselves). Mereological explanations are the most important type of identity explanations. The tradition that takes this kind of explanation seriously has a long history. I am thinking of Hobbes, for example, with his stress on the resolutive–compositive method of science, the idea that to understand something is to take it apart conceptually, and then to put it back together again conceptually. This methodology of mereological explanation reaches back before Hobbes, to 'Paduan methodology',[26] and before that, to Aristotle's material explanation and to the pre-Socratics, who wished to explain the nature of things in terms of some or all of the elements, earth, air, fire, and water. To understand something is to understand its parts or components. 'How it is' with the parts or components doesn't cause 'how it is' with the whole which is the sum of those parts or components, even though the former can explain the latter.

I think these mereological explanations are common, both in science and in ordinary life. It is important to see that explanations of the whole by its parts are not confined to the special sciences; their use in science is a refinement of a very common and ordinary idea. We take a complex and break it into its parts. Like the whole, the parts are subject to changes and are in states. We can then explain the states or changes of the whole in terms of the states or changes in the parts. Consider, for instance, an example originally due to U.T. Place: 'Her hat is a bundle of straw tied together with string.'[27] I can explain why her hat will not hold its shape, on the basis of the floppy pieces of straw which make it up.

By a quirk of intellectual fate, what I am calling mereological explanation embraces both Aristotle's material and formal explanations. He, of course, thought of these as different, but we do not. The material is the stuff out of which something is made. The form is the essence of the thing, what makes it a such rather than a particular this. But, certainly by the time of Locke's *An Essay Concerning the Human Understanding*, the real essence of gold, for example, was 'the constitution of the insensible parts of that body, on which . . . all the other properties of gold depend'.[28] Locke compares knowing the real essence of something, were this possible, to knowing 'all the springs and wheels, and other contrivances within, of the famous clock at Strasburg'. So, to know the essence becomes knowing the inner constitution of a thing, and this knowledge is inseparable from knowing the parts or material ('the contrivances') from which it is composed.

Unlike causal explanation, identity explanations cannot guarantee asymmetry. Identity is itself, of course, a symmetrical relation. As I stressed in my discussion of the irreflexivity of explanation, it is only something as conceptualized in one way that explains the same thing conceptualized in a *different* way. But the irreflexivity of explanation will not help us to ensure the asymmetry of explanation, because sometimes an event or state conceptualized in one way can explain itself conceptualized in another, *and vice versa*. These symmetric explanations typically work in virtue of there being a theory (or classificatory scheme) in which an identity claim employing both of the descriptions or conceptualizations is embedded.

Consider the mereological identity between being water and being composed of H_2O molecules (this example is also due to Achinstein). If one assumes as background the theory which identifies various ordinary substances with chemically precise compounds and mixtures, then in the appropriate circumstances, the fact that ice is water can be fully explained by the fact that ice is H_2O. In other circumstances, the fact that ice is H_2O can be fully explained by the fact that it is water. It depends on what is known and what needs explanation. In virtue of the theory and the identities it contains, a (full) explainer can move in either of two explanatory directions. The same theory permits symmetrical *full* explanations in appropriately different epistemic circumstances. In this case, unlike that of partial explanation, epistemic and pragmatic considerations do not lead us to offer *less* than a full explanation, but rather allow us to select the direction in which to give the full explanation.

Are there other non-causal singular explanations?

When an austere theorist surveys the relations in which objects or events stand in the world, he is happy with causation and identity, but is sceptical about almost everything else. The florid theorist thinks that there are other determinative relations that lie somewhere between causation and identity; they are not as strict or tightly binding as identity, but not as loose or contingent as causation. Cambridge dependency, supervenience, the by-relation (that relates actions), the relation between a disposition and its structural basis, are further suggestions advanced by various florid theorists. There is a great deal of controversy about each such alleged case. In what follows, I remain neutral between the two antagonists. The purpose of the remainder of the chapter is to argue conditionally: if there are any of these other putative relations, some may provide the basis for additional non-causal singular explanations. But I do not mean to assert unconditionally that there are any additional examples of non-causal singular explanation.

So, whether or not there are other cases of non-causal singular explanation will depend, I think, on whether or not there are determinative (or dependency) metaphysical relations between objects, events, or states other than causation and identity. Kim, certainly a florid theorist, mentions these three as examples of non-causal determinative relations: Cambridge dependency, one action being done by means of another, and event composition. The third, event composition, is similar to the ordinary mereological relation of a part to a whole, but is defined for events rather than objects, and therefore where the parthood in question is temporal rather than spatial. Examples of the first two kinds rest on highly contentious (but not obviously false) theses about event identity.

An example of Cambridge dependency is this: Xantippe became a widow in virtue of, as a consequence of, Socrates' death. An example of an action being done *by* doing another is: I open the window by turning the knob. If either of these has any consequences for a theory of explanation, it will be the Cambridge dependency case. Examples of actions done by means of other actions lend themselves to explaining-how rather than explaining-why. But the Cambridge dependency case seems to have a clear relevance for explaining-why: Socrates' dying explains why Xantippe became a widow.

Kim argues that the relation between the pair of actions related by the 'by' relation, and the relation between an event and the 'Cambridge' event which depends on it, are neither causal nor relations of identity. Let's concentrate on the Cambridge dependency case. On Kim's view, Socrates' dying and Xantippe's becoming a widow cannot be the same event, on the grounds that different properties are involved in the two descriptions. (This argument rests on the fine-grained analysis of event identity which I eschewed in chapter V.) But, even apart from this consideration, there is the problem of spatial location: the first event occurred in the prison in which Socrates was being kept; the second happened wherever Xantippe was when her husband died. Since Socrates' dying and Xantippe's becoming a widow occurred at different places, by the indiscernibility of identicals, they cannot be identical, cannot be one and the same event.

Nor, he argues, can the former be the cause of the latter. They occurred simultaneously, and even if we accept the possibility of a simultaneous cause and effect, since they happen at different spatial locations, we would also have to accept simultaneous causal action at a distance. Moreover,

> it is difficult to think of any sort of contingent empirical law to support a causal relation between the two events. In fact, the relation strikes us as more intimate than one that is mediated by contingent causal laws. Given that Socrates is the husband of Xantippe, his death is sufficient, logically for the widowing of Xantippe.... As we might say, in all possible worlds in which Socrates is the husband of Xantippe at a time t and in which Socrates dies at t, Xantippe becomes a widow at t.
>
> (Kim 1974: 42–3)

So, if Socrates' dying and Xantippe's becoming a widow are both events,[29] but are not the same event, and if there is no causal relation between them, and if the former explains the latter, then they provide an additional case of non-causal singular explanation.

Another possibility for non-causal explanation centres on the supervenience relation. Kim has also written extensively about this. If there is such a metaphysical relation as supervenience, distinct from identity (and causation), then it may provide some additional examples of non-causal explanation. Kim lists these as candidate cases of supervenience: the mental on the physical; epistemic features of beliefs on their non-epistemic features; counterfactuals on indicative facts; the causal on the non-causal; relational on non-relational properties; valuational or moral properties on natural properties; to which we can add, the social on the non-social or individual.[30] If the general idea of supervenience is to add anything 'extra' for scientific and ordinary explanation, it would be nice if examples of it had an a posteriori character. The thought is this: only those examples of supervenience which are knowable a posteriori could underpin any interesting empirical explanations.[31]

However, even if there is such a distinct metaphysical relation as supervenience, in the list of alleged examples above, the most obviously a posteriori examples, mental states on physical states, and the social properties of something on its non-social properties or features, are also the most controversial. The idea of supervenience was first introduced with regard to aesthetic and moral properties, and these least controversial examples are a priori in character.[32] Even the a priori cases would provide some sort of explanation, but not the same kind as we have considered hitherto. Why was St Francis a good man? Because he was benevolent. Why is that painting beautiful? Because of its colour composition.

I think that there are good grounds for doubting whether supervenience is distinct from identity. I am sympathetic to the view of John Bacon:

> Supervenience in most of its guises entails necessary coextension. Thus theoretical supervenience entails nomically necessary coextension. . . . I suspect that many supervenience enthusiasts would cool at necessary coextension: they didn't mean to be saying anything quite so strong. Furthermore, nomically necessary coextension can be a good reason for property identification, leading to reducibility in principle. This again is more than many supervenience theorists bargained for. They wanted supervenience without reducibility. . . .[33]

The suspicion is that the whole metaphysical truth about supervenience (e.g. of the mental on the physical) is that a supervenient property may not be identical with some single base property, but rather identical with a possibly infinite disjunction of possibly infinite conjunctions of such base properties. If reducibility is an epistemic idea, reduction in such cases will be in principle impossible. But metaphysically, supervenience would just be a specially complicated case of identity.

For the purposes of this chapter, I need not decide whether the above suspicion is well-grounded or not. My claim is conditional: if supervenience is a metaphysical relation distinct from identity (and causation), as a florid theorist would have it, and if some cases of supervenience are explanatory, then supervenience explanation would be another type of singular non-causal explanation.

Disposition explanations

A pane of glass is fragile; a lump of salt is water-soluble. In virtue of those properties, each does or might do certain things. The first breaks when struck sufficiently hard; the second dissolves when immersed in water. Both have structural features which are the *bases* for these dispositional features. In the two examples of the glass and the salt, the relevant structures are microstructures. In general, there are three things that might be considered in such explanations: the structure which is the basis for the dispositional feature, the dispositional feature itself, and actual behaviour in which the dispositional feature manifests itself.

One might mean either of two things by 'disposition explanation'. We can explain actual behaviour by dispositional features, and dispositional features by (micro)structure. I shall concentrate on the second sort of explanation, the explanation of why an object has a dispositional property in terms of its structural features. It is only this type of explanation that I shall mean by 'disposition explanation'.

Even Hugh Mellor, who doubts that there is any philosophically significant contrast between the dispositional and non-dispositional properties of things, would agree that we sometimes explain properties like the property of being water-soluble in terms of properties like the property of having some specific micro-structure: 'No doubt there are virtues in explaining properties of things in terms of other properties, especially in terms of those of their spatial parts.'[34] His doubts concern the traditional characterization of the distinction between the dispositional and the non-dispositional: 'My strategy will be to show the offending features of dispositions to be either mythical or common to other properties of things. . .' (Mellor 1974: 157). Others have defended that traditional distinction between dispositions and non-dispositional properties, in terms of which properties of the first kind, but not of the second, logically entail subjunctive conditionals.[35] We can agree that there are some such explanations, without committing ourselves concerning the nature of the distinction between dispositional and non-dispositional properties.

(These disposition or structural explanations may simply be a type of supervenience explanation, and if the latter were a type of identity explanation, then disposition explanation raises no issue distinct from the ones already discussed in the section on identity explanation. Or anyway, so the austere theorist would have it. Sugar is a molecular compound; salt, an ionic one. Both are water-soluble, but in virtue of different microstructures. Since two objects can have the same dispositional feature, like water-solubility, in virtue of two different microstructural bases, the identity, if that is what it is, would have to be between the dispositional feature and the *disjunction* of the structural ones.)

Suppose that dispositions supervene on some structural basis, and that this base–disposition relation isn't just a special case of identity. The florid theorist would add: even though these disposition explanations are not identity or mereological explanations, they cannot be causal explanations either, even if cause and effect can be coexistent. On the florid theorist's view, why can't the relation between (micro)structural base and dispositional property be causal?

Let's take as our example the explanation of the dispositional property of salt, its water-solubility, in terms of its microstructure. The answer to the above question has to do with the contingency of the causal relation. Recall (2) above. There were two grades of contingency to the causal relation, weak and strong. The dispositional–structural property relation, unlike causation, fails strong contingency. Dispositional properties like water-solubility, as a matter of meta-physical necessity, have *some* structural basis; there is no possible world in which an object can have a dispositional feature and no structural basis whatever for that feature.[36] There is no possible world in which a lump of salt is just water-soluble, and there be no structural properties of the lump of salt in virtue of which it is water-soluble. The florid theorist says that there must be, as a matter of metaphysical necessity, some structural water-solubility-making properties of the salt.

It is even more controversial whether the relation also fails weak contingency (the florid theorist need not have a view about this, in order to distinguish causation from the structure–disposition relation). Is there a metaphysically possible world in which salt has the same micro-structure as it does in this world, but in virtue of that structure, has different dispositional properties? Could it, for example, be water-insoluble in that possible world, in virtue of the same microstructure as it has in this world? That this is nomically impossible is not in dispute; the question is whether it is metaphysically possible, and this is disputable.

Still, the fact that the structure–disposition relation fails to be strongly contingent is by itself enough, for the purposes of the florid theorist, to distinguish it from the causal relation. On the florid theorist's view, the disposition-structure relation is neither the same relation as the identity relation nor the same as the causal relation, and this distinctive metaphysical relation licenses further examples of non-causal singular explanation.

227

What kind of fact is the fact that salt has a certain dispositional feature like water-solubility? I believe that this fact is a singular fact, but David Lewis disagrees. David Lewis's view is that all singular explanation is causal explanation. He would agree with the florid theorist that the explanation for why salt is water-soluble is *not* a causal explanation.[37] However, he argues that the explanation of why some object has a dispositional property is not an explanation of any *singular* fact at all. (Lewis argues that the explanation is not an explanation of a singular *event*, but I have translated his thesis about singular events into the terminology of singular facts; the point of his thesis is unaffected by the translation.) Thus, he claims that disposition explanation is no counterexample to the thesis that all explanations of *singular* facts are causal explanations.

Disposition explanation, on his view then, is not singular explanation at all. Rather, it has this structure: 'Why is it that something is F? Because A is F. An existential quantification is explained by providing an instance' (Lewis 1986: 223). Lewis's view is that, in explaining, for example, why salt is water-soluble (Lewis's example is why Walt has smallpox-immunity), I explain (what I have called) an existentially general fact (and not a singular fact). Despite appearances, according to Lewis, if I explain the fact that salt is water-soluble, I do *not* explain something with the form, 'Fa'. The explanandum has this form: the fact that $(\exists x)(Fx)$. The explanans, in order to count as an instance of the existential quantification, must therefore have the form: Fa. On Lewis's view, in a case in which I am explaining an existential quantification by providing an instance, *the property, F, whatever it is, must appear both in the explanans and the explanandum.*

How would this work for the case of the water-solubility of salt? Since the salt's micro-structure must somehow figure in the explanans, Lewis's 'a' must refer to that microstructure (Let's call that microstructure 'm'). Since the explanans is 'Fa', for what property of the microstructure does 'F' stand? There are two possibilities to be considered: the micro-property of making salt water-soluble, or the micro-property of making salt dissolve in water.

Clearly, the second possibility is not available to Lewis. If 'F' stands for the micro-property of making salt dissolve in water, the existentially general explanandum must be: the fact that there is something which makes salt dissolve in water. *This explanation is not a disposition explanation at all, because the fact being explained is not dispositional, on any view of what disposition explanation is.* Built into the idea of a

228

disposition is the possibility that the behaviour in which it is manifested may never occur. A disposition explanation explains why something would behave in a certain way, if the appropriate conditions were ever realized; that explanation may work even if there is no actual behaviour to explain. If salt never does dissolve in water, despite its being water-soluble, there is no possible explanation for why there is something in virtue of which salt dissolves in water, because it doesn't. The property F must be a dispositional property, if the explanation is to be a disposition explanation of any sort.

The first possibility was that 'F' stood for the microproperty of making salt water-soluble. On this first alternative, Lewis's 'F' stands for the dispositional property of the microstructure, makes salt water-soluble, or perhaps for a dispositional relational property, makes water-soluble (true, for example, of the ordered pair, microstructure m and salt). The explanandum would then be an existentially general *dispositional* fact: the fact that there is something which makes salt water-soluble. To explain why salt is water-soluble is really just to explain why there is something which makes salt water-soluble. So far, so good.

But, on this first possibility, what is the explanans? The explanans would be: m makes salt water-soluble. That is to say, microstructure m has the property, makes salt water-soluble. What kind of property is that? It seems to be a dispositional property of the microstructure. According to Lewis's theory, the explanans must be a singular fact, with the form, 'Fa'. But this explanans is also a dispositional fact, since it attributes a dispositional property to something, namely to the microstructure. Lewis's proposal makes this *singular dispositional* fact the explanans for salt's water-solubility: microstructure m makes salt water-soluble. Since that fact attributes a (perhaps relational) dispositional property to microstructure m, it must itself count as a singular dispositional fact.

So Lewis's view *entails* that there are some singular dispositional facts. There is no inconsistency in his holding these two theses: (1) there are some singular dispositional facts; (2) all explainable (apparently singular) dispositional facts are really only existentially general facts. But the conjunction of the two implies that all genuinely singular dispositional facts are inexplicable. The view seems entirely *ad hoc* and unmotivated. On his thesis, we know that there must be some genuinely singular dispositional facts with the form, 'Fa', which are the explanations for the genuinely existentially general dispositional facts, whatever they are. But we could never know, concerning some specific dispositional fact which appears to be singular, whether it is genuinely singular or only existentially general, unless we know whether it is in principle capable of being further explained. If an explanation is possible, it must be an existentially general dispositional fact after all, despite appearances; only if an explanation of it is impossible can we admit that it is a genuinely singular dispositional fact after all.

To my mind, this is all counterintuitive and needlessly baroque. If we accept that we can sometimes explain *singular* dispositional facts, like the fact that salt is water-soluble, the account is straightforward. The explanans for this (truly and not just apparently) singular dispositional fact is a singular structural fact: the fact that salt has microstructure m. Of course, if we do accept this, and if we retain Lewis's admission that this explanation is not causal, we would also have to accept that there are some non-causal explanations of singular facts, and that therefore Lewis's thesis that all singular explanation is causal is simply false.

Again: determinative, high, and low dependency explanations

I said in chapter I:

> It will be helpful in introducing this typology [of determinative, high, and low dependency theories of explanation] to assume something that I regard as false: all explanations of singular events or states of affairs are causal explanations. . . . I will discuss this assumption in chapter VII, and broaden the kinds of singular explanations that there can be. It will then be easy to broaden the typology to take account of this, having already introduced it on the narrower assumption. But, in the interim, I will be making this (admittedly false) assumption.

It is now time to make good my promise. In what follows, I mean the rather bland word, 'thing', to cover whatever the reader thinks there is in the world, apart from how we conceptualize or think: objects, events, states, structures, properties, relations, and so on.

In the cases of explaining singular facts so far discussed, we explained in one of at least three ways: (1) we saw what *makes* something happen, (2) we saw how what the thing is like structurally *makes* it have its dispositional features, and (3) we analysed or conceptually resolved the particular to see what *makes* it what it is. The 'makes' here is ambiguous between 'causally makes', 'is the structural basis which makes',[38] and 'mereologically makes'. All of these ideas have long traditions in the history of philosophy and of scientific thought. Causes are events which make their effects occur; structural features of a thing make it liable to behave in certain ways; parts and what they are like make up the whole and make it what it is like.

There is a unifying, if ambiguous, thought that unites all of these cases: explanations work in virtue of something determining or being responsible for something. Explanations work only in virtue of the determinative relations that exist in the world. The determinative relations may be causal, but they may also be whatever other determinative relations there are: between structure and dispositional features, between an event and the Cambridge event which it determines, between a thing or property and itself (but differently described or conceptualized).

There was an insight in the causal theory of explanation: we explain something by showing what makes it or what is responsible for it. The fault of the causal theory of explanation was to overlook the fact that there are more ways of *making* something what it is or being *responsible* for it than by causing it. The general idea is the idea of determination: we explain something by showing what determines that thing to be as it is. Causation is a particular kind of determinative relation, but not the only such determinative relation.[39] Causation was held to be a potential cure for both the ills of irrelevance and symmetry, which plagued Hempel's account of explanation. Just as the wider idea of determinative relation can cure symmetry *where* it is desirable to do so, so too the wider idea will cure explanatory irrelevance. If one thing is determined by another, the second is explanatorily relevant for the first; on the other hand, if there are no determinative (or dependency, see below) relations between the things, then they are explanatorily irrelevant to one another.

However, the above will not quite do, for reasons I have given in chapter I. I do not want to beg the question between determinative, high, and low dependency theories of explanation (and the consequent commitment to a certainty, HEP or LEP theory of explanation which depends on that choice). In terms of the argument of this book, I wish to leave this an open question. If there are nondeterministic causes and one can explain in virtue of them, then the explanatory idea of one thing making another happen is not to be understood only in a deterministic sense.

As I also said in chapter I, I do not think that there are any other nondeterminative explanations other than those which would arise on the basis of explanation by nondeterministic causes. Since identity is a metaphysically necessary relation, there is no room for mere dependency in its case. But if the reader can think of other candidates for nondeterministic relations that can be explanatory, other than nondeterministic causation, these too can be included in the view I here advance.

When I discussed Aristotle in chapter III, I said that he held (E): something can be explained only by either its matter, or its form, or its purpose, or its change-initiator. I then asked whether (E) was just an *ad hoc* disjunction, or whether Aristotle had some deeper reason for thinking that these four modes of explanation were exhaustive of the sorts of explanation there are. I agreed with Julius Moravcsik's rationale for Aristotle's (E): for Aristotle, a particular substance is a set of elements with a fixed structure that moves itself towards self-determined goals. The four elements in this definition are: element, structure, motion originator, and goal. These correspond to, and justify, the four types of explanation. Since everything else that can be said to be is an aspect of substance, the four types of explanation are both non-arbitrary and exhaustive. (E), far from being *ad hoc*, is the kernel of a theory of explanation.

Kim's remarks at the beginning of this chapter provide an analogous strategy for deciding what types of singular explanation there can be, for it is important, as I have argued throughout the book, to ground a theory of explanation on a theory of metaphysics. Metaphysically, it is this determinative (and possibly, dependency) picture of the world that grounds explanation of singular facts. This is so, even if the explanation relation itself has 'epistemicized' facts, or statements, or propositions as its relata. Explanantia fully explain explananda only in virtue of how things really are. Explanations work only because things make things happen or make things have some feature ('things' should be taken in an anodyne sense, to include whatever the reader wishes to count as a denizen of reality). And the *making* can be taken either in a deterministic or in a nondeterministic (dependency) sense.

And this, I think, is the ultimate basis for any reply to an explanation theorist who holds that full explanation is only and entirely a pragmatic or otherwise anthropomorphic conception. On my view, explanation is epistemic, but with a solid metaphysical basis. A realist theory of explanation that links the determinative (or dependency) relations in the world with explanation gets at the intuitively acceptable idea that we explain something by showing what is responsible for it or what makes it as it is. This is what, in the end, explains explanation.

Notes

Chapter I   Getting our Bearings

1 Karel Lambert and Gordon G. Brittan, Jr, *An Introduction to the Philosophy of Science*, third edition, Ridgeview Publishing Company, Atascadero, 1987, pp. 14–17.

2 Carl Hempel, *Aspects of Scientific Explanation*, Free Press, New York, 1965, pp. 335–6. Subsequent page numbers in my text following discussion of Hempel's views throughout this book refer to this title, unless otherwise indicated.

3 Michael Friedman, 'Explanation and Scientific Understanding', *Journal of Philosophy*, vol. LXXI, 1974, pp. 5–19. Quotation from p. 5.

4 Raimo Tuomela, 'Explaining Explaining', *Erkenntnis*, vol. 15, 1980, pp. 211–43. Quote from p. 217.

5 Romane Clark and Paul Welsh, *Introduction to Logic*, Van Nostrand, Princeton, 1962, pp. 153–4. The 'destruction at Rotterdam' is their example. Following Clark and Welsh, I construe 'process' sufficiently widely to include acts and activities.

6 S. Bromberger, 'An Approach to Explanation', in *Analytical Philosophy*, second series, ed. R.J. Butler, Blackwell, Oxford, 1965, pp. 72–105. Quotation from p. 104.

7 Peter Achinstein, *The Nature of Explanation*, Oxford University Press, New York, 1983; see chapters 2 and 3. I have learned a great deal from Achinstein's writings on explanation, even on issues where I do not in the end agree with what he has to say. Another example of an approach to explanation which makes explanatory acts the conceptually prior concept is to be found in Raimo Tuomela, *op. cit.*

8 An act of another illocutionary type, to be precise. For the distinction between illocutionary, locutionary, and perlocutionary acts, see J.L. Austin, *How to do Things with Words*, second edition, ed. J.O. Urmson and Marina Sbisà, Oxford University Press, Oxford, 1984. See especially Lectures VIII and IX, pp. 94–120.

9 Illocutionary acts.

10 Illocutionary product.

11 Carl Hempel, *op. cit.*, p. 412.

12 Ernest Sosa, 'The Analysis of "Knowledge that P"', *Analysis*, vol. 25, new series no. 103, October 1964, p. 1.

13 Edmund Gettier, 'Is Justified True Belief Knowledge?' *Analysis*, vol. 23, June 1963, pp. 121–3; and then, by way of selected examples: Michael Clark, 'Knowledge and Grounds', *Analysis*, vol. 24, no.2, new series no. 98, December 1963, pp. 46–8; John Turk Saunders and Narayan Champawat, 'Mr. Clark's Definition of Knowledge', *Analysis*, vol. 25, no. 1, new series no. 103, October 1964, pp. 8–9; Keith Lehrer, 'Knowledge, Truth, and Evidence', *Analysis*, vol. 25, no. 5, new series no. 107, April 1965, pp. 168–75; and of course Sosa, *op. cit.*

14 Michael Friedman, *op. cit.*, p. 13.

15 See for example Peter Unger, 'On Experience and the Development of the Understanding', *American Philosophical Quarterly*, vol. 3, 1966, pp. 48–56.

16 Karl Popper, 'Epistemology Without a Knowing Subject', in Karl Popper, *Objective Knowledge*, Oxford University Press, Oxford, 1973, pp. 106–52. For quotes, see pp. 108–11.

17 I speak in unorthodox terminology of a concept's intension (normally, it is words which have intensions). I mean by 'intension of a concept' merely its model, i.e. the analysis of it.

18 I have always liked the account of this by Stephen Toulmin, *Foresight and Understanding*, Harper, New York, 1961, and especially his sharp distinction between understanding and foresight (prediction).

19 Carl Hempel, *op. cit.*, p. 413.

20 Examples include Peter Achinstein, *op. cit.*, pp. 15–73; Arthur Collins, 'Explanation and Causality', *Mind*, vol. 75, 1966, pp. 482–500.

21 Carl Hempel, *op. cit.*, p. 412.

22 Hempel's famous Deductive-Nomological and Inductive-Statistical models are meant to provide two different sets of requirements for *full* scientific explanation. I discuss these models fully in chapter IV. Hempel speaks of a third model, the Deductive-Statistical, but I ignore it here, and elsewhere in the book.

23 Hilary Putnam, *Meaning and the Moral Sciences*, Routledge & Kegan Paul, London, 1978, pp. 41–2.

24 David Lewis, 'Causal Explanation', in his *Philosophical Papers*, vol. II, Oxford University Press, Oxford and New York, 1986, pp. 214–40. See especially pp. 217–21 and 226–8.

25 Hilary Putnam, *op. cit.*, pp. 42–3.

26 A full discussion of this issue would involve careful investigation of the differences between sentences, statements, and propositions, and of the question of which, of the three, logical relations like material implication or strict entailment hold between. But this would take us far off course; let me here assume that it is sentences which entail, etc., other sentences.

27 Almost uncontroversial, since Peter Achinstein's theory of explanation might controvert it. See my review of his *The Nature of Explanation* in the *British Journal for the Philosophy of Science*, vol. 37, 1986, pp. 377–84.

28 Carl Hempel, *op. cit.*, p. 336.

29 Wesley Salmon, *Scientific Explanation and the Causal Structure of the World*, Princeton University Press, Princeton, 1984, pp. 15–16.
30 I draw the distinctions as I do, because I think they help one to see what is at stake in deciding between different theories of explanation. Of course, there are many other (perhaps more illuminating for different purposes) ways in which to divide up the competing theories. In particular, my typology differs in important ways from a superficially similar one offered by Salmon in *Scientific Explanation and the Causal Structure of the World*, pp. 16–18.
31 Carl Hempel, *op. cit.*, p. 337.
32 See for example: Brian Skyrms, *Choice and Chance*, Dickinson Publishing Company, Encino and Belmont, California, 1975, chapters, I, VI, and VII, pp. 200–3; J.L.Mackie, *Truth, Probability, and Paradox*, Oxford University Press, Oxford, 1973, chapter 5; David Lewis, *op. cit.*, 1986, Part 5; and especially the classical source for the distinction, Rudolf Carnap, 'The Two Concepts of Probability', *Philosophy and Phenomenological Research*, vol. V, 1945, pp. 513–32.
33 G.H. von Wright, *Explanation and Understanding*, Routledge, London, 1971, p. 13. Von Wright, not surprisingly, goes on to deny that there are any non-deductive explanations: 'It seems to me better ... not to say that the inductive-probabilistic model explains what happens, but to say only that it justifies certain expectations and predications' (p. 14). See also Wolfgang Stegmüller, 'Two Successor Concepts to the Notion of Statistical Explanation', in *Logic and Philosophy*, ed. G.H. von Wright, Nijhoff, The Hague, 1980, pp. 37–52. As far as I know, the best defence of probabilistic explanation is to be found in Colin Howson, 'On a Recent Argument for the Impossibility of a Statistical Explanation of Single Events, and a Defence of a Modified Form of Hempel's Theory of Statistical Explanation', *Erkenntnis*, vol. 29, 1988, pp. 113–24.
34 Wesley Salmon, R. Jeffrey, and J. Greeno *Statistical Explanation and Statistical Relevance*, University of Pittsburgh Press, Pittsburgh, 1971, p. 64.
35 Peter Railton, 'A Deductive-Nomological Model of Probabilistic Explanation', *Philosophy of Science*, vol. 45, 1978, pp. 206–26. Quotation from p. 216.
36 Henry Kyburg, Jr, 'Conjunctivitis', in *Induction, Acceptance, and Rational Beliefs*, ed. M. Swain, Reidel, Dordrecht, 1970, pp. 55–82.
37 For example, in Wesley Salmon, *Scientific Explanation and the Causal Structure of the World*, p. 87, and in his 'A Third Dogma of Empiricism', in *Basic Problems in Methodology and Linguistics*, ed. R. Butts and J. Hintikka, Reidel, Dordrecht, 1977, pp. 152–3.
38 Colin Howson, *op. cit.*, pp. 122–3.
39 Wesley Salmon *et al.*, *Statistical Explanation and Statistical Relevance*, pp. 62–5; *Scientific Explanation and the Causal Structure of the World*, p. 46.
40 Salmon's own exposition seems to use both epistemic and physical probability; I have set out the example, trying to be clear about which probability is involved in the argument.
41 Wesley Salmon, *Statistical Explanation and Statistical Relevance*, p. 64.

42 Karl Popper, *The Logic of Scientific Discovery*, Hutchinson, London, 1972, pp. 59–60.

43 This claim might be challenged, in view of Peter Railton's D-N model of probabilistic explanation. I stand by my claim. For Railton, an explanation of why an event e 'improbably took place' is the *conjunction* of a deductive argument whose conclusion is that e had a low probability of occurrence, and 'a parenthetic addendum to the effect that' e occurred (*op. cit.*, p. 214). The conjunction of an argument and an addendum is not itself an argument.

The conclusion of the argument on its own is not a sentence that asserts that e occurred, and so the argument by itself cannot be an explanation of why e occurred. Rather, the conclusion of the deductive argument is only a sentence assigning a probability of occurrence, perhaps exceedingly small, to e's occurrence. The argument on its own, if it explains anything, only explains (with a conditional certainty) why e has some specific probability of occurrence. 'Dropping off the addendum leaves an explanation, but it is a D-N explanation of the occurrence of a particular probability, not a probabilistic explanation of the occurrence of a particular decay' (p. 217).

44 Salmon's view in 'A Third Dogma of Empiricism', pp. 149–66, is that 'an explanation is an assemblage of factors that are statistically relevant . . .' (p. 159).

45 Bas van Fraassen's view: 'An explanation is not the same as a proposition, or an argument, or a list of propositions; it is an answer.' Bas van Fraassen, *The Scientific Image*, Oxford University Press, Oxford, 1980, p. 134.

46 See for example his 'A Third Dogma of Empiricism'.

47 David Lewis, 'Postscripts to "Causation"', in *op. cit.*, pp. 175–84; Wesley Salmon, *Scientific Explanation and the Causal Structure of the World*, pp. 184–205; Patrick Suppes, *Probabilistic Metaphysics*, Blackwell, Oxford, 1984, pp. 35–75; John Mackie, *The Cement of the Universe*, Oxford University Press, Oxford, 1974, pp. 39–43.

48 Strong sufficiency is stronger than material sufficiency.

49 Wesley Salmon, *Scientific Explanation and the Causal Structure of the World*, pp. 185–90.

50 It is in this light that I understand the oft-cited case of paresis (and Salmon's example of mushroom poisoning after having ingested a certain type of mushroom). Only a very small number of those with untreated latent syphilis develop paresis, although the only way in which to get paresis is by having untreated latent syphilis. However, having untreated latent syphilis explains getting paresis, although having untreated latent syphilis confers only a low epistemic probability on that person having paresis. All of this is consistent with the certainty model, if it is a partial explanation. Presumably, we believe that it is. We believe that there is some set of conditions c, perhaps unknown, such that if one has untreated latent syphilis and is in condition c, then getting paresis is physically necessary. And a full explanation of getting paresis must refer both to untreated latent syphilis and conditions c. But there is no reason why I cannot give a partial explanation of getting paresis just in terms of having untreated latent syphilis.

51 See Salmon, *Scientific Explanation and the Causal Structure of the World*: '. . .the statistical relevance relations that are invoked . . . must be explained

in terms of causal relations. The explanation ... is incomplete until the causal components ... have been provided' (p. 22); 'It now seems to me that the statistical relationships ... constitute the statistical basis for a ... scientific explanation, but that this basis must be supplemented by certain causal factors in order to constitute a satisfactory scientific explanation' (p. 34); '... statistical relevance relations are to be explained in terms of causal relevance relations'(p. 208). But the causation so evidenced may itself be analysable in terms of statistical relevance relations: 'I cannot think of any reason to suppose that ordinary causal talk would dissolve into nonsense if Laplacian determinism turned out to be false. I shall therefore proceed on the supposition that probabilistic causality is a coherent and important philosophical concept. In advocating the notion of probabilistic causality, neither Suppes nor I intend to deny that there are sufficient causes.... On our view, sufficient causes constitute a limiting case of probabilistic causes' (p. 190).

52 References in the text to Salmon in what follows this note are to his 'A Third Dogma of Empiricism'. References to van Fraassen are to his *The Scientific Image*.

53 I have discussed contrastive explanation in 'Explaining Contrastive Facts', *Analysis*, vol. 47, January 1987, pp. 35–7. Peter Lipton's reply (in 'A Real Contrast', *Analysis*, vol. 47, October 1987, pp. 207–8) and Dennis Temple's view (in 'The Contrast Theory of Why-Questions', *Philosophy of Science*, vol. 55, 1988, pp. 141–51) are both discussed below.

54 See for example Fred Dretske, 'Contrastive Facts', *Philosophical Review*, vol. 81, 1972, pp. 411–37; Alan Garfinkel, *Forms of Explanation*, Yale University Press, New Haven, 1981, from which the Sutton story is borrowed; Bas van Fraassen, *op. cit.*; Jon Dorling, 'On Explanation in Physics: Sketch of an Alternative to Hempel's Account of the Explanation of Laws', *Philosophy of Science*, vol. 45, 1978, pp. 136–40.

55 Some (although not all) of van Fraassen's alleged cases of explaining contrastive facts can be dealt with by carefully distinguishing between different non-contrastive explananda. Consider for example the difference between explaining why Adam ate *an* apple and why Adam ate *the* apple. See van Fraassen, *op. cit.*, p. 127.

56 David Lewis, 'Causal Explanation', in *op. cit.*, pp. 229–31; see also 'Causation', *op. cit.*, p. 177. On Lewis's view, a maximally true explanatory proposition about an event is the proposition which gives the whole truth about the entire causal history of the event (presumably, stretching back to the beginning of the universe). An alternative might be to take the maximally true explanatory proposition as the one which gives the whole truth only about the whole of the *immediate* cause of the explanandum event.

57 Dennis Temple, *op. cit.*, p. 149.

Chapter II Plato on Explanation

1 I am using R.S. Bluck, *Plato's Phaedo*, Bobbs-Merrill, Indianapolis, 1955, but checking that translation against the translation by Hugh Tredennick, in

Plato: The Collected Dialogues, ed. Edith Hamilton and Huntington Cairns, Bollingen Foundation, 1966.

2 For this, I use the Cornford translation in Hamilton and Cairns, *op. cit.*

3 Gregory Vlastos, 'Reasons and Causes in the *Phaedo*', *Philosophical Review*, vol. 78, 1969, pp. 291–325.

4 E.L. Burge, 'The Ideas as *Aitiai* in the *Phaedo*', *Phronesis*, vol. 16, 1971, pp. 1–13.

5 See for example David Melling, *Understanding Plato*, Oxford University Press, Oxford, 1987, pp. 11–12, for a brief discussion of this identification.

6 Gregory Vlastos, *op. cit.*

7 I have discussed the distinction between real and so-called Cambridge change in 'A Puzzle about Posthumous Predication', *Philosophical Review*, vol. XCVII, 1988, pp. 211–36.

8 M.J. Cresswell, 'Plato's Theory of Causality: *Phaedo* 95–106', *Australasian Journal of Philosophy*, vol. 49, 1971, pp. 244–9. Remarks relevant to this point on pp. 246–7.

9 Julia Annas, 'Aristotle on Inefficient Causes', *Philosophical Quarterly*, vol. 32, 1982, pp. 311–26.

10 C.C.W. Taylor, 'Forms as Causes in the *Phaedo*', *Mind*, vol. LXVIII, 1969, pp. 45–59. His argument for this is on p. 53.

11 M.J. Cresswell, *op. cit.*, pp. 248–9.

12 E.L. Burge, *op. cit.*, p. 4.

13 One obvious restriction on what can be included in the causally relevant context and conditions is this: no explicit causal information can be included. That the token striking caused a lighting cannot be taken to be part of the conditions co-present with the token striking in other possible worlds in which it occurs. If causal information of this sort were to be included, it would become trivially impossible to ask about other causes or effects that token event has in some other possible world.

14 Mary Mackenzie, 'Plato's Analysis of Individuation', unpublished manuscript.

15 Hugh Mellor, 'Probable Explanation', *Australasian Journal of Philosophy*, vol. 54, 1976, pp. 231–41.

16 The indicative mood counterparts of (10) and (11), which I have not bothered to list, are trivial for the same sorts of reasons for which (4) and (5) were trivial. If d explains g, then g has happened, and *ex hypothesi* neither ~g nor f can have happened. One cannot explain what has not happened, just as something that has not happened cannot explain anything.

17 There are complications here that we need not go into. Since Mellor thinks that causation is a deterministic concept (see Mellor, *op. cit.*, p. 235), he thinks of high dependency explanation as explanation where there is no causation at all, or no causal explanation available.

18 By this, I mean strong sufficiency, and not just material sufficiency. See chapter I. Strong sufficiency requires the truth of certain counterfactuals.

19 To reject (10) is certainly to reject a determinative view of explanation, and hence to hold a determinative theory is to hold (10). But this does *not* follow: to reject a determinative theory is to reject (10). Mellor, unlike Plato, holds a high dependency theory and he, like Plato, subscribes to (10). Indeed,

Mellor argues (correctly) that any low dependency theory is inconsistent with (10) (and the addition of some uncontroversial further premisses). If (10) is true, then either a determinative or a high dependency theory of explanation is true, a low dependency theory is false.

20 In this and other of the more technical arguments in this chapter, I am grateful for the patient help of Peter Milne.

21 The idea of necessity here is strong necessity, not material necessity. A cause is strongly necessary for its effect iff if the cause had not, in the circumstances, occurred, the effect would not have occurred. I discuss Lewis's analysis of causal necessity and sufficiency in 'Lewis and the Problem of Causal Sufficiency', *Analysis*, vol. 41, 1981, pp. 38–41. In that article, I did not take adequate account of the possibility of nondeterministic causation, and this is a flaw in what I wrote. But I still believe that the difficulty I claimed to find in Lewis's account is still a difficulty for an analysis of deterministic causation, in the sense in which a cause is both strongly necessary and strongly sufficient in the circumstances for its effect.

22 Much discussion of whether a cause is necessary in the circumstances for its effect centres on the possibility of causal pre-emption. See, for instance, William Goosens, 'Causal Chains and Counterfactuals', *Journal of Philosophy*, vol. LXXVI 1979, pp. 489–95.

23 'c occurs, e has some chance x of occurring, and as it happens e does occur; if c had not occurred, e would still have had some chance y of occurring, but only a very slight chance since y would have been very much less than x. We cannot quite say that without the cause, the effect would not have occurred; but we can say that without the cause, the effect would have been very much less probable than it actually was' (David Lewis, 'Causation', *Philosophical Papers*, vol. II, Oxford University Press, Oxford and New York, 1986, p. 176.

24 John Watkins, *Science and Scepticism*, Princeton University Press, Princeton, 1984, pp. 227–8. I have substituted 'd' and 'g' for his 'h' and 'e'.

25 David Melling, *op. cit.*, p. 136, construes the term in this way.

26 See Gregory Vlastos, 'The Third Man Argument in the *Parmenides*', *Philosophical Review*, 1954, and reprinted in *Studies in Plato's Metaphysics*, ed. R.E. Allen, Routledge & Kegan Paul, London, 1967, pp. 231–63.

Chapter III   Aristotle on Explanation

1 Richard Sorabji, *Necessity, Cause, and Blame*, Duckworth, London, 1980, p. 42.

2 Julius Moravcsik, 'Aristotle on Adequate Explanations', *Synthese*, vol. 28, 1974, pp. 3–17. Quote from p. 4.

3 Julius Moravcsik, *ibid.*; Max Hocutt, 'Aristotle's Four Becauses', *Philosophy*, vol. 49, 1974, pp. 385–99; Julia Annas, 'Aristotle on Efficient Causes', *Philosophical Quarterly*, vol. 32, 1982, pp. 311–26.

4 References to the *Posterior Analytics*, are to the translation by Jonathan

Barnes, *Aristotle's Posterior Analytics*, Oxford University Press, Oxford, 1975, but checked against (and occasionally taken from) *The Basic Works of Aristotle*, ed. Richard McKeon, Random House, New York, 1966. Books A and B of the *Posterior Analytics* refer to the Barnes translation; Books I and II of the *Posterior Analytics* refer to the translation in McKeon. References to other of Aristotle's writings are to the McKeon edition.

5 Jonathan Barnes, trans., *op. cit.*, pp. 215–16.

6 The example comes from Karel Lambert and Gordon Brittan, Jr, *An Introduction to the Philosophy of Science*, Ridgeview Publishing Company, Atascadero, 1987, p. 12.

7 W. Wieland, 'The Problem of Teleology', reprinted in *Articles on Aristotle 1: Science*, ed. Jonathan Barnes, Malcolm Schofield, and Richard Sorabji, Duckworth, London, 1975, pp. 141–60. Quote from p. 147.

8 See Julia Annas, *op. cit.*, p. 321.

9 Peter Achinstein, *The Nature of Explanation*, Oxford University Press, New York, 1983, pp. 5–6.

10 See for example G.E.L. Owen, 'Tithenai ta Phainomena', reprinted in Jonathan Barnes, Malcolm Schofield, and Richard Sorabji, eds, *op. cit.*, pp. 113–26.

11 Julius Moravcsik, *op. cit.*

12 That the four senses of 'Why?' are non-overlapping is, I think, Wieland's view, since he calls the unity provided by 'Why?' a 'formal unity'. On the other hand, Wieland also calls the question 'Why?' 'a functional element', which suggests that it is able to provide some unity more substantive than a syntactic unity, for the four senses of 'explanation'. Perhaps he thinks that, in spite of the four-way ambiguity of 'explanation', each of the four senses of the term 'explanation' do share *part* of their meaning in common, and that this shared, overlapping part is somehow accounted for by part of the meaning of the question 'Why?' However, Wieland nowhere develops the possibility of overlapping meanings of the four senses, and there is nothing obvious in Aristotle's text to support the thought.

13 This, I take to be the insight captured by Wesley Salmon, in his *Scientific Explanation and the Causal Structure of the World*, Princeton University Press, Princeton, 1984, but neglected by both Peter Achinstein and Carl Hempel, the latter of whom concentrates almost exclusively on the epistemic rather than the metaphysical requirements of explanation.

14 Why do I add the qualification, 'if possible. . .'? Perhaps it is not logically impossible that there be a world that is inexplicable, or in which there are some inexplicable occurrences. Perhaps things could happen that we could never understand. This, as I said in chapter I, will depend on the theory of explanation one adopts. The qualification is added, in order not to beg this open question.

15 Wesley Salmon, *op. cit.*, pp. 240, 278.

16 Compare his account at *Physics* II, 5: 'But, secondly, some events are for the sake of something, others not. Again, some of the former class are in accordance with deliberate intention, others not, but both are in the class of things which are for the sake of something. Hence it is clear that even among the things which are outside the necessary and the normal, there are some in

connection with which the phrase "for the sake of something" is applicable. Things of this kind, then, when they come to pass incidentally are said to be "by chance".'

17 I am here deeply indebted to Richard Sorabji, *op. cit.*, pp. 3–13, to which work the reader is advised to refer for detailed textual support. My interpretation of these passages differs somewhat from his.

18 Richard Sorabji, *op. cit.*, p. 8. Do formal, final, and material *aitiai* also necessitate what they explain, or is this only true of motion-originators? Aristotle's claim is limited to the accidentally generated and destroyed, so the necessitation might seem to be limited to the motion-originator. However, Jonathan Barnes, trans., *op. cit.*, pp. 215–16, argues that the matter of a thing, when appropriately described, necessitates what it explains. (Aristotle says that the premises are the matter or material explanation of their conclusion, and premises necessitate their conclusion.) A thing's form necessitates its being what it is: three-sidedness necessitates something's being a triangle. Perhaps for Aristotle, then, all *per se aitiai* necessitate what they explain.

19 There is some controversy as to whether the conclusions of such arguments are propositions, or imperatives, but this does not affect my point.

20 References in the text to *PA* are to the *Posterior Analytics*.

21 The interested reader might like to consult Jonathan Barnes, trans., *op. cit.*, p. 184 and p. 229, whom I have followed fairly closely on this issue, for a discussion of these passages and further references.

22 For a discussion of this notion in Aristotle, see David Hamlyn, 'Aristotelian Epagoge', *Phronesis*, vol. XXI, 1976, pp. 167–84.

23 Closer to the truth, but not quite the truth, since Aristotle has no account at all of the scientific explanation of particular cases.

24 I deal with the difference between the non-symmetry and the asymmetry of explanation in chapters VI and VII.

25 See Jonathan Barnes, trans., *op. cit.*, pp. 98–101 for a helpful discussion of this.

26 Presumably, 'they' refers to the premises, although this is a matter of some controversy.

27 Baruch Brody, 'Towards an Aristotelian Theory of Scientific Explanation', *Philosophy of Science*, vol. 39, 1972, pp. 20–31. Discussed by Timothy McCarthy, 'On an Aristotelian Model of Scientific Explanation', *Philosophy of Science*, vol. 44, 1977, pp. 159–66; Nathan Stemmer, 'Brody's Defense of Essentialism', *Philosophy of Science*, vol. 40, 1973, pp. 393–6.

28 'For, if an explanation requires premises related to conclusion as cause to effect, and causes fall into four clearly recognizable types, then we do have a non-circular criterion of explanation' (Bas van Fraassen, 'A Re-examination of Aristotle's Philosophy of Science', *Dialogue*, vol. 19, 1980, pp. 20–45. Quote from p. 32).

Chapter IV   Mill and Hempel on Explanation

1 Carl Hempel and P. Oppenheim, 'Studies in the Logic of Explanation', in

Aspects of Scientific Explanation, Free Press, New York, 1965, p. 251. All
further page references to Hempel in my text are to this volume.

2 John Stuart Mill, *A System of Logic*, Longman, London, 1970, Book III,
chapter XII, section 1, p. 305. References in the text to Mill are to *A System
of Logic*; numbers are to book, chapter, and section (in that order) or to page
number as in the Longman edition, 1970.

3 Alan Ryan, *The Philosophy of John Stuart Mill*, Macmillan, London, second
edition, 1971, chapter 1, pp. 3–20.

4 Also in Hempel, *op. cit.*

5 See Peter Urbach, *Francis Bacon's Philosophy of Science*, Open Court, La
Salle, 1987.

6 Pierre Duhem, *The Aim and Structure of Physical Theory*, Atheneum, New
York, 1977. Quote from p. 7.

7 But Hempel ends his discussion of the problem of lawlikeness on an
optimistic note: 'Though the preceding discussion has not led to a fully
satisfactory general characterization of lawlike sentences and thus of laws,
it will, I hope, have clarified to some extent the sense in which those
concepts will be understood in the present study' (Hempel, *op. cit.*, p. 343).

8 Or invariability of coexistence, for the case of the explanation of laws? I deal
with this question below.

9 Also, of course, a particular token event of the antecedent type mentioned in
the law, for the explanation of a particular event.

10 I have discussed these issues more fully in my 'Causal Scepticism or
Invisible Cement', *Ratio*, vol. XXIV, 1982, pp. 161–72.

11 The example is Mill's. For textual accuracy, and despite my own
reservations about the offence that it might cause, I have retained it.

12 Ernest Nagel, *The Structure of Science*, Harcourt, Brace, & World, New
York, 1961, pp. 73–8.

13 Robert Nozick, in *Philosophical Explanations*, Oxford University Press,
Oxford, 1984, pp. 116–21, discusses the possibility of explanatory
self-implication for the case of laws. Suppose that the 'ultimate law' was:
(P) lawlike statements with characteristic f are true. 'f' might stand for some
feature like invariance or symmetry, so (P) would assert that the presence of
such a feature was a sufficient condition for the truth of a lawlike statement.
If, further, (P) itself has f, then we can infer that (P) itself is true. As Nozick
stresses, it is not a question of proving that (P) is true. Rather, assuming that
(P) is true it is a question of explaining why (P) is true by deducing it as an
instance of itself. Even if this sort of self-explanation of laws is logically
possible, there is, I should think, little possibility of finding 'ultimate' laws
which state sufficient conditions for the truth of lawlike statements in terms
of features which they themselves possess.

14 Robert Nozick, *op. cit.*, pp. 116–17.

15 The interested reader might consult John Skorupski, *John Stuart Mill*,
Routledge, London, 1989, chapters 3 and 4, for a detailed and illuminating
account of Mill's views on these matters.

16 John Skorupski, *ibid.*, chapter 4.

17 Robert Nozick, *op. cit.*, pp. 204–11, and 227–40.

18 Mill distinguishes between 'two parts of the process of philosophising, the

inferring part, and the registering part. . .' (Mill, *op. cit.*, p. 122). Mill believes that error will arise if we ascribe to the latter some of the functions of the former: 'The mistake is that of referring a person to his own notes for the origin of his knowledge.' For Mill, uninformative deductive inference has a function, but its function is not the same as that of real inference, the gaining of new knowledge of the conclusions of those inferences. The function of uninformative inference (which, to repeat, is not *real* inference for Mill) is to *register* knowledge that one already possesses. 'And so in all cases, the general propositions, whether called definitions, axioms, or laws of nature, which we lay down at the beginning of our reasonings, are merely abridged statements, in a kind of shorthand, of the particular facts, which, as occasion arises, we either think we may proceed on as proved, or intend to assume. . . . General propositions are merely registers of such inferences already made, and short formulae for making more: The major premiss of a syllogism, consequently, is a formula of this description; and the conclusion is not an inference drawn from the formula, but an inference drawn according to the formula. . .'(*ibid.*, p. 126).

19 Hempel, *op. cit.*, p. 335.
20 Although I will work with this assumption, it is not finally clear whether it is correct so to interpret him. In his *The Philosophy of Natural Science* (1966), Hempel is careful not to claim necessity or sufficiency for the conditions he offers in the analysis of scientific explanation.
21 See Rolf Eberle, David Kaplan, and Richard Montague, 'Hempel and Oppenheim on Explanation', *Philosophy of Science*, vol. 28, 1961, pp. 418–28; David Kaplan, 'Explanation Revisited', *Philosophy of Science*, vol. 28, 1961, pp. 429–36; Jaegwon Kim, 'Discussion: On the Logical Conditions of Deductive Explanation', *Philosophy of Science*, vol. 30, 1963, pp. 286–91; Robert Ackermann, 'Discussions: Deductive Scientific Explanation', *Philosophy of Science*, vol. 32, 1965, pp. 155–67.
22 Ardon Lyon, 'The Relevance of Wisdom's Work for the Philosophy of Science', in *Wisdom: Twelve Essays*, ed. Renford Bambrough, Blackwell, Oxford, 1974, pp. 218–48. See especially pp. 232–48.
23 These various kinds of partiality are carefully distinguished by Hempel, *op. cit.*, pp. 415–25.
24 Compare R. Carnap, 'The Two Concepts of Probability', *Philosophy and Phenomenological Research*, vol. V, 1945, pp. 513–32: 'The problem of probability may be regarded as the task of finding an adequate definition of the concept of probability that can provide a basis for a theory of probability. This task is not one of defining a new concept but rather of redefining an old one. Thus we have here an instance of that kind of problem . . . where a concept already in use is to be made more exact, or, rather, is to be replaced by a more exact new concept. Let us call these problems . . . problems of *explication*; in each case of an explication, we call the old concept, used in a more or less vague way either in every-day language or in an earlier stage of scientific language, the *explicandum*; the new, more exact concept which is proposed to take the place of the old one the *explicatum*' (p. 513). Carnap is adopting a version of the language users' approach, on which he avails himself of the possibility of 'tidying up the discourse'.

25 See the discussion of this by Roy Bhaskar, *A Realist Theory of Science*, Harvester, Brighton, 1978, pp. 63–79.

26 S. Bromberger, 'Why-Questions', in *Mind and Cosmos: Essays in Contemporary Science and Philosophy*, ed. Robert Colodny, University of Pittsburgh Press, Pittsburgh, 1966, pp. 86–111. The counterexample mentioned in the text, with four others, can be found on pp. 92–3.

27 This isn't quite true, but the qualifications don't matter here. Imagine a deterministic world in which e occurs. Event e might be described in terms of, and explicable within, two different languages, L and L'. Its explanation in L might be an I-S explanation, and e might have *only* an I-S explanation in L. There may be no way within the conceptual resources of L to convert the I-S explanation into a D-N explanation. To get a complete D-N explanation of e, one might have to switch to L'. The explanation of e in L is thus not part of any D-N explanation.

28 I agree with the gist of Peter Railton's remarks, that genuine statistical explanation 'properly so called, is the explanation of things that happen by chance. . .' ('Probability, Explanation, and Information', *Synthese*, vol. 48, 1981, pp. 233–56), but unlike Railton, I do not believe that this is Hempel's view (as distinct from being implied by certain things he says). Indeed, how could one reconcile the quotation from Hempel in my text with the view? If statistical explanation were *independent* of the assumption of strictly universal laws, as Hempel says, then it would be consistent with that assumption as well. See Peter Railton, 'A Deductive-Nomological Model of Probabilistic Explanation', *Philosophy of Science*, vol. 45, 1978, pp. 206–26. In the quotation, Hempel means by 'universal', 'universally quantified'.

29 In Hempel, *op. cit.*, but he has refined the idea further, in the light of subsequent criticism.

30 J. Alberto Coffa, 'Hempel's Ambiguity', *Synthese* vol. 28, 1974, pp. 141–63.

31 Hempel's treatment of the epistemic ambiguity of I-S explanation must be further evidence against Railton's attribution to Hempel of the explicit avowal of the contrary view in n. 28.

Chapter V   The Ontology of Explanation

1 P.F. Strawson, 'Causation and Explanation', in B. Vermazen and J. Hintikka, eds, *Essays on Davidson*, Oxford University Press, Oxford, 1985.

2 As I indicated in chapter I, the distinction I draw between metaphysics and epistemology is only intended to be rough and ready; certainly, it may be that some things or relations belong to both provinces. Facts are, on my view, just that sort of thing.

3 Susan Haack, *Philosophy of Logic*, Cambridge University Press, Cambridge, 1978, p. 246.

4 The argument is credited originally to Frege. It has also been used by Gödel, Quine ('Three Grades of Modal Involvement'), and Church. It is discussed by Robert Cummins and Dale Gottlieb, 'On an Argument for Truth-Functionality', *American Philosophical Quarterly*, vol. IX, 1972,

pp. 265–9; John Mackie, *The Cement of the Universe*, Oxford University Press, Oxford, 1974; Kenneth Russell Olson, *An Essay on Facts*, Center for the Study of Language and Information, Leland Stanford Junior College, Stanford, California, 1987; Martin Davies, *Meaning, Necessity, and Quantification*, Routledge & Kegan Paul, London, 1981, pp. 209–13; G.E.M. Anscombe, 'Causality and Extensionality', *Journal of Philosophy*, vol. LXVI, 1969, pp. 152–9. My statement of the slingshot is taken from Mackie, *op. cit.*

5 So Martin Davies tells me. See Davies, *op. cit.*

6 What about phenomena? I have always found it somewhat surprising that the term 'phenomenon' occurs so frequently in the philosophy of explanation literature. Its only other frequent occurrence is in the Kantian literature. I do not know what a phenomenon is, at least in the explanation literature, if it is not simply an event.

7 Zeno Vendler discusses the mixed case of facts and events as the relata for the causal relation. See Zeno Vendler, 'Causal Relations', *Journal of Philosophy*, vol. LXIV, 1967, pp. 704–13.

8 David Lewis, 'Causal Explanation', *Philosophical Papers*, vol. II, Oxford University Press, Oxford and New York, 1986, pp. 214–40.

9 James Woodward, 'A Theory of Singular Causal Explanation', *Erkenntnis*, vol. 21, 1984, pp. 231–62; 'Are Singular Causal Explanations Implicit Covering Law Explanations?' *Canadian Journal of Philosophy*, vol. 16, 1986, pp. 253–80. Page references in text to the last article.

10 John Mackie, *op. cit.*, p.260.

11 Hilary Putnam discusses a case in which there is both a geometric 'macroexplanation' and a 'microexplanation' in terms of the laws of particle physics, for the fact that a peg 1 inch square goes through a 1 inch square hole and not through a 1 inch round hole, in his *Meaning and the Moral Sciences*, Routledge & Kegan Paul, London, 1978, pp. 42–3. I referred to this example in chapter I.

12 Carl Hempel, *Aspects of Scientific Explanation*, Free Press, New York, 1965, quote from p. 423.

13 How does one know what a sentence (or fact) is about? See Nelson Goodman, 'About', *Mind*, vol. LXX, 1961, pp. 1–24.

14 Peter Achinstein, *The Nature of Explanation*, chapters 2 and 3, *passim*.

15 Donald Davidson, 'Causal Relations', *Journal of Philosophy*, vol. LXIV, no. 21, 1967, pp. 691–703; reprinted in *Causation and Conditionals*, ed. Ernest Sosa, Oxford University Press, Oxford, 1975, pp. 82–94. My page references are to the Sosa collection.

16 Donald Davidson, *op. cit.*, pp. 84–6.

17 Donald Davidson, 'True to the Facts', *Journal of Philosophy*, vol. LXVI, 1969, pp. 748–64.

18 Compare Russell's view of facts in his 'The Philosophy of Logical Atomism', in *Russell's Logical Atomism*, ed. David Pears, Fontana/Collins, London, 1972, pp. 51–72, and *passim*. 'The simplest imaginable facts are those which consist in the possession of a quality by some particular thing' (p. 53). Zeno Vendler also insists on the fact/proposition distinction on metaphysical grounds: 'Propositions belong to the people who make or

entertain them, but facts are not owned. . . . The facts of the case, however, do not belong to anybody; they are, objectively, "there" to be found, discovered, or arrived at' (Zeno Vendler, *op. cit.*, p. 710). The unordinary facts needed for explanation will not be quite as objective as Vendler says, but this qualification will not erase all the metaphysical differences Vendler mentions between facts and propositions.

19 N.L. Wilson, 'Facts, Events, and Their Identity Conditions', *Philosophical Studies*, vol. 25, 1974, pp. 303–21. Page references in my text to his views are to this article. On his view, which identifies true propositions and facts, he must say that entities, things, can be constituents of true propositions: 'the notion of an entity being a constituent of a proposition may be baffling. It is, however, definable' (p. 308). Wilson's 'definition' does not lessen my bafflement at the idea.

20 J.L. Austin, 'Truth', *Proceedings of the Aristotelian Society*, supp. vol. XXIV, 1950; reprinted in *Truth*, ed. George Pitcher, Prentice-Hall, Englewood Cliffs, NJ, 1964, pp. 18–31. Quote from p. 24.

21 Suppose we had agreed earlier to a fine-grained criterion of event identity, to obtain a conception of an event which could cope with the ways in which properties matter to explanation. We would now need 'epistemicized' events, which would, I think, take us to a conception of event unsuited to play the role for which events are introduced.

22 Nathan Salmon, *Frege's Puzzle*, MIT Press, Cambridge, Mass., 1986, p. 111. Page references in the text are to this.

23 Barry Taylor, 'States of Affairs', in *Truth and Meaning: Essays in Semantics*, ed. Gareth Evans and John McDowell, Oxford University Press, Oxford, 1976, pp. 263–84. Taylor uses intensions as the predicative element he requires in constructing facts, whereas I use properties (for ordinary facts) and properties as conceptualized (for special or epistemicized facts). Clearly, there are similarities in our approaches. Taylor's facts are useless for a theory of truth (see p. 280). Taylor mentions other possible uses for states of affairs (and facts), but he does not mention their employment in a theory of explanation.

24 Zeno Vendler, *op. cit.*, quotation in text from p. 710; N.L. Wilson, *op. cit.*, quotation in text from p. 305.

25 'BCE' and 'CE' (standing for 'before the common era' and 'the common era') provide a good way for non-Christians to give dates non-ideologically.

26 Stephen Schiffer, *Remnants of Meaning*, MIT Press, Cambridge, Mass., 1987. See especially p. 51, chapter 6 (pp. 139–78), and pp. 234–9.

Chapter VI Arguments, Laws, and Explanation

1 See for example: William Kneale, 'Natural Laws and Contrary-to-Fact Conditionals', *Analysis*, vol. 10, 1950, pp. 121–5; Karl Popper, *The Logic of Scientific Discovery*, Hutchinson, London, 1972, Appendix *10, pp. 420–41; Milton Fisk, 'Are There Necessary Connections in Nature?' *Philosophy of Science*, vol. 37, 1970, pp. 385–404.

2 Richard Braithwaite, *Scientific Explanation*, Cambridge University Press,

Cambridge, 1964, chapter IX, pp. 293–318; Ernest Nagel, *The Structure of Science*, Harcourt, Brace, & World, New York, 1961, chapter 4, pp. 47–78; D.H. Mellor, 'Necessities and Universals in Natural Laws', in D.H. Mellor, ed., *Science, Belief, and Behaviour*, Cambridge University Press, Cambridge, 1980, pp. 105–19.

3 Fred Dretske, 'Laws of Nature', *Philosophy of Science*, vol. 44, 1977, pp. 248–68; for a reply to Dretske, see Ilkka Niiniluoto, *Philosophy of Science*, vol. 45, 1978, pp. 431–9; David Armstrong, *What is a Law of Nature?* Cambridge University Press, Cambridge, 1987.

4 Ardon Lyon, 'The Relevance of Wisdom's Work for the Philosophy of Science: A Study of the Concept of Scientific Explanation', in *Wisdom: Twelve Essays*, ed. Renford Bambrough, Blackwell, Oxford, 1974, pp. 218–48.

5 Baruch Brody, 'Towards an Aristotelian Theory of Explanation', *Philosophy of Science*, vol. 39, 1972, pp. 20–31.

6 Peter Achinstein, *The Nature of Explanation*, Oxford University Press, New York, 1983. Discussion of this example on pp. 168 and 170–1.

7 The case of causal pre-emption presents some difficulty for any analysis of deterministic and/or nondeterministic causation which makes a cause necessary in the circumstances for its effect. As discussed in chapters I and II, David Lewis does not think that a nondeterministic cause is necessary in the circumstances for its effect, but he does think that a deterministic cause is. Lewis deals (on p.191) with the case of pre-emption in 'Causation', reprinted in Ernest Sosa, *Causation and Conditionals*, Oxford University Press, Oxford, 1975, pp. 180–91; his treatment is discussed by William Goosens, 'Causal Chains and Counterfactuals', *Journal of Philosophy*, 1979, pp. 489–95.

8 Michael Redhead suggests this reply in a paper, 'Explanation' (unpublished): '. . . we need to attend to all the relevant circumstances . . . . Again the scientific ideal assumes that all the relevant circumstances are being cited' (p. 5). Redhead's reply to my argument is that I neglect the relevant microphysical circumstances linking the bus, but not the arsenic, with the death. On this sort of view, at best only microphysical explanation will meet Hempel's requirements for explanation.

9 In private discussion.

10 Wesley Salmon, 'A Third Dogma of Empiricism', in *Basic Problems in Methodology and Linguistics*, ed. Robert Butts and Jaako Hintikka, Reidel, Dordrecht, 1977, pp. 149–66. Readers can learn about the nervous husband and the religious explainer on p. 150. Also section 2 of Wesley Salmon, 'Statistical Explanation', in R. Colodny, ed., *The Nature and Function of Scientific Theories*, University of Pittsburgh Press, Pittsburgh, 1970, pp. 173–231, reprinted in W. Salmon, R. Jeffrey, and J. Greeno, *Statistical Explanation and Statistical Relevance*, University of Pittsburgh Press, Pittsburgh, 1971, pp. 29–88.

11 John Meixner, 'Homogeneity and Explanatory Depth', *Philosophy of Science*, vol. 46, 1979, pp. 366–81.

12 There are two principles of explanation which might be thought to be true. The first is a closure principle and the second has a certain similarity to a

closure principle: (P1) if p explains q and q entails r, then p explains r; (P2) if p entails q, and if q explains r, then p explains r. As it stands (P1) can't be right, since it implies that everything explains a tautology. I do not know whether a suitably modified version of (P1) is true, but I pointed out above in the text that Hempel's account of explanation cannot accept (P1), even if suitably modified to rule out this absurd implication about explanation of tautologies. According to Hempel's D-N model, explanation is not closed under logical entailment.

(P2) says that a statement explains everything that anything it entails explains. (P2) is of course not available to the statistical relevance theorist, to use in his own defence against Meixner. On the statistical relevance theory, no statistically irrelevant information can be included in an explanans. But since the premiss p will typically be information-richer than q, p may contain some additional information statistically irrelevant to the truth of r. So, on the statistical relevance theory, p cannot explain r, just because q does and p entails q.

(P2) is unsound in any case, since it falls foul of Salmon's original irrelevance objection. Sometimes, as Meixner says, we are happy with statistically irrelevant information (like the fact that the substance is salt), but of course sometimes we are not, as in the original counterexamples. The original counterexamples provide cases in which p entails q, q explains r, and yet p fails to explain r.

13 James Woodward, 'Explanatory Asymmetries', *Philosophy of Science*, vol. 51, 1984, pp. 421–42. See also Evan Jobe, 'A Puzzle Concerning D-N Explanation', *Philosophy of Science*, vol. 43, 1976, pp. 542–9, and Clark Glymour, 'Two Flagpoles are More Paradoxical Than One', *Philosophy of Science*, vol. 45, 1978, pp. 118–19. Peter Achinstein, *op. cit.*, p. 236: 'It is possible to explain the presence of a macro-property by appeal to the presence of an identical micro-property; or vice-versa.' Achinstein does not draw the conclusion explicitly that explanation is not asymmetric, but the conclusion follows from what he does say.

14 Aristotle's example of vines which are deciduous because broad-leaved provides a 'symmetry' counterexample to Hempel's account of the explanation of laws.

15 Wesley Salmon, 'A Third Dogma of Empiricism', p. 150.

16 Wesley Salmon, *Scientific Explanation and the Causal Structure of the World*, Princeton University Press, Princeton, 1984, p. 192, p. 96.

17 Baruch Brody, *op. cit*, pp. 23–4.

18 Timothy McCarthy, 'On an Aristotelian Model of Scientific Explanation', *Philosophy of Science*, vol. 44, 1977, pp. 159–66.

19 Jaegwon Kim 'Discussion: On the Logical Conditions of Deductive Explanation', *Philosophy of Science*, vol. 30, 1963, pp. 286–91. The conjunctive normal form requirement is introduced on p. 288.

20 McCarthy, *op. cit.*, pp. 161–2. Can we strengthen the causal requirements, to rule out a McCarthy-style counterexample? In the arguments so far, the law, even though it might be a causal law, is 'irrelevant' to the explanation (although it is not irrelevant for the derivation). The law may be a causal law, but it does not *join* the cause of the explanandum event with the

explanandum event. The law premiss and the description of the explanandum's cause don't mesh together. In McCarthy's example, the law (let's assume that it is an irrelevant *causal* law) was: $(x)(Ax \supset Bx)$, but the description of the explanandum's cause was 'Ce'. As McCarthy says: 'Let "$(x)(Ax \supset Bx)$" represent any law irrelevant to the occurence of e' (p. 161). In the second example, the law relates blackness and crows, but the cause of o's turning black has nothing to do with the law; the cause of o's turning black is having been immersed in black paint. No law in the derivation related black paint immersion and turning black. Perhaps a bit of tinkering is all that is needed. Can we impose a further requirement, and thereby escape the counterexample to Hempel's theory as supplemented by the causal requirement?

Suppose we impose the additional requirement that not only must there be a premiss essential to the argument which describes C, the particular cause of the event to be explained, but that there also must be a law premiss essential to the argument such that c(o) and the event to be explained, in this case, o's turning black, are covered by *that* law. That is to say, the law itself must not be 'irrelevant'; it must bring together the event to be explained and the cause of that event. Thus, the additional 'relevance' needed can be cashed out as 'the law must be a covering law which covers the token cause and effect mentioned in the explanatory argument'. If there is one law which covers both the token cause and the token effect, the law will be a causal law.

We must not require that the explanandum event and the cause be covered by the *same* law, as the above suggests. This would be too strong, for surely there are occasions on which we can explain an effect by its cause mediately, rather than immediately, via two or more laws. Perhaps we should require that however many laws there are, not only must the premisses contain a description of the cause of the event to be explained, but that both the cause and the explanandum event must be covered by relevant laws, which may relate the cause with the effect only mediately, so that the cause and effect can each be covered by a different law. No doubt, at least one of the laws will be a causal law; but it would be too strong to require that all of the 'interconnecting' laws be causal: I can explain the period of a metal pendulum at t' by citing the fact that heat was applied to the pendulum at t, the causal law that heat causes metal to expand, and the (non-causal) law that relates the length and period of a pendulum.

Even this additional condition will not let us deal with McCarthy's third case, which is as follows. I shall first sketch the third example informally, in order to make it fully intuitive. Suppose o's being F causes o to be G. One would imagine that the explanation of o's being G is o's being F, via the *causal* law (for let us suppose that it is a causal law) that whatever is F is G. But, with certain other assumptions about the case, we can construct an argument which meets all of the Mill–Hempel conditions, even supplemented in all the required causal ways I have suggested, but which still fails to explain.

As we have already specified, o's being F causes o to be G. What we are to imagine is a case in which the cause of an event to be explained is also the cause of the prediction of that event: If a machine of type T is brought into contact with an object which is F, the object's being F causes the machine to predict that the object is G, as well as causing the object to be G. Moreover, the machines are to be of type T, which are 'infallible predictors': if it predicts that an object is G, it follows that the object is G. We can now obtain the following argument, noting that (2) states a causal law:

(1) If a machine is of type T and if it predicts that an object is G, it follows that the object is G.

(2) If an object is F, and if a machine of type T is in the right relationship with the object, the machine will predict that the object is G.

(3) Object o is F.

(4) The machine of type t is in the right relationship with object o.

(5) Object o is G.

This argument meets all the conditions we have laid down. The premisses include essentially a description of the cause of o's being G, namely o's being F. Further, the premisses include laws which cover and connect the cause and effect, and at least one of which is a causal law. But still, I believe, the argument is not an explanation of why o is G. The object o is G *because* it is F, and nothing in the derivation reflects this.

21 My suggestion for remedying the difficulty McCarthy points out is taken from, or anyway inspired by, Peter Achinstein, *op. cit.*, pp. 159–62, 188–92.

22 This idea is close to Peter Achinstein's conception of a complete content-giving proposition. I do not believe, though, that any purely grammatical characterization of this idea is possible. See Peter Achinstein, *ibid.*, pp. 28–48, and my review of his book in the *British Journal for the Philosophy of Science*, vol. 37, 1986, pp. 377–84.

23 Peter Achinstein, *op. cit.*, pp. 78–83.

24 Wesley Salmon, 'A Third Dogma of Empiricism', pp. 159–62.

25 That there must be a lawlike generalization among the premisses in an explanatory argument does not follow simply from the assumption that explanations are arguments, for there are sound arguments with no such premiss. But the additional assumptions that would be needed in the case of arguments that are explanations are straightforward and uncontroversial to the question at hand.

26 Gilbert Ryle, '"If," "So," and "Because"', in Max Black, ed., *Philosophical Analysis: A Collection of Essays*, Prentice-Hall, Englewood Cliffs, NJ, 1963, pp. 302–18; Michael Scriven, in a series of contributions, but perhaps especially in 'Truisms as the Grounds for Historical Explanations' in *Theories of History*, ed. Patrick Gardiner, Free Press, New York, 1959, pp. 443–75 (see p. 446; page references in the text are to 'Truisms. . .'); Wesley Salmon, 'A Third Dogma of Empiricism', pp. 158–9; Peter Achinstein, *op. cit.*, pp. 81–3, and also in 'The Object of Explanation', in *Explanation*, ed. Stephan Korner, Blackwell, Oxford, 1975, pp. 1–45.

27 See Thomas Nickles, 'Davidson on Explanation', *Philosophical Studies*, vol. 31, 1977, pp. 141–5, where the idea that 'strict' covering laws may be 'non-explanatory' is developed.

28 Scriven's distinction is similar to Donald Davidson's, between homonomic and heteronomic generalizations. See Davidson, 'Mental Events', reprinted in his *Essays on Actions and Events*, Oxford University Press, Oxford, 1980, pp. 207–27; see especially pp. 218–20.

29 Note that I say '. . .that the following is *a* full explanation'. It is no part of my view that there can be at most only one full explanation for a singular fact. To take just one possibility: suppose one wants to explain why o is G. Suppose it is a law that all D are F, and a law that all F are G. The fact that o is G can be fully explained both by the fact that o is F, and the fact that o is D.

30 I do not deny that there can be cases of explanation in which explanatory relevance is borne by names; indeed, I said as much in chapter V. But I do not deal with these cases here.

31 David Hume, *A Treatise of Human Nature*, ed. L.A. Selby-Bigge, Oxford University Press, Oxford, 1965, p. 88. I think that much of the motivation for the inclusion of a generalization in every full explanation stems from the Humeian analysis of causation.

32 See Michael Friedman, 'Theoretical Explanation', in *Reduction, Time, and Reality*, ed. Richard Healey, Cambridge University Press, Cambridge, 1981, pp. 1–16. See also his 'Explanation and Scientific Understanding', *Journal of Philosophy*, vol. LXXI, 1974, pp. 5–19, and the reply by Philip Kitcher, 'Explanation, Conjunction, and Unification', *Journal of Philosophy*, vol. LXXIII, 1976, pp. 207–12.

Chapter VII A Realist Theory of Explanation

1 Jaegwon Kim, 'Noncausal Connections', *Nous*, vol. 8, 1974, pp. 41–52. Kim's own examples of non-causal determinative relations include compositional determination of one event by another, which is the event-analogue of what I have called 'mereological determination', and two others which I do not discuss, Cambridge determination and agency determination. I have discussed Cambridge determination in my 'A Puzzle About Posthumous Predication', *Philosophical Review*, vol. XCVII, 1988, pp. 211–36.

2 Bas van Fraassen, *The Scientific Image*, Oxford University Press, Oxford, 1980, p. 124.

3 John Forge, 'Physical Explanation: With Reference to the Theories of Scientific Explanation of Hempel and Salmon', in Robert McLaughlin, ed., *What? Where? When? Why?* Reidel, Dordrecht, 1982, pp. 211–29. Quotation from p. 228.

4 Wesley Salmon, *Scientific Explanation and the Causal Structure of the World*, Princeton University Press, Princeton, 1984, p. 132. See also pp. 242–59.

5 Richard Miller, *Fact and Method*, Princeton University Press, Princeton, 1987, p.60.

6 Philip Kitcher, 'Salmon on Explanation and Causality: Two Approaches to Explanation', *Journal of Philosophy*, vol. LXXXII, 1985, pp. 632–9. Examples are given on pp. 636–7.

7 Nancy Cartwright, *How the Laws of Physics Lie*, Oxford University Press, Oxford, 1983, p. 21.

8 Clark Glymour, 'Causal Inference and Causal Explanation', in Robert McLaughlin, *op. cit.*, pp, 179–91. Quotation from p. 184. His examples are from pp. 184–6.

9 Peter Railton, 'A Deductive-Nomological Model of Probabilistic Explanation', *Philosophy of Science*, vol. 45, 1978, pp. 206–26. Quotation from p. 207.

10 John Forge, 'The Instance Theory of Explanation', *Australasian Journal of Philosophy*, vol. 64, 1986, p. 132.

11 Either a relational fact that c and e stand in some relation, or a conditional fact, the fact that if c, then e. I do not bother to distinguish relations from sentence connectives here, since it makes no difference to my argument.

12 Peter Achinstein, *The Nature of Explanation*, Oxford University Press, New York, 1983, pp. 228–48; also his 'A Type of Non-Causal Explanation', in *Midwest Studies in Philosophy*, vol. IX, 1984, University of Minnesota Press, Minneapolis, pp. 221–43.

13 Or, as I would prefer to put it, some explanations of a singular fact about an event invoke as explanans a singular fact about another event contemporaneous with the first.

14 For example, see the discussion in Tom Beauchamp and Alexander Rosenberg, *Hume and the Problem of Causation*, Oxford University Press, New York, 1981, pp. 236–40. They offer a 'micro' reply to such cases.

15 J.L. Mackie, *The Cement of the Universe*, Oxford University Press, Oxford, 1974, pp. 154–9. For a view contrary to Mackie's, see Robert Cummins, 'States, Causes, and the Law of Inertia', *Philosophical Studies*, vol. 29, 1976, pp. 21–36. The crux of Cummins's argument seems to be: 'a state is a condition of changelessness', and all effects are changes. A system which *remains* in a state of inertia during an interval is one in which there is no change, and hence one in which there is no effect during that interval. But if there is no effect in such a system during that interval, there can be nothing which is a cause of an effect in that system during that interval (*ibid.*, pp. 22–4). The dubious premiss in the argument is that all effects are changes; presumably, it is this which Mackie would deny.

16 James Woodward, 'Explanatory Asymmetries', *Philosophy of Science*, vol. 51, 1984, pp. 421–42. Quotation from p. 436.

17 Einstein, Podolsky, and Rosen, 'Can Quantum-Mechanical Description of Physical Reality Be Considered Complete?' *Physical Review*, vol. 47, 1935, pp. 777–80; J.S. Bell, 'On the Einstein Podolsky Rosen Paradox', *Physics*, vol. I, 1964, pp. 195–200, and 'On the Problem of Hidden Variables in Quantum Mechanics', *Review of Modern Physics*, vol. 38, 1966, pp. 447–52. I rely on Salmon, *op. cit.*, and Patrick Suppes, *Probabilistic Metaphysics*, Blackwell, Oxford, 1984, for my (scanty) knowledge of this problem.

18 See, for example, O. Costa de Beauregard, 'Two Lectures on the Direction of Time', *Synthese*, vol. 35, 1977, pp. 129–54.

19 Bernard d'Espagnat, 'The Quantum Theory and Reality', *Scientific American*, vol. 241, no. 5, 1979, pp. 158–81.

20 My indebtedness in this section and the following to Peter Achinstein's work will be obvious to anyone who knows his writings.

21 I add 'thing', because I have in mind the thesis that God is *causa sui*. I have no reason to dispute the thesis; it falls outside the purview of my claims here.

22 I don't use the contingency claim (2) here because I want to leave it open whether the identities are contingent or necessary.

23 Peter Achinstein, *The Nature of Explanation*, pp. 233–7.

24 Paul Oppenheim and Hilary Putnam, 'Unity of Science as a Working Hypothesis', *Minnesota Studies in the Philosophy of Science*, ed. H. Feigl, M. Scriven, and G. Maxwell, University of Minnesota Press, Minneapolis, 1958, pp. 3–36.

25 David-Hillel Ruben, *The Metaphysics of the Social World*, Routledge & Kegan Paul, London, 1985.

26 See, for example, J.W.N. Watkins, *Hobbes' System of Ideas*, Hutchinson, London, 1973, chapter 3, 'Scientific Tradition', pp. 28–42.

27 U.T. Place, 'Is Consciousness a Brain Process?' *British Journal of Psychology*, vol. XLVII, 1956, pp. 44–50, and reprinted in *The Philosophy of Mind*, ed. V.C. Chappell, Prentice-Hall, Englewood Cliffs, NJ, 1962, pp. 101–9.

28 John Locke, *An Essay Concerning the Human Understanding*, ed. A.S. Pringle-Pattison, Oxford University Press, London, 1964, p. 243.

29 David Lewis would deny this: see his 'Events', in *Philosophical Papers*, vol. II, Oxford University Press, Oxford and New York, 1986, pp. 241–69. On pp. 262–6, Lewis deals explicitly with Kim's Socrates–Xantippe example.

30 Jaegwon Kim, 'Supervenience and Supervenient Causation', in *Spindel Conference 1983: Supervenience*, ed. Terence Horgan, vol. XXII, Supplement to *Southern Journal of Philosophy*, pp. 45–61.

31 See Cynthia and Graham Macdonald, 'Mental Causes and the Explanation of Action', *Philosophical Quarterly*, vol. 36, 1986, pp. 145–58, and especially p. 157, where they argue that since the supervenience of the mental on the physical is likely to be stipulated on a priori grounds, there will not, or may not, be any explanations of the mental by the physical.

32 R.M. Hare, *Philosophical Review*, vol. 68, 1959, pp. 421–56: 'First, let us take the characteristic of "good" which has been called its supervenience. Suppose that we say St. Francis was a good man. It is logically impossible to say this and to maintain at the same time that there might have been another man placed exactly in the same circumstances as St. Francis, and who behaved in exactly the same way but who differed from St. Francis in this respect only, that he was not a good man.'

33 John Bacon, 'Supervenience, Necessary Coextension, and Reducibility', *Philosophical Studies*, vol. 49, 1986, pp. 163–76. Quotation from p. 175.

34 D.H. Mellor, 'In Defense of Dispositions', *Philosophical Review*, vol. LXXXIII, 1974, pp. 157–81. Quotation from p. 172.

35 Elizabeth Prior, *Dispositions*, Aberdeen University Press, Aberdeen, 1985, p.62: '...the commonly accepted view that dispositional properties can be distinguished from categorical ones because dispositional ascription sentences possess a relationship to certain subjunctive conditionals not

possessed by categorical ascription sentences, survives unscathed'.

36 *Pace* Mellor: 'Explanatory dispositions require some independent basis for their ascriptions between displays; but the basis need only be another disposition' (*op. cit.*, p. 174).

37 David Lewis, 'Causal Explanation', in *op. cit.*, pp. 214–40. Page references in my text are to this article. Lewis's own example of small-pox immunity misleads him, because the 'F' in his example is '. . .protects. . .', which can have either a dispositional or a non-dispositional sense.

38 Assuming of course that the austere theorist is wrong, and that this is a distinctive metaphysical relation.

39 The idea of determination can perhaps even be extended to the relation between a general law(s) and the less general regularities or particular occurrences that the former explains. There is a sense of determination, described by Professor Anscombe, in which the rules of chess might determine the next move in a game. The chess rules create specific move possibilities, and the current position of the pieces, in conjunction with the rules, may reduce the possibilities to one. Similarly, the existence of a regularity in a system S may be determined by a set of laws governing that system (G.E.M. Anscombe, 'Causality and Determination', reprinted in *Causation and Conditionals*, ed. Ernest Sosa, Oxford University Press, Oxford, 1975, pp. 63–81). More general regularities determine less general ones. A determinative theory of explanation can also hope to capture explanation of laws by more general laws.

Bibliography

Achinstein, Peter, 1975, 'The Object of Explanation', in *Explanation*, ed. Stephan Körner, Blackwell, Oxford.
— 1983, *The Nature of Explanation*, Oxford University Press, New York.
— 1984, 'A Type of Non-Causal Explanation', in *Midwest Studies in Philosophy* IX, University of Minnesota Press, Minneapolis.
Ackermann, Robert, 1965, 'Discussions: Deductive Scientific Explanation', *Philosophy of Science*, 32.
Annas, Julia, 1982, 'Aristotle on Inefficient Causes', *Philosophical Quarterly*, 32.
Anscombe, G.E.M., 1969, 'Causality and Extensionality', *Journal of Philosophy*, LXVI.
— 1975, 'Causality and Determination', reprinted in *Causation and Conditionals*, ed. Ernest Sosa, Oxford University Press, Oxford.
Aristotle, 1966, *The Basic Works of Aristotle*, ed. Richard McKeon, Random House, New York.
— 1975, *Posterior Analytics*, trans. Jonathan Barnes, Oxford University Press, Oxford.
Armstrong, David, 1987, *What Is a Law of Nature?*, Cambridge University Press, Cambridge.
Austin, J. L., 1984, *How To Do Things With Words*, second edition, ed. J.O. Urmson and Marina Sbisà, Oxford University Press, Oxford.
— 1964, 'Truth', reprinted in *Truth*, ed. George Pitcher, Prentice-Hall, Englewood Cliffs, NJ.
Bacon, John, 1986, 'Supervenience, Necessary Coextension, and Reducibility', *Philosophical Studies*, 49.
Beauchamp, Tom and Alexander Rosenberg, 1981, *Hume and the Problem of Causation*, Oxford University Press, New York.
Bell, J.S., 1964, 'On the Einstein Podolsky Rosen Paradox', *Physics*, I.
— 1966, 'On the Problem of Hidden Variables in Quantum Mechanics', *Review of Modern Physics*, 38.
Bhaskar, Roy, 1978, *A Realist Theory of Science*, Harvester, Brighton.
Braithwaite, Richard, 1964, *Scientific Explanation*, Cambridge University Press, Cambridge.

Bibliography

Brody, Baruch, 1972, 'Towards an Aristotelian Theory of Scientific
  Explanation', *Philosophy of Science*, 39.
Bromberger, Sylvain, 1965, 'An Approach to Explanation', in *Analytical
  Philosophy*, second series, ed. R.J. Butler, Blackwell, Oxford.
— 1966, 'Why-Questions', in *Mind and Cosmos: Essays in Contemporary
  Science and Philosophy*, ed. Robert Colodny, University of Pittsburgh
  Press, Pittsburgh.
Burge, E.L., 1971, 'The Ideas as *Aitiai* in the *Phaedo*', *Phronesis*, 16.
Carnap, Rudolf, 1945, 'The Two Concepts of Probability', *Philosophy and
  Phenomenological Research*, V.
Cartwright, Nancy, 1983, *How the Laws of Physics Lie*, Oxford University
  Press, Oxford.
Clark, Romane, and Paul Welsh, 1962, *Introduction to Logic*, Van Nostrand,
  Princeton.
Coffa, J. Alberto, 1974, 'Hempel's Ambiguity', *Synthese*, 28.
Collins, Arthur, 1966, 'Explanation and Causality', *Mind*, LXXV.
Cresswell, M. J., 1971, 'Plato's Theory of Causality: *Phaedo* 95–106',
  Australasian Journal of Philosophy, 49.
Cummins, Robert, 1976, 'States, Causes, and the Law of Inertia',
  Philosophical Studies, 29.
— and Dale Gottlieb, 1972, 'On an Argument for Truth-Functionality',
  American Philosophical Quarterly, IX.
Davidson, Donald, 1969, 'True to the Facts', *Journal of Philosophy*, LXVI.
— 1975, 'Causal Relations', reprinted in *Causation and Conditionals*, ed.
  Ernest Sosa, Oxford University Press, Oxford.
— 1980, 'Mental Events', reprinted in his *Essays on Actions and Events*,
  Oxford University Press, Oxford.
Davies, Martin, 1981, *Meaning, Necessity, and Quantification*, Routledge &
  Kegan Paul, London.
de Beauregard, O. Costa, 1977, 'Two Lectures on the Direction of Time',
  Synthese, 35.
d'Espagnat, Bernard, 1979, 'The Quantum Theory and Reality', *Scientific
  American*, 241, 5.
Dorling, John, 1978, 'On Explanation in Physics: Sketch of an Alternative to
  Hempel's Account of the Explanation of Laws', *Philosophy of Science*, 45.
Dretske, Fred, 1972, 'Contrastive Facts', *Philosophical Review*, 81.
— 1977, 'Laws of Nature', *Philosophy of Science*, 44.
Duhem, Pierre, 1977, *The Aim and Structure of Physical Theory*, Atheneum,
  New York.
Eberle, Rolf, David Kaplan, and Richard Montague, 1961, 'Hempel and
  Oppenheim on Explanation', *Philosophy of Science*, 28.
Einstein, Podolsky, and Rosen, 1935, 'Can Quantum-Mechanical Description
  of Physical Reality Be Considered Complete?', *Physical Review*, 47.
Fisk, Milton, 1970, 'Are There Necessary Connections in Nature?',
  Philosophy of Science, 37.
Forge, John, 1982, 'Physical Explanation: With Reference to the Theories of
  Scientific Explanation of Hempel and Salmon', in Robert McLaughlin, ed.,

What? Where? When? Why?, Reidel, Dordrecht.
— 1986, 'The Instance Theory of Explanation', *Australasian Journal of Philosophy*, 64.

Friedman, Michael, 1974, 'Explanation and Scientific Understanding', *Journal of Philosophy*, LXXI.
— 1981, 'Theoretical Explanation', in *Reduction, Time, and Reality*, ed. Richard Healey, Cambridge University Press, Cambridge.

Garfinkel, Alan, 1981, *Forms of Explanation*, Yale University Press, New Haven.

Gettier, Edmund, 1963, 'Is Justified True Belief Knowledge?', *Analysis*, 23.

Glymour, Clark, 1978, 'Two Flagpoles Are More Paradoxical Than One', *Philosophy of Science*, 45.
— 1982, 'Causal Inference and Causal Explanation', in Robert McLaughlin, ed., *What? Where? When? Why?*, Reidel, Dordrecht.

Goodman, Nelson, 1961, 'About', *Mind*, LXX.

Goosens, William, 1979, 'Causal Chains and Counterfactuals', *Journal of Philosophy*, vol. LXXVI.

Haack, Susan, 1978, *Philosophy of Logic*, Cambridge University Press, Cambridge.

Hamlyn, David, 1976, 'Aristotelian Epagoge', *Phronesis*, XXI.

Hare, R. M., 1959, 'Aesthetic Concepts', *Philosophical Review*, 68.

Hempel, Carl, 1965, *Aspects of Scientific Explanation*, The Free Press, New York. (I have in fact used the 1970 paperback, with the same pagination.)
— 1966, *Philosophy of Natural Science*, Prentice-Hall, Englewood Cliffs, NJ.

Hocutt, Max, 1974, 'Aristotle's Four Becauses', *Philosophy*, 49.

Howson, Colin, 1988, 'On a Recent Argument for the Impossibility of a Statistical Explanation of Single Events, and a Defence of a Modified Form of Hempel's Theory of Statistical Explanation', *Erkenntnis*, 29.

Jobe, Evan, 1976, 'A Puzzle Concerning D-N Explanation', *Philosophy of Science*, 43.

Kaplan, David, 1961, 'Explanation Revisited', *Philosophy of Science*, 28.

Kim, Jaegwon, 1963, 'Discussion: On the Logical Conditions of Deductive Explanation', *Philosophy of Science*, 30.
— 1974, 'Noncausal Connections', *Nous*, 8.
— 1983, 'Supervenience and Supervenient Causation', in *Spindel Conference 1983: Supervenience*, ed., Terence Horgan, XXII, Supplement to *Southern Journal of Philosophy*.

Kitcher, Philip, 1976, 'Explanation, Conjunction, and Unification', *Journal of Philosophy*, 73.
— 1985, 'Salmon on Explanation and Causality: Two Approaches to Explanation', *Journal of Philosophy*, LXXXII.

Kneale, William, 1950, 'Natural Laws and Contrary-to-Fact Conditionals', *Analysis*, 10.

Kyburg, Henry, Jr, 1970, 'Conjunctivitis', in M. Swain, ed., *Induction, Acceptance, and Rational Beliefs*, Reidel, Dordrecht.

Lambert, Karel and Gordon G. Brittan, Jr, 1987, *An Introduction to the Philosophy of Science*, third edition, Ridgeview Publishing Company, Atascadero.

Lewis, David, 1986, *Philosophical Papers*, vol. II, Oxford University Press, New York.

Lipton, Peter, 1987, 'A Real Contrast', *Analysis*, 47.

Lyon, Ardon, 1974, 'The Relevance of Wisdom's Work for the Philosophy of Science', in *Wisdom: Twelve Essays*, ed. Renford Bambrough, Blackwell, Oxford.

McCarthy, Timothy, 1977, 'Discussion: on an Aristotelian Model of Scientific Explanation', *Philosophy of Science*, 44.

Macdonald, Cynthia and Graham, 1986, 'Mental Causes and the Explanation of Action', *Philosophical Quarterly*, 36.

Mackenzie, Mary, 'Plato's Analysis of Individuation', unpublished manuscript.

Mackie, John, 1973, *Truth, Probability, and Paradox*, Oxford University Press, Oxford.

— 1974, *The Cement of the Universe*, Oxford University Press, Oxford.

Meixner, John, 1979, 'Homogeneity and Explanatory Depth', *Philosophy of Science*, 46.

Melling, David, 1987, *Understanding Plato*, Oxford University Press, Oxford.

Mellor, D. H., 1974, 'In Defense of Dispositions', *Philosophical Review*, LXXXIII.

— 1976, 'Probable Explanation', *Australasian Journal of Philosophy*, 54.

— 1980, 'Necessities and Universals in Natural Laws', in Mellor, ed., *Science, Belief, and Behaviour*, Cambridge University Press, Cambridge.

Mill, John Stuart, 1970, *A System of Logic*, Longman, London.

Miller, Richard, 1987, *Fact and Method*, Princeton University Press, Princeton.

Moravcsik, Julius, 1974, 'Aristotle on Adequate Explanations', *Synthese*, 28.

Nagel, Ernest, 1961, *The Structure of Science*, Harcourt, Brace & World, New York.

Nickles, Thomas, 1977, 'Davidson on Explanation', *Philosophical Studies*, 31.

Niiniluoto, Ilkka, 1978, 'Dretske on Laws of Nature', *Philosophy of Science*, 45.

Nozick, Robert, 1984, *Philosophical Explanations*, Oxford University Press, Oxford.

Olson, Kenneth Russell, 1987, *An Essay on Facts*, Center for the Study of Language and Information, Leland Stanford Junior College, Stanford, California.

Oppenheim, Paul and Hilary Putnam, 1958, 'Unity of Science as a Working Hypothesis', *Minnesota Studies in the Philosophy of Science*, ed. Feigl, Scriven, and Maxwell, University of Minnesota Press, Minneapolis.

Owen, G.E.L., 1975, 'Tithenai ta Phainomena', reprinted in *Articles on Aristotle 1: Science*, ed. Jonathan Barnes, Malcolm Schofield, and Richard Sorabji, Duckworth, London.

Place, U.T., 1962, 'Is Consciousness a Brain Process?', reprinted in *The Philosophy of Mind*, ed. V.C. Chappell, Prentice-Hall, Englewood Cliffs, NJ.

Plato, 1955, The *Phaedo*, trans. R.S. Bluck, Bobbs-Merrill, Indianapolis.

— 1966, *Plato: The Collected Dialogues*, ed. Edith Hamilton and Huntington Cairns, Bollingen Foundation.

Popper, Karl, 1972, *The Logic of Scientific Discovery*, Hutchinson, London.

— 1973, 'Epistemology Without a Knowing Subject', in *Objective Knowledge*, Oxford University Press, Oxford.

Prior, Elizabeth, 1985, *Dispositions*, Aberdeen University Press, Aberdeen.

Putnam, Hilary, 1978, *Meaning and the Moral Sciences*, Routledge & Kegan Paul, London.

Railton, Peter, 1978, 'A Deductive-Nomological Model of Probabilistic Explanation', *Philosophy of Science*, 45.

— 1981, 'Probability, Explanation, and Information', *Synthese*, 48.

Redhead, Michael, 1989, 'Explanation' (unpublished but delivered as a paper at the Royal Institute of Philosophy Conference on Explanation in Glasgow, and to be published in a volume of conference proceedings by Cambridge University Press).

Ruben, David-Hillel, 1981, 'Lewis and the Problem of Causal Sufficiency', *Analysis*, 4.

— 1982, 'Causal Scepticism or Invisible Cement', *Ratio*, XXIV.

— 1985, *The Metaphysics of the Social World*, Routledge & Kegan Paul, London.

— 1986, 'Review of Peter Achinstein's *The Nature of Explanation*', *British Journal for the Philosophy of Science*, 37.

— 1987, 'Explaining Contrastive Facts', *Analysis*, 47.

— 1988, 'A Puzzle about Posthumous Predication', *Philosophical Review*, XCVII.

Russell, Bertrand, 1972, 'The Philosophy of Logical Atomism', in *Russell's Logical Atomism*, ed. David Pears, Fontana/Collins, London.

Ryan, Alan, 1987, *The Philosophy of John Stuart Mill*, Macmillan, London, second edition.

Ryle, Gilbert, 1963, '"If," "So," and "Because"', in Max Black, ed., *Philosophical Analysis: A Collection of Essays*, Prentice-Hall, Englewood Cliffs, NJ.

Salmon, Nathan, 1986, *Frege's Puzzle*, MIT Press, Cambridge, Mass.

Salmon, Wesley, 1970, 'Statistical Explanation', in R. Colodny, ed., *The Nature and Function of Scientific Theories*, University of Pittsburgh Press, Pittsburgh.

— 1977, 'A Third Dogma of Empiricism', in Butts and Hintikka, eds, *Basic Problems in Methodology and Linguistics*, Reidel, Dordrecht.

— 1984, *Scientific Explanation and the Causal Structure of the World*, Princeton University Press, Princeton.

— Richard Jeffrey, and James Greeno, 1971, *Statistical Explanation and Statistical Relevance*, University of Pittsburgh Press, Pittsburgh.

Schiffer, Stephen, 1987, *Remnants of Meaning*, MIT Press, Cambridge, Mass.

Scriven, Michael, 1959, 'Truisms as the Grounds for Historical Explanation', in *Theories of History*, ed. Patrick Gardiner, The Free Press, New York.

Skorupski, John, 1989, *John Stuart Mill*, Routledge, London.

Skyrms, Brian, 1975, *Choice and Chance*, Dickinson Publishing Company,

Bibliography

Encino and Belmont, California.

Sorabji, Richard, 1980, *Necessity, Cause, and Blame*, Duckworth, London.

Sosa, Ernest, 1964, 'The Analysis of "Knowledge that P"', *Analysis*, 25.

Stegmüller, Wofgang, 1980, 'Two Successor Concepts to the Notion of Statistical Explanation', in *Logic and Philosophy*, ed. G.H. von Wright, Nijhoff, The Hague.

Stemmer, Nathan, 1973, 'Brody's Defense of Essentialism', *Philosophy of Science*, 40.

Strawson, Peter, 1985, 'Causation and Explanation', in Vermazen and Hintikka, eds, *Essays on Davidson*, Oxford University Press, Oxford.

Suppes, Patrick, 1984, *Probabilistic Metaphysics*, Blackwell, Oxford.

Taylor, Barry, 1976, 'States of Affairs', in *Truth and Meaning: Essays in Semantics*, ed. Gareth Evans and John McDowell, Oxford University Press, Oxford.

Taylor, C.C.W., 1969, 'Forms as Causes in the *Phaedo*', *Mind*, LXVIII.

Temple, Denis, 1988, 'The Contrast Theory of Why–Questions', *Philosophy of Science*, 55.

Toulmin, Stephen, 1961, *Foresight and Understanding*, Harper, New York.

Tuomela, Raimo, 1980, 'Explaining Explaining', *Erkenntnis*, 15.

Urbach, Peter, 1987, *Francis Bacon's Philosophy of Science*, Open Court, La Salle.

van Fraassen, Bas, 1980, 'A Re-examination of Aristotle's Philosophy of Science', *Dialogue*, 19.

— 1980, *The Scientific Image*, Oxford University Press, Oxford.

Vendler, Zeno, 1967, 'Causal Relations', *Journal of Philosophy*, LXIV, 21.

Vlastos, Gregory, 1954, 'The Third Man Argument in the *Parmenides*,' *Philosophical Review* and reprinted in *Studies in Plato's Metaphysics*, R.E. Allen, ed., Routledge & Kegan Paul, London, 1967.

— 1969, 'Reasons and Causes in the *Phaedo*', *Philosophical Review*, 78.

von Wright, Georg Henrik, 1971, *Explanation and Understanding*, Routledge & Kegan Paul, London.

Watkins, John, 1973, *Hobbes' System of Ideas*, Hutchinson, London.

— 1984, *Science and Scepticism*, Princeton University Press, Princeton.

Wieland, W., 1975, 'The Problem of Teleology', reprinted in *Articles on Aristotle I: Science*, ed., Jonathan Barnes, Malcolm Schofield, and Richard Sorabji, Duckworth, London.

Wilson, N.L., 1974, 'Facts, Events, and Their Identity Conditions', *Philosophical Studies*, 25.

Woodward, James, 1984, 'A Theory of Singular Causal Explanation', *Erkenntnis*, 21.

— 1984, 'Explanatory Asymmetries', *Philosophy of Science*, 51.

— 1986, 'Are Singular Causal Explanations Implicit Covering Law Explanations?', *Canadian Journal of Philosophy*, 16.

Name Index

Name Index

Salmon, N. 176–7
Salmon, W. 24–5, 27–31, 38–9, 87, 153, 187–9, 193–4, 199, 211, 213
Schiffer, S. 179–80
Scriven, M. 191, 199–200, 202
Skorupski, J. 132–3
Sorabji, R. 77, 93
Strawson, P. 155–6, 164

Taylor, C. 51
Temple, D. 41–2

Tuomela, R. 5

van Fraassen, B. 29, 38, 40, 211, 217
Vendler, Z. 177–8
Vlastos, G. 45, 49–51

Watkins, J. W. N. 67–8
Welsh, P. 7
Wieland, W. 80–1, 84–6
Wilson, N. 168, 174, 177–8
Woodward, J. 160–2, 168, 191

Subject index

ambiguity of 'explanation' 16, 28, 80–1

Cambridge change 50, 222–4, 230–3
causal explanation 35–9, 45–6, 105–8,
    140–1, 192–4, 209–33
causation 50, 113–14, 185, 211–18, 230–3
closure under conjunction 29–31, 42–3
closure under implication 131–3, 187,
    248 fn. 12
contrastives 39–44

deterministic v non-deterministic
    causation 35–7, 46–7, 49, 64–70,
    116–17, 149–54
dispositions 225–33

emptiness, explanatory 67–71
explaining that 15–16, 79–80
explanation, complete and partial 16–21,
    143–5, 149–51, 202–4
explanation, good and bad 21–3, 32,
    163–4, 190
explanation, ordinary and scientific 5–6,
    16–19, 95–108, 206
explanation, theories of: argument and
    non-argument theories 33–5, 45, 97,
    197–9; certainty, high, and low
    epistemic probability theories 27–32,
    33–9; deductivism 33–9, 97–108,
    110–11, 116–17, 129–38;
    determinative, high, and low
    dependency theories 36–9, 45, 49,
    61–2, 64–70, 93–5, 116–17, 151,
    230–3; probabilism 33–9, 100, 138,
    149–54

facts v events 23–5, 39, 51–2, 115,

139–40, 156, 160–80
fallacy of composition/decomposition 73

identity 157–8, 165, 174–6, 218–22,
    230–3
intensionality (non-extensionality) 57, 78,
    87–93, 155–80, 205–6

knowledge 6, 10, 11–12, 72–5, 96–7,
    130–8

language users' v technical approach
    11–15, 77, 84–7, 140–4
laws, explanation of and by 4–5, 58, 89,
    93–5, 97–8, 113–14, 115, 117, 118–23,
    181–2, 186–7, 197, 199–208

mereology 218–22, 230–3

paradox of analysis 10
pragmatism, explanatory 21–3, 180
probability 26, 63–72, 131
process/product ambiguity 6–9

quantum mechanics 216–17

realism, explanatory 23–4, 160, 167–8,
    209–11, 230–3
reduction 122–3, 218–22, 230–3
reflexivity of explanation relation 129,
    138, 175, 219–20, 221
regress of explanation 73–4, 102–4, 125–9
relevance/irrelevance 23, 162–4, 170–1,
    183–90

self-explanation 129, 138, 175, 219–20,
    221

264